THE BIG BOOK OF ILLUSTRATION IDEAS: 2

THE BIG BOOK OF ILLUSTRATION

IDEAS:2

general editors:
roger walton + jen cogliantry

COLLINS | DESIGN

An Imprint of HarperCollinsPublishers

THE BIG BOOK OF ILLUSTRATION IDEAS: 2
Copyright © 2008 by COLLINS DESIGN and DUNCAN BAIRD PUBLISHERS

HarperCollins books may be purchased for educational, business, or sales promotional use. For information, please write to: Special Markets Department, HarperCollins*Publishers*, 10 East 53rd Street, New York, NY 10022.

First published in 2008 by:
Collins Design
An Imprint of HarperCollins*Publishers*
10 East 53rd Street
New York, NY 10022
Tel: (212) 207-7000
Fax: (212) 207-7654
collinsdesign@harpercollins.com
www.harpercollins.com

Distributed throughout the world by:
HarperCollins*Publishers*
10 East 53rd Street
New York, NY 10022
Fax: (212) 207-7654

Conceived, created, and designed by:
Duncan Baird Publishers, Ltd.
Sixth Floor, Castle House
75–76 Wells Street
London W1T 3QH
United Kingdom

Library of Congress Control Number: 2007939259

ISBN: 978-0-06-121514-8

Designer: Jen Cogliantry
Project Coordinator & Editor: Julia Szczuka

Printed in Thailand by Imago
First Printing, 2008

NOTE
The caption information, and artwork in this book have been supplied by the illustrators and/or their agents. All works have been reproduced on the condition that this is with the knowledge and prior consent of the illustrators, designers, client company, publication, and/or other interested parties. No responsibility is accepted by the Publishers for any infringement of copyright arising out of the publication.

All caption material, including contact details, is based upon information received from the illustrators and/or their agents. Where caption information is missing, no information has been received despite all efforts to contact all parties. The term N/A (not applicable) is used where the illustrators and/or their agents felt the category is not relevant. While every effort has been made to ensure the accuracy of information, the Publishers cannot under any circumstances accept responsibility for inaccuracies, errors, or omissions.

All measurements are provided in width x height format and are rounded to the nearest 1/8 of an inch or millimeter.

The captions for pages 1-5 appear at the back of the book.

Front jacket image (top) by Séverine Scaglia (Costume 3 Pièces) is reproduced with permission of Lalique "Mythic Garden" collection (agency: Atelier Pernet).

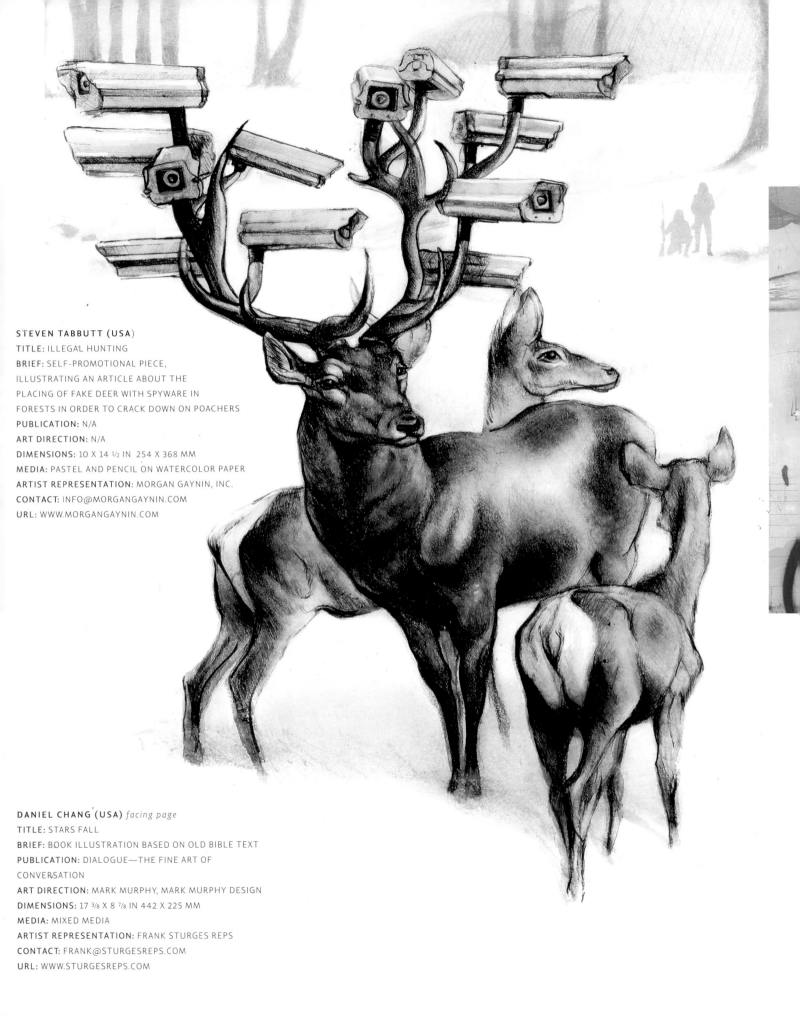

STEVEN TABBUTT (USA)
TITLE: ILLEGAL HUNTING
BRIEF: SELF-PROMOTIONAL PIECE,
ILLUSTRATING AN ARTICLE ABOUT THE
PLACING OF FAKE DEER WITH SPYWARE IN
FORESTS IN ORDER TO CRACK DOWN ON POACHERS
PUBLICATION: N/A
ART DIRECTION: N/A
DIMENSIONS: 10 X 14 ½ IN 254 X 368 MM
MEDIA: PASTEL AND PENCIL ON WATERCOLOR PAPER
ARTIST REPRESENTATION: MORGAN GAYNIN, INC.
CONTACT: INFO@MORGANGAYNIN.COM
URL: WWW.MORGANGAYNIN.COM

DANIEL CHANG (USA) *facing page*
TITLE: STARS FALL
BRIEF: BOOK ILLUSTRATION BASED ON OLD BIBLE TEXT
PUBLICATION: DIALOGUE—THE FINE ART OF
CONVERSATION
ART DIRECTION: MARK MURPHY, MARK MURPHY DESIGN
DIMENSIONS: 17 ³⁄₈ X 8 ⁷⁄₈ IN 442 X 225 MM
MEDIA: MIXED MEDIA
ARTIST REPRESENTATION: FRANK STURGES REPS
CONTACT: FRANK@STURGESREPS.COM
URL: WWW.STURGESREPS.COM

contents

COLE GERST (USA) *facing page*
TITLE: KILOWATT
BRIEF: SELF-PROMOTIONAL PIECE FOR OPTION-G STUDIOS
PUBLICATION: N/A
ART DIRECTION: COLE GERST / OPTION-G
DIMENSIONS: 13 X 19 IN 330 X 483 MM
MEDIA: ARCHIVAL GICLEE PRINT
ARTIST REPRESENTATION: ART DEPARTMENT
CONTACT: STEPHANIEP@ART-DEPT.COM
URL: WWW.ART-DEPT.COM

foreword

THE BIG BOOK OF ILLUSTRATION IDEAS: 2 is a unique collection of some of the best illustration work from around the world.

So if you're a designer, an art director, an illustrator or an illustrators' agent, or if you work in magazines or book publishing, in the theater, TV or the movies, or in any form of visual communication, this book is for you.

Why, do I hear you ask? Well, a quick leaf through these pages will reveal to you, among other things, the man with the antelope horns, astonished fish, some very interesting tattoos, the wild double bass player, the man with the bullhorn who shouts at cars, a map made out of rusty metal, the "object-swallowing sideshow" and a sign saying "love for sale" composed entirely out of drawings of legs, not to mention many other very beautiful, haunting, and surprising images.

So, what are you waiting for? Just jump right in: it's bound to be a rewarding, illuminating, and improving experience. But, more than that—it's just downright fun!

Richard Wilkinson

RICHARD WILKINSON (UK)
TITLE: BIODYNAMIC BEAUTY
BRIEF: ILLUSTRATION TO ACCOMPANY AN ARTICLE ON NEW TRENDS
IN ORGANIC AND "BIODYNAMIC" BEAUTY PRODUCTS
PUBLICATION: THE TELEGRAPH MAGAZINE, UK
ART DIRECTION: GARY COCHRAN, THE TELEGRAPH MAGAZINE
DIMENSIONS: 3 7/8 X 5 1/4 IN 97 X 132 MM
MEDIA: MIXED MEDIA, ADOBE PHOTOSHOP
ARTIST REPRESENTATION: CENTRAL ILLUSTRATION AGENCY (CIA)
CONTACT: INFO@CENTRALILLUSTRATION.COM
URL: WWW.CENTRALILLUSTRATION.COM

people

WELL, WHO'S HERE? The antler guy, the skinny party people who aren't really talking to each other, the other party people who are having a ball, the wild dancing couple who are always dancing, that nice transparent lady, the very thin lady with almost no clothes on, that guy who isn't feeling so well (page 30, don't dwell), the snooty girls, the very dreamy (and slightly odd?) girls, urban types, rural types, the girl with the crocodiles, the guy who's been drawn on wood is also here, and you on page 36 get a shave, why don't you, or the guy on page 38 with the dog who'll come looking for you. There's the huge fellow with birds flying round his head, those crazy tattooed gals, Bionic Brian's here, the kissing couples who are riding bicycles (how do they do that?). They're all here, and many, many more ...

DAMIEN WEIGHILL (UK)
TITLE: CHRISTMAS CELEBRATION
BRIEF: LEAVING CARD ILLUSTRATION
PUBLICATION: N/A
ART DIRECTION: N/A
DIMENSIONS: 8 ¼ X 11 ¾ IN 210 X 297 MM
MEDIA: LINE DRAWING
ARTIST REPRESENTATION: JELLY LONDON
CONTACT: INFO@JELLYLONDON.COM
URL: WWW.JELLYLONDON.COM

ANNIKA WESTER (FRANCE)
TITLE: KITTY
BRIEF: A T-SHIRT ILLUSTRATION FEATURING
A CAT-GIRL'S HEAD
PUBLICATION: N/A
ART DIRECTION: N/A
DIMENSIONS: 6 ¾ X 9 IN 170 X 230 MM
MEDIA: PEN AND INK
ARTIST REPRESENTATION: CWC INTERNATIONAL
CONTACT: AGENT@CWC-I.COM
URL: WWW.CWC-I.COM

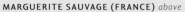

MARGUERITE SAUVAGE (FRANCE) *above*
TITLE: I PREFER THE GIRL COMING FROM NORTH EUROPE
BRIEF: TO ILLUSTRATE AN ARTICLE ABOUT A MAN WHO
DESCRIBES HIS FASCINATION AND OBSESSION WITH A
YOUNG SWEDISH GIRL IN THE 1970S
PUBLICATION: SENSO
ART DIRECTION: V. CHAHINE, SENSO
DIMENSIONS: 4 X 6 ¼ IN 100 X 160 MM
MEDIA: PENCIL, ADOBE PHOTOSHOP
ARTIST REPRESENTATION: MAGNET REPS
CONTACT: ART@MAGNETREPS.COM
URL: WWW.MAGNETREPS.COM /
WWW.MARGUERITESAUVAGE.COM

GEORGINA FEARNS (UK) *above*
TITLE: PAMPERED
BRIEF: A HIGH-MAINTENANCE WOMAN BEING FUSSED OVER
AND PAMPERED AS SHE PREPARES FOR A NIGHT OUT
PUBLICATION: N/A
ART DIRECTION: N/A
DIMENSIONS: 6 ¼ X 10 IN 159 X 254 MM
MEDIA: MIXED MEDIA, PEN AND INK, ADOBE PHOTOSHOP
ARTIST REPRESENTATION: THE INKSHED
CONTACT: ABBY@INKSHED.CO.UK
URL: WWW.INKSHED.CO.UK

CHARLES WILKIN (USA) *facing page*
TITLE: DAY OF LUXURY
BRIEF: EDITORIAL ILLUSTRATION
PUBLICATION: VOGUE AUSTRALIA
ART DIRECTION: PAUL MEANE, VOGUE MAGAZINE
DIMENSIONS: 8 X 11 IN 203 X 279 MM
MEDIA: MIXED MEDIA / DIGITAL
ARTIST REPRESENTATION: MAGNET REPS
CONTACT: ART@MAGNETREPS.COM
URL: WWW.MAGNETREPS.COM

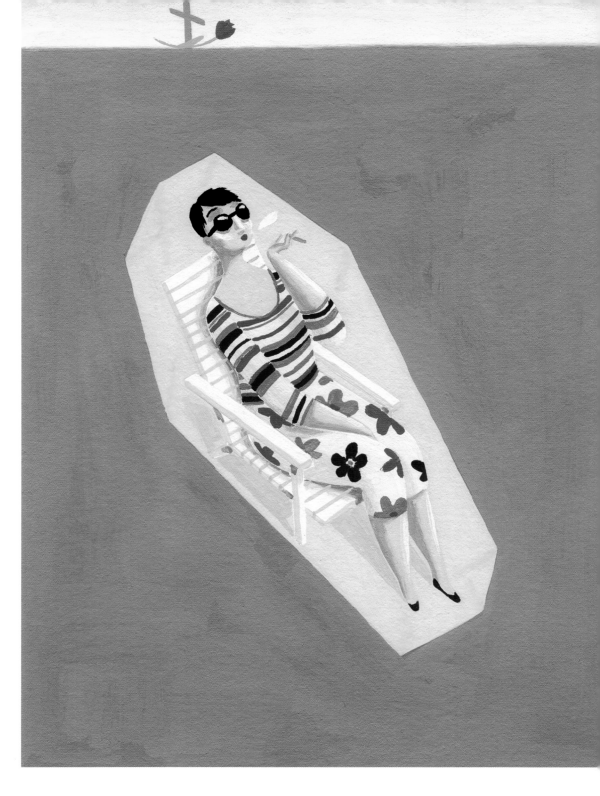

PIETER VAN EENOGE (BELGIUM)
TITLE: COUGHIN/COFFIN
BRIEF: TO ILLUSTRATE THE DEVELOPMENT OF
MEDICATION THAT MAKES US ALMOST IMMORTAL
PUBLICATION: TRENDS MAGAZINE
ART DIRECTION: TRENDS MAGAZINE
DIMENSIONS: 5 5/8 X 7 7/8 IN 143 X 200 MM
MEDIA: GOUACHE
ARTIST REPRESENTATION: EYE CANDY
ILLUSTRATION AGENCY
CONTACT: INFO@EYECANDY.CO.UK
URL: WWW.EYECANDY.CO.UK

LISA YARDLEY (UK)
TITLE: CUPPA TEA ANGEL
BRIEF: TO CREATE A PICTURE OUT OF A RANDOM PIECE
OF CUT-OUT PAPER. THIS PIECE INSPIRED A QUIRKY
CHARACTER, ABUNDANT WITH TEA
PUBLICATION: N/A
ART DIRECTION: N/A
DIMENSIONS: 9 7/8 X 9 7/8 IN 250 X 250 MM
MEDIA: MIXED MEDIA
ARTIST REPRESENTATION: N/A
CONTACT: YARDLEYLISA@YAHOO.CO.UK

RALPH (UK) *below*
TITLE: THE SINGER
BRIEF: PERSONAL PIECE
PUBLICATION: N/A
ART DIRECTION: N/A
DIMENSIONS: 5 1/8 X 5 3/4 IN 131 X 145 MM
MEDIA: PENCIL AND DIGITAL
ARTIST REPRESENTATION: JELLY LONDON
CONTACT: INFO@JELLYLONDON.COM
URL: WWW.JELLYLONDON.COM

GIANLUCA FOLÌ (ITALY) *facing page*
TITLE: ADIDAS
BRIEF: SELF-PROMOTIONAL PIECE
PUBLICATION: N/A
ART DIRECTION: N/A
DIMENSIONS: N/A
MEDIA: PENCIL, WATERCOLOR
ARTIST REPRESENTATION: ANNA GOODSON MANAGEMENT
CONTACT: ANNA@AGOODSON.COM
URL: WWW.AGOODSON.COM

JOANNA WALSH (UK) *below*
TITLE: ORLISTAT
BRIEF: EDITORIAL ILLUSTRATION DEPICTING PEOPLE IN
AN INCREASINGLY OBESE SOCIETY TAKING ANTI-OBESITY
PILLS IN PURSUIT OF A HEALTHY IDEAL
PUBLICATION: N/A
ART DIRECTION: GLAXO WELLCOME
DIMENSIONS: 9 7/8 X 10 3/8 IN 252 X 264 MM
MEDIA: DIGITAL (ADOBE ILLUSTRATOR)
ARTIST REPRESENTATION: EASTWING
CONTACT: ANDREA@EASTWING.CO.UK
URL: WWW.EASTWING.CO.UK

JUSTINE BECKETT (NEW ZEALAND) *above*
TITLE: GUILT 1
BRIEF: ILLUSTRATION TO ACCOMPANY AN ARTICLE ABOUT
GUILT ENTITLED "ARE YOU TOO HARD ON YOURSELF?"
PUBLICATION: PSYCHOLOGIES MAGAZINE
ART DIRECTION: VANESSA GRZYWACZ (ART EDITOR),
HACHETTE FILIPACCHI UK LTD
DIMENSIONS: 10 7/8 X 8 1/2 IN 275 X 215 MM
MEDIA: PEN AND INK, ADOBE PHOTOSHOP
ARTIST REPRESENTATION: FRANK STURGES REPS
CONTACT: FRANK@STURGESREPS.COM
URL: WWW.STURGESREPS.COM

KATIE WOOD (UK) *right*
TITLE: PURPLE FLOWERS
BRIEF: SELF-PROMOTIONAL PIECE
PUBLICATION: N/A
ART DIRECTION: N/A
DIMENSIONS: 11 ¼ X 11 IN 286 X 278 MM
MEDIA: DIGITAL / MIXED MEDIA
ARTIST REPRESENTATION: NEW DIVISION
CONTACT: INFO@NEWDIVISION.COM
URL: WWW.NEWDIVISION.COM

SUZANNE BARRETT (UK) *above*
TITLE: PARK SKIRT
BRIEF: PERSONAL WORK—A SKIRT WITH A PRINT
DEPICTING PEOPLE PLAYING IN THE PARK
PUBLICATION: N/A
ART DIRECTION: N/A
DIMENSIONS: 3 ⅛ X 3 ⅝ IN 80 X 92 MM
MEDIA: ACRYLIC / GOUACHE
ARTIST REPRESENTATION: N/A
CONTACT: SUZE.BARRETT@VIRGIN.NET
URL: WWW.MONSTERS.CO.UK

PIETER VAN EENOGE (BELGIUM) *facing page, bottom*

TITLE: FESTIVAL FRESH

BRIEF: SELF-PROMOTIONAL PIECE

PUBLICATION: N/A

ART DIRECTION: N/A

DIMENSIONS: 6 5/8 X 11 1/8 IN 168 X 283 MM

MEDIA: SCREEN PRINT

ARTIST REPRESENTATION: EYE CANDY
ILLUSTRATION AGENCY

CONTACT: INFO@EYECANDY.CO.UK

URL: WWW.EYECANDY.CO.UK

TRACY WALKER (CANADA) *above*

TITLE: WOMAN IN A CROWD

BRIEF: ILLUSTRATION TO ACCOMPANY MAGAZINE
ARTICLE ON HEART HEALTH, ENTITLED "WOMEN
AND HEART DISEASE"

PUBLICATION: HEART HEALTHY LIVING, SPRING 2006

ART DIRECTION: MICHELLE BILYEU, HEART HEALTHY
LIVING MAGAZINE

DIMENSIONS: 8 X 10 IN 203 X 254 MM

MEDIA: ACRYLIC

ARTIST REPRESENTATION: I2I ART, INC.

CONTACT: INFO@I2IART.COM

URL: WWW.I2IART.COM

BARBARA SPOETTEL (GERMANY) *facing page*
TITLE: BEAUTIFUL BACK
BRIEF: EDITORIAL ILLUSTRATION FOR A FEATURE ON BODY
CARE—DRAWING ON A RETRO CHIC AESTHETIC
PUBLICATION: MADAME MAGAZINE, GERMANY
ART DIRECTION: KATHRIN HORN, MADAME MAGAZINE
DIMENSIONS: 4 ½ X 6 ¼ IN 115 X 160 MM
MEDIA: DIGITAL
ARTIST REPRESENTATION: NEW DIVISION
CONTACT: INFO@NEWDIVISION.COM
URL: WWW.NEWDIVISION.COM

ADRIAN VALENCIA (UK) *left*
TITLE: "THE DEVIL IN THE JUNIOR LEAGUE"
BRIEF: A SAMPLE BOOK COVER FOR "THE DEVIL IN THE
JUNIOR LEAGUE" (SELF-PROMOTIONAL WORK)
PUBLICATION: N/A
ART DIRECTION: N/A
DIMENSIONS: 3 ¾ X 6 ⅜ IN 95 X 161 MM
MEDIA: DIGITAL
ARTIST REPRESENTATION: EASTWING
CONTACT: ANDREA@EASTWING.CO.UK
URL: WWW.EASTWING.CO.UK

PAULA MCNAMARA (UK) *below*
TITLE: GIRLS ON SOFA
BRIEF: PERSONAL WORK INSPIRED BY ARCHITECTS'
DRAWINGS AND THE FASHION AND INTERIORS OF
THE ART DECO PERIOD
PUBLICATION: N/A
ART DIRECTION: N/A
DIMENSIONS: 42 X 32 IN 1067 X 813 MM
MEDIA: PEN AND INK
ARTIST REPRESENTATION: THE ARTWORKS
CONTACT: STEPH@THEARTWORKSINC.COM
URL: WWW.THEARTWORKSINC.COM

JASON STAVROU (UK) *above*
TITLE: DROP SOME ACID
BRIEF: EDITORIAL ILLUSTRATION OF SOMEONE WITH
THE ACID REFLEX CONDITION
PUBLICATION: MEN'S HEALTH MAGAZINE
ART DIRECTION: MEN'S HEALTH MAGAZINE
DIMENSIONS: 16 ½ X 11 ⅝ IN 420 X 296 MM
MEDIA: MIXED MEDIA
ARTIST REPRESENTATION: EYE CANDY ILLUSTRATION AGENCY
CONTACT: INFO@EYECANDY.CO.UK
URL: WWW.EYECANDY.CO.UK

KARINE FAOU (FRANCE) *facing page*
TITLE: PLAY AT THE POWER STATION
BRIEF: TO CREATE VISUALS ADVERTISING THE NEW DEVELOPMENT
OF THE BATTERSEA POWER STATION, LONDON
PUBLICATION: THE POWER STATION MAGAZINE
ART DIRECTION: DEEP CREATIVE, THE POWER STATION MAGAZINE
DIMENSIONS: 9 7/8 X 13 3/4 IN 250 X 350 MM
MEDIA: DIGITAL
ARTIST REPRESENTATION: EYE CANDY ILLUSTRATION AGENCY
CONTACT: INFO@EYECANDY.CO.UK
URL: WWW.EYECANDY.CO.UK

SIEGELBAUM (FRANCE) *above*
TITLE: FASHION CROCODILE
BRIEF: EDITORIAL ILLUSTRATION
PUBLICATION: IO, DONNA
ART DIRECTION: IO, DONNA
DIMENSIONS: 6 1/8 X 8 5/8 IN 155 X 219 MM
MEDIA: DIGITAL
ARTIST REPRESENTATION: TRAFFIC NYC
CONTACT: INFO@TRAFFICNYC.COM
URL: WWW.TRAFFICNYC.COM

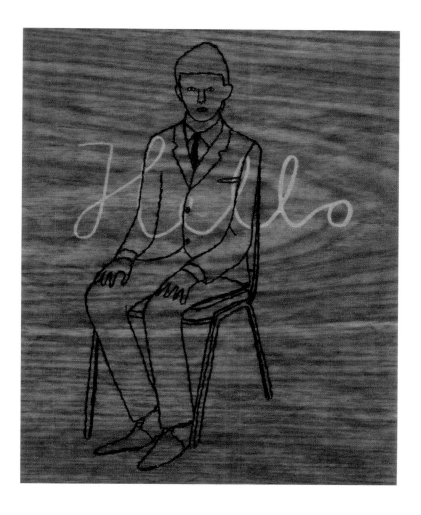

HANNA MELIN (SWEDEN) *above left*
TITLE: MAN ON CHAIR
BRIEF: SELF-PROMOTIONAL PIECE SHOWING A MAN
IMPOSED ON WOOD-LIKE FABRIC
PUBLICATION: N/A
ART DIRECTION: N/A
DIMENSIONS: 8 5/8 X 9 IN 220 X 228 MM
MEDIA: EMBROIDERY, DRAWING
ARTIST REPRESENTATION: PRIVATE VIEW, UK
CONTACT: CREATE@PVUK.COM
URL: WWW.PVUK.COM

PIETER VAN EENOGE (BELGIUM) *above right*
TITLE: HYPERVENTILATION
BRIEF: ILLUSTRATION TO ACCOMPANY AN ARTICLE ABOUT
HYPERVENTILATION
PUBLICATION: WEEKEND KNACK (MAGAZINE)
ART DIRECTION: WEEKEND KNACK (MAGAZINE)
DIMENSIONS: 7 7/8 X 11 IN 200 X 280 MM
MEDIA: COLOR PENCIL, RUBBER STAMPS
ARTIST REPRESENTATION: EYE CANDY ILLUSTRATION AGENCY
CONTACT: INFO@EYECANDY.CO.UK
URL: WWW.EYECANDY.CO.UK

NICK DEWAR (UK) *facing page*
TITLE: N/A
BRIEF: TO PORTRAY A YOUNG FOREIGN WRITER WHO
MOVED TO NEW YORK. THE PICTURE SHOWS A MAN
DIPPING HIS TOES IN US CULTURE WHILE RETAINING HIS
ROOTS IN PALESTINE
PUBLICATION: THE GUARDIAN, UK
ART DIRECTION: ROGER BROWNING, THE GUARDIAN, UK
DIMENSIONS: 9 5/8 X 10 5/8 243 X 271MM
MEDIA: ACRYLIC ON BOARD
ARTIST REPRESENTATION: KATE LARKWORTHY (USA) /
EASTWING (UK)
CONTACT: KATE@LARKWORTHY.COM /
ANDREA@EASTWING.CO.UK
URL: WWW.LARKWORTHY.COM / WWW.EASTWING.CO.UK

[PH]ILIPPE NEUMAGER (FRANCE) *left*

[TI]TLE: DIZZY LIVE AT THE SAHARAN

[BR]IEF: "LOCATED ON SANTA MONICA BOULEVARD, THE [SA]HARAN MOTOR HOTEL IS THE PERFECT PLACE TO STAY [ON] A BUDGET IN HOLLYWOOD." A CROPPED VERSION OF [TH]IS ILLUSTRATION APPEARED IN TRAX MAGAZINE

[PU]BLICATION: TRAX MAGAZINE

[AR]T DIRECTION: N/A

[DI]MENSIONS: 5 7/8 X 5 7/8 IN 150 X 150 MM

[ME]DIA: PEN AND INK, PHOTOGRAPH, DIGITAL

[AR]TIST REPRESENTATION: COSTUME 3 PIÈCES

[CO]NTACT: CONTACT@COSTUME3PIECES.COM

[UR]L: WWW.COSTUME3PIECES.COM

KIM ROSEN (USA) *above*
TITLE: THE CELEBRATION
BRIEF: SELF-PROMOTIONAL PIECE DEPICTING PEOPLE OF
DIFFERENT AGES AT A WEDDING CELEBRATION
PUBLICATION: N/A
ART DIRECTION: N/A
DIMENSIONS: 11 X 17 IN 279 X 432 MM
MEDIA: DIGITAL
ARTIST REPRESENTATION: ANNA GOODSON MANAGEMENT
CONTACT: INFO@AGOODSON.COM
URL: WWW.AGOODSON.COM

OWEN SHERWOOD (USA) *left*
TITLE: N/A
BRIEF: BUILDING CONTRACTORS TRYING TO GET PAID
PUBLICATION: BUILDING MAGAZINE
ART DIRECTION: BUILDING MAGAZINE
DIMENSIONS: 5 1/8 X 5 1/8 IN 130 X 130 MM
MEDIA: PENCIL, ADOBE PHOTOSHOP
ARTIST REPRESENTATION: NB ILLUSTRATION
CONTACT: INFO@NBILLUSTRATION.CO.UK
URL: WWW.NBILLUSTRATION.CO.UK

MARLENA ZUBER (CANADA) *below*
TITLE: GROWTH PATTERN
BRIEF: ILLUSTRATION FOR A CORPORATE MAGAZINE.
"PATTON BOGGS IS NO LONGER A SMALL FIRM, BUT IT
STILL THINKS THAT WAY. THE RESULT IS GREATER
AGILITY—AND A GROWTH PATTERN THAT FITS
CLIENTS' NEEDS"
PUBLICATION: PATTON BOGGS LLP ANNUAL REVIEW
(INTERNAL PUBLICATION)
ART DIRECTION: JAMES VAN FLETEREN, PATTON BOGGS
DIMENSIONS: 8 X 11 IN 203 X 279 MM
MEDIA: ACRYLIC INKS AND PAINT
ARTIST REPRESENTATION: MARLENA AGENCY
CONTACT: MARLENA@MARLENAAGENCY.COM
URL: WWW.MARLENAAGENCY.COM

VIDHA SAUMYA (INDIA) *facing page*
TITLE: MY MAN
BRIEF: PERSONAL WORK REPRESENTING THE ARTIST'S
OBSERVATIONS OF THE RELATIONSHIP BETWEEN MEN
AND WOMEN IN HER SOCIETY. THE PICTURE SHOWS
THE PASSIVE ROLE OF THE MAN AS HUSBAND, LOVER,
FATHER OR SON
PUBLICATION: N/A
ART DIRECTION: N/A
DIMENSIONS: 11 X 14 IN 279 X 356 MM
MEDIA: PEN AND INK, ACRYLIC PAINT, DIGITAL TEXT
AND BACKGROUND
ARTIST REPRESENTATION: N/A
CONTACT: VIDHASAUMYA@REDIFFMAIL.COM

BJORN RUNE LIE (NORWAY) *above*
TITLE: WILDER THAN ANYTHING ON WHEELS!
BRIEF: A PERSONAL PIECE SHOWING PEOPLE AND SNOWMOBILES
PUBLICATION: N/A
ART DIRECTION: N/A
DIMENSIONS: 35 ⅜ X 35 ⅜ IN 900 X 900 MM
MEDIA: ACRYLIC ON BOARD
ARTIST REPRESENTATION: EYE CANDY ILLUSTRATION AGENCY
CONTACT: INFO@EYECANDY.CO.UK
URL: WWW.EYECANDY.CO.UK

Laud you I will all the time. In your happiness lays mine.
I do not lie to myself, I really care.
Care to launder all your mess.
This is what I am born for. This is what I have vowed for.
Rest upon me all your lethargy.
Rest for one moment more.

42   **RENAUD PERRIN (FRANCE)**
TITLE: THE MASKED FARMER
BRIEF: UNPUBLISHED PERSONAL PIECE, FROM A SERIES
INSPIRED BY MASKS IN BULGARIA
PUBLICATION: N/A
ART DIRECTION: N/A
DIMENSIONS: 8 ¾ X 8 ¾ IN 221 X 221 MM
MEDIA: LINOCUT
ARTIST REPRESENTATION: COSTUME 3 PIÈCES
CONTACT: CONTACT@COSTUME3PIECES.COM
URL: WWW.COSTUME3PIECES.COM

VALERIA PETRONE (ITALY) *below*
TITLE: THE GIANT AND THE TAILOR
BRIEF: IMAGE FOR AN EXHIBITION ON THE FAIRY
TALES OF THE BROTHERS GRIMM
PUBLICATION: N/A
ART DIRECTION: N/A
DIMENSIONS: N/A
MEDIA: DIGITAL
ARTIST REPRESENTATION: MORGAN GAYNIN, INC.
CONTACT: INFO@MORGANGAYNIN.COM
URL: WWW.MORGANGAYNIN.COM

SUSAN ESTELLE KWAS (USA) *right*
TITLE: JANET IN THE SNOW
BRIEF: SELF-PROMOTIONAL PIECE, SHOWING A GIRL AND A
LITTLE BLACK CAT WALKING IN THE SNOW
PUBLICATION: N/A
ART DIRECTION: N/A
DIMENSIONS: 6 X 9 IN 152 X 229 MM
MEDIA: GOUACHE
ARTIST REPRESENTATION: MORGAN GAYNIN, INC.
CONTACT: INFO@MORGANGAYNIN.COM
URL: WWW.MORGANGAYNIN.COM

ERIC GIRIAT (FRANCE) *facing page, top*
TITLE: THE WOMEN ON THE PARIS–NY BUS
BRIEF: INVITATION CARD AND CALENDAR POSTER FOR AN
EXHIBITION ABOUT FRENCH ILLUSTRATORS IN NEW YORK
PUBLICATION: N/A
ART DIRECTION: ALAIN LACHARTRE, VUE SUR LA VILLE
DIMENSIONS: 8 ¼ X 5 ⅝ IN 210 X 142 MM
MEDIA: PAINT ON PHOTOGRAPHIC BACKGROUND
ARTIST REPRESENTATION: VIRGINIE
CONTACT: VIRGINIE@VIRGINIE.FR
URL: WWW.VIRGINIE.FR

SUSAN MCKENNA (UK) *facing page, bottom*
TITLE: BEAUTY PAGEANT
BRIEF: PERSONAL PIECE
PUBLICATION: N/A
ART DIRECTION: N/A
DIMENSIONS: 8 X 11 ½ IN 203 X 292 MM
MEDIA: GOUACHE
ARTIST REPRESENTATION: LILLA ROGERS
CONTACT: LILLA@LILLAROGERS.COM
URL: WWW.LILLAROGERS.COM

BELLA PILAR (USA) *below*
TITLE: BIRTHDAY CONE
BRIEF: DEVELOPMENTAL ILLUSTRATION FOR
A CHILDREN'S BOOK (UNPUBLISHED)
PUBLICATION: N/A
ART DIRECTION: N/A
DIMENSIONS: 8 X 11 IN 203 X 279 MM
MEDIA: GOUACHE
ARTIST REPRESENTATION: MAGNET REPS
CONTACT: ART@MAGNETREPS.COM
URL: WWW.MAGNETREPS.COM

EMILIANO PONZI (ITALY) *below*
TITLE: I HATE BUTTERFLY TATTOOS
BRIEF: A SATIRICAL LOOK AT A CURRENT TREND
PUBLICATION: RCS MAGAZINE
ART DIRECTION: OLIDIO SUDDI, RCS
DIMENSIONS: 8 X 11 IN 203 X 279 MM
MEDIA: DIGITAL
ARTIST REPRESENTATION: MAGNET REPS
CONTACT: ART@MAGNETREPS.COM
URL: WWW.MAGNETREPS.COM

Beauty Pageant......

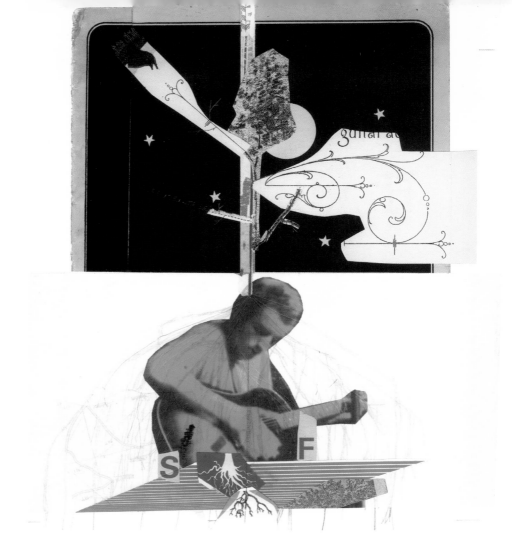

48 **ANJA KROENCKE (AUSTRIA)** *previous page*
TITLE: FLOATING SISTERS
BRIEF: EDITORIAL ILLUSTRATION
PUBLICATION: SQUINT MAGAZINE
ART DIRECTION: SQUINT MAGAZINE
DIMENSIONS: N/A
MEDIA: MIXED MEDIA
ARTIST REPRESENTATION: TRAFFIC NYC
CONTACT: INFO@TRAFFICNYC.COM
URL: WWW.TRAFFICNYC.COM

MARK LAZENBY (UK) *right*
TITLE: BEAUTIFUL TREE
BRIEF: ILLUSTRATION FOR MUSICIAN STEPHEN
FRETWELL—INSPIRED BY THE LYRICS, "A
BEAUTIFUL TREE, A BEAUTIFUL TREE, IT'S A
SHAME THE ROOT OF IT IS ME"
PUBLICATION: DAZED & CONFUSED MAGAZINE
ART DIRECTION: DAZED & CONFUSED MAGAZINE
DIMENSIONS: 7 7/8 X 9 1/2 IN 200 X 241 MM
MEDIA: GOUACHE, MIXED MEDIA
ARTIST REPRESENTATION: EYE CANDY
ILLUSTRATION AGENCY
CONTACT: INFO@EYECANDY.CO.UK
URL: WWW.EYECANDY.CO.UK

ILANA KOHN (USA) *left*
TITLE: N/A
BRIEF: SELF-PROMOTIONAL PIECE
PUBLICATION: N/A
ART DIRECTION: N/A
DIMENSIONS: 9 X 12 IN 229 X 305 MM
MEDIA: ACRYLIC, COLLAGE
ARTIST REPRESENTATION: ANNA GOODSON MANAGEMENT
CONTACT: INFO@AGOODSON.COM
URL: WWW.AGOODSON.COM

MARCO MARELLA (ITALY) *above*
TITLE: MOSCOW–GROZNY
BRIEF: BOOK COVER ART FOR A REPORTER'S TALE OF A TRIP
FROM MOSCOW TO GROZNY, CHECHNYA
PUBLICATION: "MOSCA-GROZNY," SALERNO EDITORE, ROME, ITALY
ART DIRECTION: ANDREA BAYER, ROME
DIMENSIONS: 16 ¼ X 11 ¼ IN 413 X 286 MM
MEDIA: MIXED MEDIA
ARTIST REPRESENTATION: LILLA ROGERS
CONTACT: LILLA@LILLAROGERS.COM
URL: WWW.LILLAROGERS.COM

SUSAN FARRINGTON (USA) *left*
TITLE: THE TROUBLE WITH SCIENCE
BRIEF: COVER ART FOR A BOOK ABOUT HOW THE LEFT AND RIGHT BRAIN
FUNCTION DIFFERENTLY; A MAN WEARS A HAT REPRESENTING THE TWO SIDES
OF THE BRAIN AND HOLDS A PAPER WITH SCIENTIFIC ICONOGRAPHY
PUBLICATION: "THE TROUBLE WITH SCIENCE," HARVARD UNIVERSITY PRESS
ART DIRECTION: HARVARD UNIVERSITY PRESS
DIMENSIONS: 18 X 24 IN 457 X 610 MM
MEDIA: MIXED MEDIA
ARTIST REPRESENTATION: LILLA ROGERS
CONTACT: LILLA@LILLAROGERS.COM
URL: WWW.LILLAROGERS.COM

MAYUMI FUJIMOTO (JAPAN) *facing page, top left*
TITLE: YURARI
BRIEF: UNPUBLISHED PIECE
PUBLICATION: N/A
ART DIRECTION: N/A
DIMENSIONS: 7 1/4 X 5 IN 182 X 125 MM
MEDIA: N/A
ARTIST REPRESENTATION: CWC INTERNATIONAL
CONTACT: AGENT@CWC-I.COM
URL: WWW.CWC-I.COM

OLIVIER KUGLER (GERMANY) *above*
TITLE: ORANGE
BRIEF: AN IMAGE OF A GROUP OF PEOPLE FOR AN
IN-HOUSE BOOKLET FOR THE COMPANY ORANGE
PUBLICATION: ORANGE INTERNAL PUBLICATION
ART DIRECTION: ANDI GEORGIOU, CONRAN DESIGN
DIMENSIONS: N/A
MEDIA: PEN AND INK, DIGITAL
ARTIST REPRESENTATION: THE ARTWORKS
CONTACT: STEPH@THEARTWORKSINC.COM
URL: WWW.THEARTWORKSINC.COM

LEIF PARSONS (USA) *facing page, bottom left*
TITLE: LOVE
BRIEF: MAGAZINE ILLUSTRATION
PUBLICATION: N/A
ART DIRECTION: GRAFUCK
DIMENSIONS: 11 X 3 5/8 IN 279 X 93 MM
MEDIA: N/A
ARTIST REPRESENTATION: N/A
CONTACT: LEIF@LEIFPARSONS.COM
URL: WWW.LEIFPARSONS.COM

ERIC GIRIAT (FRANCE) *left*
TITLE: FONDUE ATTITUDE
BRIEF: AN IMAGE OF THE ART OF LIVING, A TRENDY FUN
FASHION DINNER PARTY FOR A CALENDAR (JANUARY)
PUBLICATION: 2007 VUE SUR LA VILLE CALENDAR
ART DIRECTION: ALAIN LACHARTRE, VUE SUR LA VILLE
DIMENSIONS: 14 ¾ X 10 ⅝ IN 376 X 270 MM
MEDIA: N/A
ARTIST REPRESENTATION: VIRGINIE
CONTACT: VIRGINIE@VIRGINIE.FR
URL: WWW.VIRGINIE.FR

GISELLE POTTER (USA) *facing page*
TITLE: BRIDE
BRIEF: PORTRAIT OF A YOUNG BRIDE (UNPUBLISHED)
PUBLICATION: N/A
ART DIRECTION: N/A
DIMENSIONS: 11 ⅜ X 15 ½ IN 290 X 394 MM
MEDIA: GOUACHE AND COLLAGE ON PAPER
ARTIST REPRESENTATION: FRIEND AND JOHNSON
CONTACT: BJOHNSON@FRIENDANDJOHNSON.COM
URL: WWW.FRIENDANDJOHNSON.COM

MARTIN HAAKE (GERMANY) *below*
TITLE: BOAT
BRIEF: A PERSONAL PIECE
PUBLICATION: N/A
ART DIRECTION: N/A
DIMENSIONS: 23 ⅝ X 31 ½ IN 600 X 800 MM
MEDIA: MIXED MEDIA
ARTIST REPRESENTATION: LINDGREN & SMITH (USA) /
CENTRAL ILLUSTRATION AGENCY (UK)
CONTACT: INFO@LSILLUSTRATION.COM /
INFO@CENTRALILLUSTRATION.COM

SCOTT CHAMBERS (UK) *facing page*
TITLE: CANDY FLOSS
BRIEF: SELF-PROMOTIONAL PIECE FEATURING A
BOY EATING COTTON CANDY (CANDY FLOSS)
PUBLICATION: N/A
ART DIRECTION: N/A
DIMENSIONS: 8 ¼ X 11 ¾ IN 210 X 300 MM
MEDIA: MIXED MEDIA
ARTIST REPRESENTATION: SYNERGY
CONTACT: INFO@SYNERGYART.CO.UK
URL: WWW.SYNERGYART.CO.UK

CECILY LANG (USA) *above*
TITLE: SURPRISE
BRIEF: SELF-PROMOTIONAL PIECE—A GIRL WITH A BIRD
AND FLOWERS
PUBLICATION: N/A
ART DIRECTION: N/A
DIMENSIONS: 8 X 11 IN 203 X 279 MM
MEDIA: CUT PAPER WITH WATERCOLOR, INK, GOUACHE
ARTIST REPRESENTATION: N/A
CONTACT: CLANG@NYC.RR.COM
URL: WWW.CECILYLANG.COM

ALEXANDRA HIGLETT (UK) *above*
TITLE: GIRL CONTROLS HOME
BRIEF: SELF-PROMOTIONAL PICTURE OF A GIRL TOWERING
OVER HER HOME AND PLAYING WITH HER CAR
PUBLICATION: N/A
ART DIRECTION: N/A
DIMENSIONS: 11 ¼ X 17 ⅜ IN 286 X 442 MM
MEDIA: PAINTING AND COLLAGE / CUT PAPER ON ENDPAPER
ARTIST REPRESENTATION: N/A
CONTACT: ALEXHIGLETT@HOTMAIL.COM
URL: WWW.ALEXANDGEORGE.CO.UK

JESSIE FORD (UK) *facing page*
TITLE: MEDITATION WITH CHILDREN
BRIEF: BOOK COVER ART—TWO CHILDREN'S SILHOUETTES
WITH PATTERNS AND TEXTURE
PUBLICATION: "TEACHING MEDITATION TO CHILDREN",
DUNCAN BAIRD PUBLISHERS, LONDON
ART DIRECTION: ROGER WALTON, DUNCAN BAIRD PUBLISHERS
DIMENSIONS: 7 ½ X 11 ¾ IN 191 X 297 MM
MEDIA: MIXED MEDIA
ARTIST REPRESENTATION: BERNSTEIN & ANDRIULLI (USA) /
CENTRAL ILLUSTRATION AGENCY (UK)
CONTACT: LOUISA@BA-REPS.COM
URL: WWW.BA-REPS.COM / WWW.CENTRALILLUSTRATION.COM

DANIEL HASKETT (UK) *above*
TITLE: OUTKAST RECORD COVER
BRIEF: N/A
PUBLICATION: N/A
ART DIRECTION: N/A
DIMENSIONS: 5 ⅞ X 8 ½ IN 150 X 215 MM
MEDIA: DIGITAL
ARTIST REPRESENTATION: JELLY LONDON
CONTACT: INFO@JELLYLONDON.COM
URL: WWW.JELLYLONDON.COM

CHRIS KEEGAN (UK) *right*
TITLE: DARFUR
BRIEF: EDITORIAL PIECE ABOUT THE
UNDER-REPORTED WAR IN SUDAN
PUBLICATION: THE FINANCIAL TIMES
SATURDAY MAGAZINE, UK
ART DIRECTION: ANDREW LEE,
THE FINANCIAL TIMES, UK
DIMENSIONS: 4 ¾ X 7 ⅞ IN 120 X 200 MM
MEDIA: PHOTOMONTAGE, PEN AND INK
ARTIST REPRESENTATION: SYNERGY
CONTACT: INFO@SYNERGYART.CO.UK
URL: WWW.SYNERGYART.CO.UK

58

CLEMENTINE HOPE (UK) *above*
TITLE: CHEERS
BRIEF: A PIECE FOR ADVERTISING PURPOSES
ILLUSTRATING THE DIFFERENT COUNTRIES
INVOLVED IN THE COFFEE INDUSTRY
PUBLICATION: N/A
ART DIRECTION: THIRD PERSON, ALLIANCE COFFEE
DIMENSIONS: 9 ½ X 9 ½ IN 240 X 240 MM
MEDIA: PEN AND INK, ADOBE PHOTOSHOP
ARTIST REPRESENTATION: NB ILLUSTRATION
CONTACT: INFO@NBILLUSTRATION.CO.UK
URL: WWW.NBILLUSTRATION.CO.UK

GUSTAF VON ARBIN (SWEDEN) *center*
TITLE: THE BAND
BRIEF: DOCUMENTATION OF A TOUR OF THE SWEDISH
BAND, "SHOUT OUT LOUDS"—SHOWN HERE ON STAGE IN
AUSTIN, TEXAS
PUBLICATION: N/A
ART DIRECTION: N/A
DIMENSIONS: 11 X 15 ⅜ IN 280 X 390 MM
MEDIA: INK ON PINK CONSTRUCTION PAPER
ARTIST REPRESENTATION: ART DEPARTMENT
CONTACT: STEPHANIEP@ART-DEPT.COM
URL: WWW.ART-DEPT.COM

I DO BELIEVE THAT WE HAVE

MICHAEL FISH

IL PLEUT SUX

ADAM GRAFF (UK) *above*
TITLE: LOOKS LIKE RAIN
BRIEF: A SAMPLE OF AN ONGOING, TRANSATLANTIC VISUAL
CORRESPONDENCE HIGHLIGHTING THE POSITIVE ASPECTS
OF LIVING IN LONDON AND NEW YORK. A SELF-INITIATED
AUTHORIAL PROJECT
PUBLICATION: N/A
ART DIRECTION: N/A
DIMENSIONS: 8 1/4 X 11 7/8 IN 210 X 297 MM
MEDIA: PEN AND INK, MIXED MEDIA, DIGITAL
ARTIST REPRESENTATION: EYE CANDY ILLUSTRATION AGENCY
CONTACT: INFO@EYECANDY.CO.UK
URL: WWW.EYECANDY.CO.UK

JOAQUIN GONZALES (SPAIN) *above*
TITLE: AUTUMN
BRIEF: A PERSONAL PIECE SHOWING A YOUNG WOMAN IN
NEW YORK ON A WINDY AUTUMN DAY
PUBLICATION: N/A
ART DIRECTION: N/A
DIMENSIONS: 8 1/8 X 11 1/4 IN 205 X 286 MM
MEDIA: DIGITAL
ARTIST REPRESENTATION: NEW DIVISION
CONTACT: INFO@NEWDIVISION.COM
URL: WWW.NEWDIVISION.COM

LAURE FOURNIER (FRANCE) *above*
TITLE: WAKING PRAYER 02
BRIEF: ILLUSTRATION FOR A PRAYER BOOK FOR
CHILDREN—AN ENGLISH PRAYER FOR THE WAKING
PUBLICATION: "MY FIRST PRAYER BOOK"
ART DIRECTION: FRANCES LINCOLN, UK
DIMENSIONS: 9 1/2 X 9 1/2 IN 240 X 240 MM
MEDIA: ACRYLIC ON PAPER
ARTIST REPRESENTATION: THE ORGANISATION
CONTACT: INFO@ORGANISART.CO.UK
URL: WWW.ORGANISART.CO.UK

GEZ FRY (JAPAN) *facing page*
TITLE: POPLIN
BRIEF: AN IMAGE FOR AN ADVERTISEMENT
OF FIRETRAP FASHION
PUBLICATION: N/A
ART DIRECTION: N/A
DIMENSIONS: N/A
MEDIA: DIGITAL
ARTIST REPRESENTATION: FOLIO
CONTACT: ALL@FOLIOART.CO.UK
URL: WWW.FOLIOART.CO.UK

JOHN JAY CABUAY (USA) *above left*
TITLE: N/A
BRIEF: SELF-PROMOTIONAL PIECE
PUBLICATION: N/A
ART DIRECTION: N/A
DIMENSIONS: 11 X 14 IN 279 X 356 MM
MEDIA: GREASE PENCIL, ADOBE PHOTOSHOP
ARTIST REPRESENTATION: SHANNON ASSOCIATES
CONTACT: INFORMATION@SHANNONASSOCIATES.COM
URL: WWW.SHANNONASSOCIATES.COM

REINHARD SCHLEINING (AUSTRIA) *center*
TITLE: CROSSING SHADOWS
BRIEF: ONE OF SIX IMAGES FOR A MAGAZINE FASHION SPREAD. THE SERIES WAS
INFLUENCED BY THE 1970S AND TITLED, "ZABRISKIE POINT SHOREDITCH" IN
HOMAGE TO ANTONIONI'S CULT MOVIE.
PUBLICATION: 125 MAGAZINE, THE DECADES ISSUE, 2005
ART DIRECTION: MARTIN YATES, 125 MAGAZINE
DIMENSIONS: N/A
MEDIA: PENCIL ON PAPER, INK ON TRACING PAPER, ADOBE PHOTOSHOP (COLOR)
ARTIST REPRESENTATION: SYNERGY
CONTACT: INFO@SYNERGYART.CO.UK
URL: WWW.SYNERGYART.CO.UK

MARIA CARDELLI (ITALY) *above right*
TITLE: WEDDING DRESS
BRIEF: PERSONAL PORTFOLIO PIECE
PUBLICATION: N/A
ART DIRECTION: N/A
DIMENSIONS: 7 3/4 X 11 5/8 IN 198 X 295 MM
MEDIA: TRADITIONAL, COLLAGE AND DIGITAL
ARTIST REPRESENTATION: WANDA NOWAK
CREATIVE ILLUSTRATORS' AGENCY
CONTACT: WANDA@WANDANOW.COM
URL: WWW.WANDANOW.COM

JOHN JAY CABUAY (USA) *facing page*
TITLE: N/A
BRIEF: SELF-PROMOTIONAL PIECE
PUBLICATION: N/A
ART DIRECTION: N/A
DIMENSIONS: 11 X 14 IN 279 X 356 MM
MEDIA: GREASE PENCIL, ADOBE PHOTOSHOP
ARTIST REPRESENTATION: SHANNON ASSOCIATES
CONTACT: INFORMATION@SHANNONASSOCIATES.COM
URL: WWW.SHANNONASSOCIATES.COM

MARIA CARDELLI (ITALY) *right*
TITLE: THE RED HAT
BRIEF: PERSONAL PORTFOLIO PIECE
PUBLICATION: N/A
ART DIRECTION: N/A
DIMENSIONS: 8 ½ X 13 IN 216 X 330 MM
MEDIA: DIGITAL
ARTIST REPRESENTATION: WANDA NOWAK
CREATIVE ILLUSTRATORS' AGENCY
CONTACT: WANDA@WANDANOW.COM
URL: WWW.WANDANOW.COM

JASON BROOKS (UK) *below*
TITLE: PERSONAL
BRIEF: N/A
PUBLICATION: N/A
ART DIRECTION: N/A
DIMENSIONS: N/A
MEDIA: DIGITAL
ARTIST REPRESENTATION: FOLIO ART
CONTACT: ALL@FOLIOART.CO.UK
URL: WWW.FOLIOART.CO.UK

MATT CROFT (UK) *below*
TITLE: BALLET
BRIEF: SELF-INITIATED DRAWING
PUBLICATION: N/A
ART DIRECTION: N/A
DIMENSIONS: 6 X 8 5/8 IN 151 X 220 MM
MEDIA: COLLAGE, PHOTOSHOP, LINE DRAWING
ARTIST REPRESENTATION: N/A
CONTACT: MATT@ILLUSTRATIONZOO.CO.UK
URL: WWW.ILLUSTRATIONZOO.CO.UK

PAUL BOMMER (UK) *below*
TITLE: BORED IN CLASS
BRIEF: EDITORIAL ILLUSTRATION TO ACCOMPANY AN EDUCATIONAL
ARTICLE ABOUT THE POINTLESSNESS OF DISCUSSING LESSON
OBJECTIVES WITH PUPILS
PUBLICATION: THE GUARDIAN, EDUCATION SUPPLEMENT, UK
ART DIRECTION: JOHN-HENRY BARAC, THE GUARDIAN, UK
DIMENSIONS: 6 3/4 X 11 1/4 IN 172 X 286 MM
MEDIA: MIXED MEDIA, DIGITAL (ADOBE PHOTOSHOP)
ARTIST REPRESENTATION: N/A
CONTACT: PAUL@PAULBOMMER.COM
URL: WWW.PAULBOMMER.COM

GÉRARD DUBOIS (FRANCE) *facing page*
TITLE: THE BEST PICKS
BRIEF: AN IMAGE USED AS AN OPENER FOR AN ARTICLE LISTING
THE BEST PICKS OF THE YEAR IN THE FINANCIAL BUSINESS
PUBLICATION: PLANSPONSOR MAGAZINE
ART DIRECTION: SOOJIN BUZELLI, ASSET INTERNATIONAL
DIMENSIONS: 9 1/2 X 12 1/2 IN 240 X 316 MM
MEDIA: ACRYLIC ON PAPER
ARTIST REPRESENTATION: MARLENA AGENCY (N.AMERICA) /
COSTUME 3 PIÈCES (EUROPE)
CONTACT: MARLENA@MARLENAAGENCY.COM /
CONTACT@COSTUME3PIECES.COM
URL: WWW.MARLENAAGENCY.COM / WWW.COSTUME3PIECES.COM

ADRIAN D'ALIMONTE (CANADA) *above*

TITLE: JOYRIDE

BRIEF: PROMOTIONAL POSTCARD IMAGE FOR SUNGLASS HUT

PUBLICATION: N/A

ART DIRECTION: STELLA NILSEN, HAGGIN MARKETING

DIMENSIONS: N/A

MEDIA: VECTOR / DIGITAL

ARTIST REPRESENTATION: N/A

CONTACT: MAIL@ADRIANDD.COM

URL: WWW.ADRIANDD.COM

SCOTT KENNEDY (NEW ZEALAND) *left*
TITLE: HAPPY TEETH
BRIEF: DENTIST'S ID, SHOWING KIDS WITH "HAPPY TEETH"
PUBLICATION: N/A
ART DIRECTION: KATHERINE HABERSHON
DIMENSIONS: 8 1/4 X 11 3/8 IN 210 X 290 MM
MEDIA: DIGITAL
ARTIST REPRESENTATION: THREE EYES LTD
CONTACT: THREEEYES@PARADISE.NET.NZ
URL: WWW.THREEEYES.CO.NZ

PAUL BOMMER (UK) *right*
TITLE: TRAIN ROBBER
BRIEF: TO ILLUSTRATE AN ARTICLE ABOUT THE SANCTITY AND MERIT OF
PLAY IN CLASSROOMS. THE ARTIST CHOSE AN ANECDOTE ABOUT A BURGLAR
WHO BROKE INTO A SCHOOL AT NIGHT, APPARENTLY TO PLAY WITH THE TOYS
PUBLICATION: THE TIMES EDUCATIONAL SUPPLEMENT (TES), UK
ART DIRECTION: LAWRENCE BOGLE, TIMES EDUCATIONAL SUPPLEMENT
DIMENSIONS: 7 7/8 X 10 1/4 IN 199 X 260 MM
MEDIA: MIXED MEDIA, DIGITAL (ADOBE PHOTOSHOP)
ARTIST REPRESENTATION: N/A
CONTACT: PAUL@PAULBOMMER.COM
URL: WWW.PAULBOMMER.COM

JONATHAN CROFT (UK) *above left*
TITLE: FIGHT NIGHT
BRIEF: SELF-PROMOTIONAL PIECE
PUBLICATION: N/A
ART DIRECTION: N/A
DIMENSIONS: 8 X 11 ¼ IN 202 X 286 MM
MEDIA: MIXED MEDIA, DIGITAL
ARTIST REPRESENTATION: N/A
CONTACT: JONATHAN.CROFT@BTINTERNET.COM
URL: WWW.JONATHANCROFT.COM

SCOTT CHAMBERS (UK) *above right*
TITLE: BIONIC BRIAN
BRIEF: SELF-PROMOTIONAL ILLUSTRATION
PUBLICATION: N/A
ART DIRECTION: N/A
DIMENSIONS: 7 ⅞ X 7 ⅞ IN 200 X 200 MM
MEDIA: MIXED MEDIA
ARTIST REPRESENTATION: SYNERGY
CONTACT: INFO@SYNERGYART.CO.UK
URL: WWW.SYNERGYART.CO.UK

OLAF HAJEK (GERMANY) *facing page*
TITLE: PLAYGROUND
BRIEF: PERSONAL PIECE FOR THE "ILLUSTRATIVE 2008" EXHIBITION
PUBLICATION: N/A
ART DIRECTION: N/A
DIMENSIONS: N/A
MEDIA: ACRYLIC ON BOARD
ARTIST REPRESENTATION: BERNSTEIN & ANDRIULLI
CONTACT: LOUISA@BA-REPS.COM
URL: WWW.BA-REPS.COM

INGI ERLINGSSON (UK)
TITLE: PEOPLE
BRIEF: PERSONAL WORK
PUBLICATION: N/A
ART DIRECTION: N/A
DIMENSIONS: 10 ⅞ X 9 ⅝ IN 275 X 243 MM
MEDIA: DIGITAL
ARTIST REPRESENTATION: JELLY LONDON
CONTACT: INFO@JELLYLONDON.COM
URL: WWW.JELLYLONDON.COM

STÉPHANE GAMAIN (FRANCE) *facing page*
TITLE: LONDON
BRIEF: MAGAZINE PIECE, A PORTRAIT OF FRENCH
PEOPLE LIVING IN LONDON
PUBLICATION: SENSO MAGAZINE
ART DIRECTION: SENSO MAGAZINE
DIMENSIONS: 11 X 16 ⅝ IN 280 X 423 MM
MEDIA: TRADITIONAL AND DIGITAL
ARTIST REPRESENTATION: NB ILLUSTRATION
CONTACT: INFO@NBILLUSTRATION.CO.UK
URL: WWW.NBILLUSTRATION.CO.UK

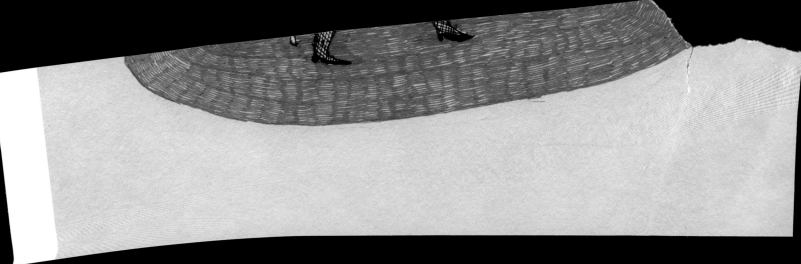

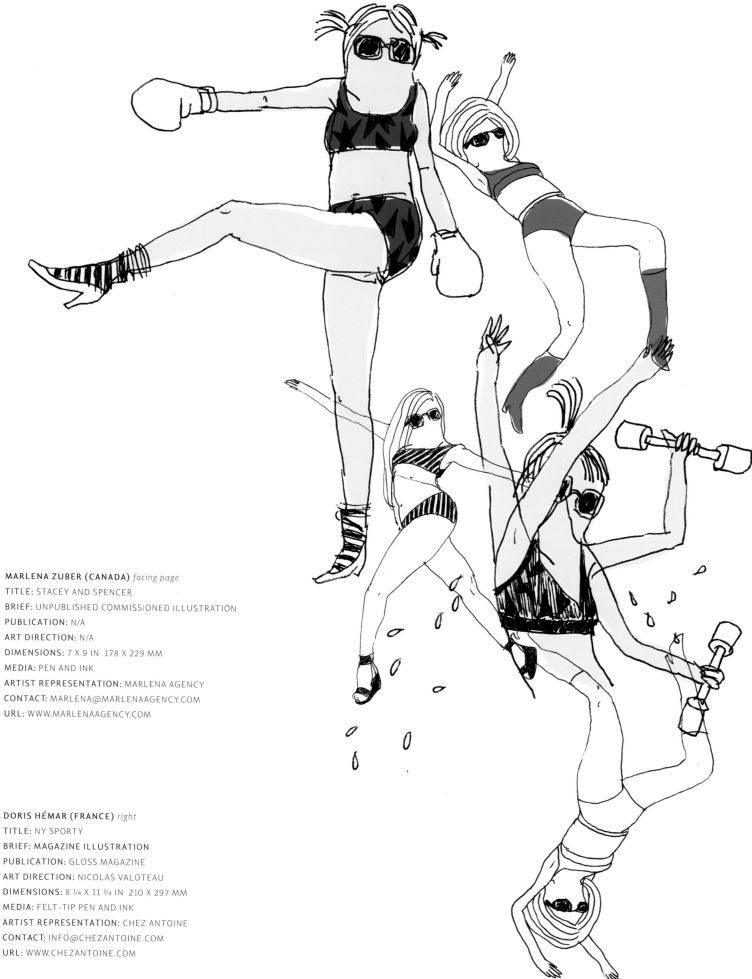

MARLENA ZUBER (CANADA) *facing page*
TITLE: STACEY AND SPENCER
BRIEF: UNPUBLISHED COMMISSIONED ILLUSTRATION
PUBLICATION: N/A
ART DIRECTION: N/A
DIMENSIONS: 7 X 9 IN 178 X 229 MM
MEDIA: PEN AND INK
ARTIST REPRESENTATION: MARLENA AGENCY
CONTACT: MARLENA@MARLENAAGENCY.COM
URL: WWW.MARLENAAGENCY.COM

DORIS HÉMAR (FRANCE) *right*
TITLE: NY SPORTY
BRIEF: MAGAZINE ILLUSTRATION
PUBLICATION: GLOSS MAGAZINE
ART DIRECTION: NICOLAS VALOTEAU
DIMENSIONS: 8 ¼ X 11 ¾ IN 210 X 297 MM
MEDIA: FELT-TIP PEN AND INK
ARTIST REPRESENTATION: CHEZ ANTOINE
CONTACT: INFO@CHEZANTOINE.COM
URL: WWW.CHEZANTOINE.COM

docteur... j'ai un problème

CARINE ABRAHAM (FRANCE)
TITLE: ALLO DOCTEUR!
BRIEF: MAGAZINE ILLUSTRATION FOR AN ARTICLE ENTITLED
"PRETTY UNREAL: THE COMEBACK OF COLLAGES"
PUBLICATION: FORM MAGAZINE
ART DIRECTION: FORM MAGAZINE
DIMENSIONS: 11 ¾ X 18 ⅛ IN 300 X 460 MM
MEDIA: COLLAGE
ARTIST REPRESENTATION: ABRAKA DESIGN / TRAFFIC NYC (US)
CONTACT: CARINE.ABRAHAM@FREE.FR / INFO@TRAFFICNYC.COM
URL: WWW.ABRAKA.COM / WWW.TRAFFICNYC.COM

portraits

LET ME INTRODUCE the French kid who's calling the doctor, the poet types, some superheroes, Mozart (you speak German, don't you?), Alfred E. Neuman, Woody Allen, the girl who seems to have forgotten to put her top on, the man whose head is made out of a wooden handle, Russell Brand, Bob Dylan, the big lonely guy (I think he might soon pick a fight), the woman who is very beautiful and sad, Dr. Who, Albert Einstein, Flora with the flowers in her hair, Andy Warhol, Twiggy, Philip Seymour Hoffman as Truman Capote, that guy whose nose is being pecked by a pink budgie ... I could go on ...

KIM ROSEN (USA) *above*
TITLE: A RIVER RUNS THROUGH HER
BRIEF: NEWSPAPER ILLUSTRATION FOR A BOOK REVIEW
OF LORNA GOODINSON'S FAMILY MEMOIR OF HER
ROOTS IN JAMAICA
PUBLICATION: THE GLOBE AND MAIL
ART DIRECTION: DEVIN SLATER, THE GLOBE AND MAIL
DIMENSIONS: 10 ½ X 10 ½ IN 267 X 267 MM
MEDIA: DIGITAL
ARTIST REPRESENTATION: ANNA GOODSON MANAGEMENT
CONTACT: INFO@AGOODSON.COM
URL: WWW.AGOODSON.COM

BRIAN GRIMWOOD (UK) *below*
TITLE: MOZART
BRIEF: PORTRAIT FOR THE BOOK COVER
OF "COFFEE WITH MOZART"
PUBLICATION: "COFFEE WITH MOZART,"
DUNCAN BAIRD PUBLISHERS
ART DIRECTION: ROGER WALTON,
DUNCAN BAIRD PUBLISHERS
DIMENSIONS: N/A
MEDIA: MIXED MEDIA
ARTIST REPRESENTATION: CENTRAL
ILLUSTRATION AGENCY (CIA)
CONTACT: INFO@CENTRALILLUSTRATION.COM
URL: WWW.CENTRALILLUSTRATION.COM

REBECCA BRADLEY (UK) *above*
TITLE: FACES
BRIEF: UNPUBLISHED PERSONAL PIECE
PUBLICATION: N/A
ART DIRECTION: N/A
DIMENSIONS: 5 3/4 X 7 3/8 IN 145 X 188 MM
MEDIA: PEN AND INK
ARTIST REPRESENTATION: LILLA ROGERS / EYE CANDY
ILLUSTRATION AGENCY
CONTACT: LILLA@LILLAROGERS.COM /
INFO@EYECANDY.CO.UK
URL: WWW.LILLAROGERS.COM / WWW.EYECANDY.CO.UK

BEN HASLER (UK) *facing page*
TITLE: SUPERHEROES
BRIEF: UNPUBLISHED WORK
PUBLICATION: N/A
ART DIRECTION: N/A
DIMENSIONS: 11 X 10 ⅜ IN 280 X 263 MM
MEDIA: ADOBE ILLUSTRATOR
ARTIST REPRESENTATION: NB ILLUSTRATION
CONTACT: INFO@NBILLUSTRATION.CO.UK
URL: WWW.NBILLUSTRATION.CO.UK

REILLY (UK) *below*
TITLE: GET OFF THE FLOOR
BRIEF: ART FOR AN INSTALLATION PROMOTING A NEW
KIM JONES MENSWEAR COLLECTION LAUNCH AT THE
VOID, TOPMAN STORE, LONDON
PUBLICATION: N/A
ART DIRECTION: N/A
DIMENSIONS: N/A
MEDIA: DIGITAL PRINT ON PVC
ARTIST REPRESENTATION: ART DEPARTMENT
CONTACT: STEPHANIEP@ART-DEPT.COM
URL: WWW.ART-DEPT.COM

MARIA RAYMONDSDOTTER (SWEDEN) *above*
TITLE: RALPH AND WILLIAM
BRIEF: SELF-PROMOTIONAL PIECE
PUBLICATION: N/A
ART DIRECTION: N/A
DIMENSIONS: N/A
MEDIA: PEN AND INK, DIGITAL
ARTIST REPRESENTATION: CENTRAL ILLUSTRATION AGENCY (CIA)
CONTACT: INFO@CENTRALILLUSTRATION.COM
URL: WWW.CENTRALILLUSTRATION.COM

AMELIE HEGARDT (SWEDEN) *above*
TITLE: BRONZE
BRIEF: EDITORIAL ILLUSTRATION SHOWING A TREND
FOR BRONZE EYESHADOW
PUBLICATION: GLAMOUR MAGAZINE, SWEDEN,
DECEMBER 2006
ART DIRECTION: GLAMOUR MAGAZINE, SWEDEN
DIMENSIONS: 7 5/8 X 11 5/8 IN 195 X 295 MM
MEDIA: INK AND PASTEL
ARTIST REPRESENTATION: TRAFFIC NYC
CONTACT: INFO@TRAFFICNYC.COM
URL: WWW.TRAFFICNYC.COM

J. DAVID MCKENNEY (USA) *left*
TITLE: BINDING IN BLUE
BRIEF: SELF-PROMOTIONAL ILLUSTRATION
PUBLICATION: N/A
ART DIRECTION: N/A
DIMENSIONS: 11 X 17 IN 279 X 432 MM
MEDIA: MARKERS, ADOBE PHOTOSHOP
ARTIST REPRESENTATION: ARTS COUNSEL, INC.
CONTACT: INFO@ARTSCOUNSELINC.COM
URL: WWW.ARTSCOUNSELINC.COM

ANJA KROENCKE (AUSTRIA) *below*
TITLE: POPPY GIRL
BRIEF: EDITORIAL ILLUSTRATION
PUBLICATION: SQUINT MAGAZINE
ART DIRECTION: SQUINT MAGAZINE
DIMENSIONS: N/A
MEDIA: N/A
ARTIST REPRESENTATION: TRAFFIC NYC
CONTACT: INFO@TRAFFICNYC.COM
URL: WWW.TRAFFICNYC.COM

SARAH BEETSON (UK) *above*
TITLE: KAYA
BRIEF: PORTRAIT OF A CHILD LYING ON A RUG IN A COTTON
TOP, COMMISSIONED BY ITALIAN CLOTHING COMPANY
TEZENIS, FOR USE ON BAGS AND IN-STORE PACKAGING
PUBLICATION: N/A
ART DIRECTION: TEZENIS INTIMO
DIMENSIONS: 17 ¾ X 14 ⅝ IN 450 X 370 MM
MEDIA: MIXED MEDIA ON PAPER
ARTIST REPRESENTATION: I2I ART (USA & CANADA) /
ILLUSTRATION WEB (EUROPE)
CONTACT: INFO@I2IART.COM /
TEAM@ILLUSTRATIONWEB.COM
URL: WWW.I2IART.COM / WWW.ILLUSTRATIONWEB.COM

DANIEL F. BIRCH (USA) *facing page, top*
TITLE: ALFRED E. NEUMAN
BRIEF: PORTRAIT OF ALFRED E. NEUMAN IN FRONT OF
ASYLUM MEDICAL RECORDS LOG (SELF-PROMOTIONAL PIECE)
PUBLICATION: N/A
ART DIRECTION: N/A
DIMENSIONS: 8 ½ X 11 IN 216 X 280 MM
MEDIA: MIXED MEDIA, COLLAGE
ARTIST REPRESENTATION: N/A
CONTACT: DFBIRCH@GMAIL.COM
URL: WWW.DFBIRCH.COM

WALSHWORKS (UK) *below left*
TITLE: EDGAR ALLAN POE
BRIEF: SELF-PROMOTIONAL PORTRAIT
PUBLICATION: N/A
ART DIRECTION: N/A
DIMENSIONS: 7 ½ X 8 ⅛ IN 191 X 205 MM
MEDIA: COLLAGE, ADOBE PHOTOSHOP
ARTIST REPRESENTATION: EASTWING
CONTACT: ANDREA@EASTWING.CO.UK
URL: WWW.EASTWING.CO.UK

RUSS TUDOR (UK) *below center*
TITLE: WOODY
BRIEF: CARICATURE OF WOODY ALLEN
(SELF-PROMOTIONAL PIECE)
PUBLICATION: N/A
ART DIRECTION: N/A
DIMENSIONS: N/A
MEDIA: GOUACHE, INK
ARTIST REPRESENTATION: N/A
CONTACT: CARTOONS@RUSSTUDOR.WANADOO.CO.UK

A. SKWISH (USA) *below right*
TITLE: TED LEO
BRIEF: MAGAZINE ILLUSTRATION OF TED LEO
(PLAYING GUITAR AND BREATHING FIRE) TO
ACCOMPANY AN INTERVIEW WITH THE MUSICIAN
PUBLICATION: N/A
ART DIRECTION: GREG PEREZ
DIMENSIONS: 7 X 13 ¾ IN 178 X 350 MM
MEDIA: ADOBE PHOTOSHOP
ARTIST REPRESENTATION: N/A
CONTACT: ILLUSTRATION@SKWISH.COM
URL: WWW.SKWISH.COM

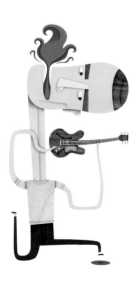

DAVID HUMPHRIES (UK) *above*
TITLE: QUANTUM READING
BRIEF: "QUANTUM READING (...) TAKES TWO TO FIVE
DAYS TO ACHIEVE EXTRAORDINARY FEATS OF SPEED AND
COMPREHENSION—UP TO TEN NON-FICTION BOOKS A DAY."
PUBLICATION: HOW TO SPEND IT, FINANCIAL TIMES MAGAZINE
ART DIRECTION: GRAHAM BLACK, THE FINANCIAL TIMES, UK
DIMENSIONS: 8 1/8 X 8 IN 206 X 203 MM
MEDIA: DIGITAL
ARTIST REPRESENTATION: MONSTERS
CONTACT: DAVID@MONSTERS.CO.UK
URL: WWW.MONSTERS.CO.UK

RINA DONNERSMARCK (GERMANY) *above*
TITLE: LOUISE
BRIEF: PERSONAL WORK
PUBLICATION: N/A
ART DIRECTION: N/A
DIMENSIONS: 5 ⅜ X 8 IN 137 X 203 MM
MEDIA: PEN AND INK
ARTIST REPRESENTATION: N/A
CONTACT: RINAHD@ANOTHER.COM
URL: WWW.RINADONNERSMARCK.CO.UK

ESTHER WATSON (USA) *above*
TITLE: THE DAY THE CHICKENS DIED
BRIEF: PAINTING FOR A GALLERY SHOW
PUBLICATION: N/A
ART DIRECTION: N/A
DIMENSIONS: 24 X 30 IN 610 X 762 MM
MEDIA: ACRYLIC ON PANEL
ARTIST REPRESENTATION: N/A
CONTACT: FUNCHICKEN@EARTHLINK.NET
URL: WWW.ESTHERWATSON.COM

AMELIE HEGARDT (SWEDEN)
TITLE: CAROLINA HERRERA
BRIEF: NEW YORK FASHION WEEK BEAUTY TRENDS FOR MAC
PUBLICATION: N/A
ART DIRECTION: MAC COSMETICS
DIMENSIONS: 16 1/4 X 11 1/4 IN 412 X 286 MM
MEDIA: INK AND WATERCOLOR ON PAPER
ARTIST REPRESENTATION: TRAFFIC NYC
CONTACT: INFO@TRAFFICNYC.COM
URL: WWW.TRAFFICNYC.COM

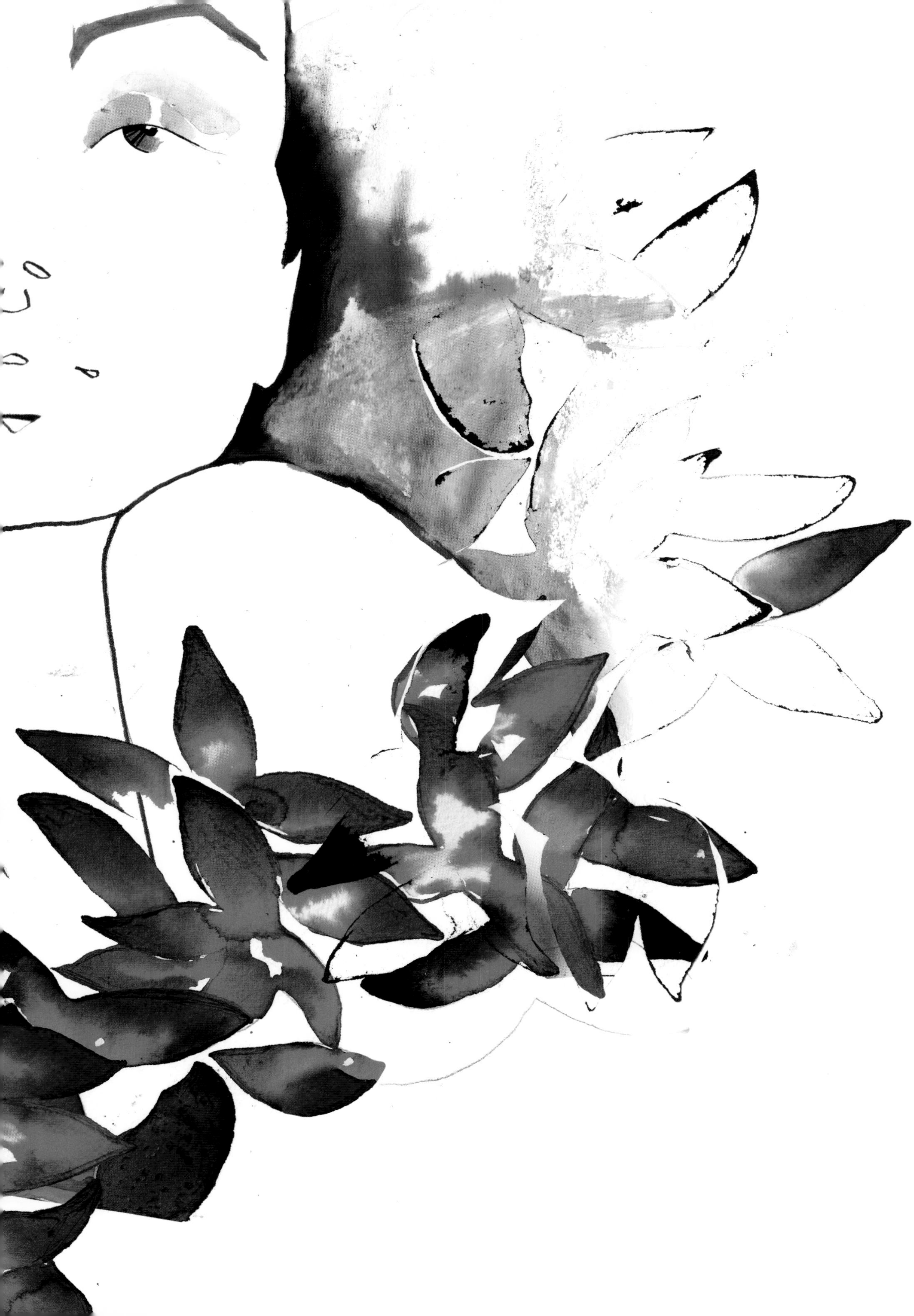

KERASCOËT (FRANCE)
TITLE: N/A
BRIEF: PERSONAL PIECE
PUBLICATION: N/A
ART DIRECTION: N/A
DIMENSIONS: N/A
MEDIA: N/A
ARTIST REPRESENTATION: COSTUME 3 PIÈCES
CONTACT: CONTACT@COSTUME3PIECES.COM
URL: WWW.COSTUME3PIECES.COM

OLIVIER GOKA (FRANCE) *facing page, top*
TITLE: THE FRENCH BUTCHER
BRIEF: PERSONAL PIECE MADE BY REASSEMBLING PLASTIC
OBJECTS INTO FIGURATIVE ENTITIES AND PLACING THEM
IN A NEW ENVIRONMENT
PUBLICATION: N/A
ART DIRECTION: N/A
DIMENSIONS: N/A
MEDIA: FOUND OBJECTS, PLASTIC
ARTIST REPRESENTATION: COSTUME 3 PIÈCES
CONTACT: CONTACT@COSTUME3PIECES.COM
URL: WWW.COSTUME3PIECES.COM

MIKE LAUGHEAD (USA) *below*
TITLE: HELLBOY JUMPING
BRIEF: SELF-PROMOTIONAL PORTRAIT
PUBLICATION: N/A
ART DIRECTION: N/A
DIMENSIONS: 9 ¼ X 9 ¼ IN 235 X 235 MM
MEDIA: DIGITAL
ARTIST REPRESENTATION: SHANNON ASSOCIATES
CONTACT: INFORMATION@SHANNONASSOCIATES.COM
URL: WWW.SHANNONASSOCIATES.COM

TOM GENOWER (UK) *facing page, top*
TITLE: JOHN PEEL
BRIEF: EDITORIAL ILLUSTRATION: A PORTRAIT OF DJ JOHN
PEEL PAINTED ON THE BACK OF AN LP COVER
PUBLICATION: LOOSE LIPS SINK SHIPS MAGAZINE
ART DIRECTION: LOOSE LIPS SINK SHIPS MAGAZINE
DIMENSIONS: N/A
MEDIA: ACRYLIC AND INK
ARTIST REPRESENTATION: MONSTERS
CONTACT: TOMGENOWER@YAHOO.CO.UK
URL: WWW.TOMMYGENOWER.COM / WWW.MONSTERS.CO.UK

DANIEL HASKETT (UK) *above*
TITLE: HOWARD MOON—JAZZ MAVERICK
BRIEF: ILLUSTRATION BASED ON THE EFFECTS THAT
HURRICANE KATRINA HAD ON NEW ORLEANS
(SELF-PROMOTIONAL PIECE)
PUBLICATION: N/A
ART DIRECTION: N/A
DIMENSIONS: 12 5/8 X 7 IN 320 X 179 MM
MEDIA: MIXED MEDIA
ARTIST REPRESENTATION: N/A
CONTACT: DANIELHASKETT@GMAIL.COM
URL: WWW.DANHASKETT.CO.UK

VICKY WOODGATE (UK) *facing page, bottom*
TITLE: ATOMIC SWING
BRIEF: 2006 PROMOTIONAL IMAGE FOR THE SWEDISH
POP GROUP "ATOMIC SWING," USED ON WEBSITE, TOUR
MATERIALS, ETC.
PUBLICATION: N/A
ART DIRECTION: N/A
DIMENSIONS: 10 1/4 X 5 1/8 IN 260 X 130 MM
MEDIA: DIGITAL (VECTOR)
ARTIST REPRESENTATION: N/A
CONTACT: VICKYWOODGATE@MAC.COM
URL: WWW.VICKYWOODGATE.COM

94

BONNIE DAIN (USA) *above*
TITLE: GIRLS IN COLOR
BRIEF: A SERIES MADE FOR STARBUCKS COFFEE AND I-POD
PUBLICATION: N/A
ART DIRECTION: GEORGE GARCIA, STARBUCKS COFFEE
DIMENSIONS: N/A
MEDIA: INK, PAINT
ARTIST REPRESENTATION: LILLA ROGERS
CONTACT: LILLA@LILLAROGERS.COM
URL: WWW.LILLAROGERS.COM

GUSTAF VON ARBIN (SWEDEN) *above*
TITLE: MOMENTS
BRIEF: SKETCHBOOK IMAGES, DOCUMENTING A TOUR
WITH THE SWEDISH BAND, "SHOUT OUT LOUDS"
PUBLICATION: N/A
ART DIRECTION: N/A
DIMENSIONS: 11 ¼ X 15 ½ IN 286 X 395 MM
MEDIA: INK, PENCIL, WHITE-OUT, VARIOUS PAPER
ARTIST REPRESENTATION: ART DEPARTMENT
CONTACT: STEPHANIEP@ART-DEPT.COM
URL: WWW.ART-DEPT.COM

IZAK ZENOU (USA) *facing page*
TITLE: SUNGLASSES
BRIEF: ADVERTISEMENT
PUBLICATION: HENRI BENDEL ADVERTISEMENT
ART DIRECTION: N/A
DIMENSIONS: N/A
MEDIA: INDIA INK, WATERCOLOR
ARTIST REPRESENTATION: TRAFFIC NYC (USA) /
VIRGINIE (EUROPE) / TAIKO AND ASSOCIATES (JAPAN)
CONTACT: INFO@TRAFFICNYC.COM /
VIRGINIE@VIRGINIE.FR / TAIKO@UA-NET.COM
URL: WWW.TRAFFICNYC.COM / WWW.VIRGINIE.FR /
WWW.UA-NET/TAIKO

124

NELLY DIMITRANOVA (UK) *left*
TITLE: RUSSELL BRAND
BRIEF: UNPUBLISHED LINE DRAWING OF THE BRITISH
COMEDIAN RUSSELL BRAND
PUBLICATION: N/A
ART DIRECTION: N/A
DIMENSIONS: 7 ½ X 11 ⅝ IN 191 X 295 MM
MEDIA: PEN AND INK ON PAPER
ARTIST REPRESENTATION: EASTWING
CONTACT: ANDREA@EASTWING.CO.UK
URL: WWW.EASTWING.CO.UK

KEVIN MCBRIDE (CANADA) *right*
TITLE: ANDY
BRIEF: UNPUBLISHED PORTRAIT OF THE CHARACTER ANDY
FROM THE TV SERIES "LITTLE BRITAIN"
PUBLICATION: N/A
ART DIRECTION: N/A
DIMENSIONS: 8 X 7 IN 203 X 178 MM
MEDIA: INK AND WATERCOLOR ON ILLUSTRATION BOARD
ARTIST REPRESENTATION: N/A
CONTACT: KMCBRIDE@SYMPATICO.CA
URL: WWW.KEVMCBRIDE.COM

JOY GOSNEY (UK) *left*
TITLE: BOB DYLAN
BRIEF: UNPUBLISHED PIECE ILLUSTRATING BOB DYLAN
IN CONVERSATION
PUBLICATION: N/A
ART DIRECTION: ROGER WALTON, DUNCAN BAIRD PUBLISHERS
DIMENSIONS: 5 7/8 X 5 7/8 IN 150 X 150 MM
MEDIA: HAND DRAWING, DIGITAL
ARTIST REPRESENTATION: EYE CANDY
ILLUSTRATION AGENCY
CONTACT: INFO@EYECANDY.CO.UK
URL: WWW.EYECANDY.CO.UK

RICK TULKA (FRANCE) *right*
TITLE: OSAMA BIN LADEN
BRIEF: SELF-PROMOTIONAL CARICATURE
PUBLICATION: N/A
ART DIRECTION: N/A
DIMENSIONS: 8 3/4 X 11 3/4 IN 222 X 299 MM
MEDIA: WATERCOLOR
ARTIST REPRESENTATION: MORGAN GAYNIN, INC.
CONTACT: INFO@MORGANGAYNIN.COM
URL: WWW.MORGANGAYNIN.COM

AMELIE HEGARDT (SWEDEN) *left*
TITLE: BOHÈME
BRIEF: UNPUBLISHED PIECE
PUBLICATION: N/A
ART DIRECTION: N/A
DIMENSIONS: 11 X 13 5/8 IN 280 X 345 MM
MEDIA: INK AND PASTEL ON PAPER
ARTIST REPRESENTATION: TRAFFIC NYC
CONTACT: INFO@TRAFFICNYC.COM
URL: WWW.TRAFFICNYC.COM

ESTHER WATSON (USA) *above*
TITLE: DRINKER
BRIEF: EDITORIAL ILLUSTRATION FOR A STORY ABOUT
A HEAVY DRINKER
PUBLICATION: THE NEW YORK TIMES MAGAZINE
ART DIRECTION: THE NEW YORK TIMES MAGAZINE
DIMENSIONS: N/A
MEDIA: DIGITAL
ARTIST REPRESENTATION: N/A
CONTACT: FUNCHICKEN@EARTHLINK.NET
URL: WWW.ESTHERWATSON.COM

REBECCA BRADLEY (UK) *left*
TITLE: CHECK SHIRT
BRIEF: UNPUBLISHED PIECE
PUBLICATION: N/A
ART DIRECTION: N/A
DIMENSIONS: 3 5/8 X 4 7/8 IN 91 X 124 MM
MEDIA: PEN AND INK, COLLAGE
ARTIST REPRESENTATION: LILLA ROGERS /
EYE CANDY ILLUSTRATION AGENCY
CONTACT: LILLA@LILLAROGERS.COM /
INFO@EYECANDY.CO.UK
URL: WWW.LILLAROGERS.COM /
WWW.EYECANDY.CO.UK

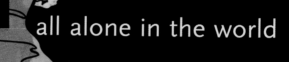

all alone in the world • mother told me i am all alone in t
the world • mother told me i am all alone in the world • m
other told me i am all alone in the world • mother told me
i am all alone in the world • mother told me i am all alone
lone in the world • mother told me i am all alone in the wo
told me i am all alone in the world • mother told me i am
all alone in the world • mother told me i am all alone in the
me i am all alone in the world • mother told me i am all al
world • mother told me i am all alone in the world • moth

all alone in the world

a.bihari 2

AARON BIHARI (CANADA)
TITLE: EDDIE (ALL ALONE IN THE WORLD)
BRIEF: SELF-PROMOTIONAL PIECE DEPICTING LONELINESS
AND A DESTROYED SENSE OF SELF-WORTH. A POT-BELLIED
MAN WALKS AGAINST A BACKGROUND OF HIS THOUGHTS
PUBLICATION: N/A
ART DIRECTION: N/A
DIMENSIONS: 14 5/8 X 11 IN 373 X 279 MM
MEDIA: DIGITAL
ARTIST REPRESENTATION: I2I ART
CONTACT: INFO@I2IART.COM
URL: WWW.I2IART.COM

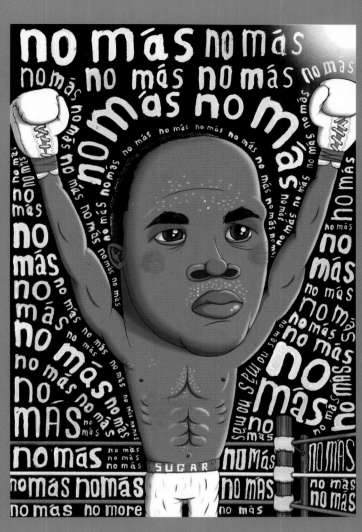

JULIA BRECKENREID (CANADA)
TITLE: BILLIE HOLIDAY
BRIEF: PERSONAL WORK
PUBLICATION: N/A
ART DIRECTION: N/A
DIMENSIONS: 8 X 11 IN 203 X 279 MM
MEDIA: GOUACHE
ARTIST REPRESENTATION: MAGNET REPS
CONTACT: ART@MAGNETREPS.COM
URL: WWW.MAGNETREPS.COM

ANDY WARD (UK)
TITLE: SUGAR RAY LEONARD
BRIEF: PORTRAIT OF SUGAR RAY LEONARD CLAIMING
VICTORY IN THE INFAMOUS "NO MÁS" FIGHT AGAINST
ROBERTO DURAN
PUBLICATION: THE OBSERVER SPORTS MONTHLY
MAGAZINE, UK
ART DIRECTION: NICK GREENSLADE, THE OBSERVER
SPORTS MONTHLY MAGAZINE, UK
DIMENSIONS: N/A
MEDIA: MIXED MEDIA, DIGITAL
ARTIST REPRESENTATION: NB ILLUSTRATION
CONTACT: INFO@NBILLUSTRATION.CO.UK
URL: WWW.NBILLUSTRATION.CO.UK

AGNES DECOURCHELLE (FRANCE) *above*
TITLE: N/A
BRIEF: MAGAZINE PORTRAIT OF THE
MAGAZINE'S CONTRIBUTORS
PUBLICATION: WALLPAPER* MAGAZINE, UK
ART DIRECTION: TONY CHAMBERS, WALLPAPER* MAGAZINE
DIMENSIONS: 11 7/8 X 8 5/8 IN 300 X 220 MM
MEDIA: MIXED MEDIA
ARTIST REPRESENTATION: EYE CANDY ILLUSTRATION AGENCY
CONTACT: INFO@EYECANDY.CO.UK
URL: WWW.EYECANDY.CO.UK

RACHEL GOSLIN (UK) *facing page*
TITLE: TOM BAKER
BRIEF: MAGAZINE ILLUSTRATION FOR A FEATURE
ON THE CAREER OF THE ACTOR TOM BAKER
PUBLICATION: THE GUARDIAN, UK
ART DIRECTION: SARAH HABERSHON, THE GUARDIAN, UK
DIMENSIONS: 6 X 7 1/4 IN 153 X 183 MM
MEDIA: MIXED MEDIA
ARTIST REPRESENTATION: EYE CANDY ILLUSTRATION AGENCY
CONTACT: INFO@EYECANDY.CO.UK
URL: WWW.EYECANDY.CO.UK

MIKAEL KANGAS (SWEDEN) *facing page*
TITLE: KRISTINA LUGN
BRIEF: THE FAMOUS SWEDISH POET, KRISTINA LUGN,
PORTRAYED AS A STRONG AND BEAUTIFUL WOMAN
PUBLICATION: BON MAGAZINE, NO.35
ART DIRECTION: CHRISTOPHER WESSEL, BON MAGAZINE
DIMENSIONS: 8 7/8 X 11 3/8 IN 225 X 290 MM
MEDIA: MIXED MEDIA
ARTIST REPRESENTATION: SYNERGY
CONTACT: INFO@SYNERGYART.CO.UK
URL: WWW.SYNERGYART.CO.UK

JIM LAURENCE (UK) *right*
TITLE: GENERAL PATTERN
BRIEF: SELF-PROMOTIONAL ILLUSTRATION REPRESENTING
"GENERAL PATTERN" IN THE IMAGE OF GENERAL PATTON
PUBLICATION: N/A
ART DIRECTION: N/A
DIMENSIONS: N/A
MEDIA: DRAWING, DIGITAL
ARTIST REPRESENTATION: NEW DIVISION
CONTACT: INFO@NEWDIVISION.COM
URL: WWW.NEWDIVISION.COM

GREG STEVENSON (CANADA) *left*
TITLE: EINSTEIN
BRIEF: SELF-PROMOTIONAL PORTRAIT OF ALBERT EINSTEIN
PUBLICATION: N/A
ART DIRECTION: N/A
DIMENSIONS: 12 X 12 IN 305 X 305 MM
MEDIA: TRADITIONAL, DIGITAL
ARTIST REPRESENTATION: I2I ART
CONTACT: INFO@I2IART.COM
URL: WWW.I2IART.COM

CHRIS RUBINO (USA) *right*
TITLE: QUESTLOVE
BRIEF: A PORTRAIT SKETCH OF "THE ROOTS" DRUMMER, QUESTLOVE
PUBLICATION: FUTURE MUSIC MAGAZINE
ART DIRECTION: TURTLE BURKYBILE, FUTURE MUSIC MAGAZINE
DIMENSIONS: 8 X 10 IN 203 X 254 MM
MEDIA: PEN AND INK, DIGITAL COLOR
ARTIST REPRESENTATION: ART DEPARTMENT
CONTACT: STEPHANIEP@ART-DEPT.COM
URL: WWW.ART-DEPT.COM

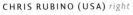

GISELLE POTTER (USA) *above*
TITLE: FLORA
BRIEF: PORTRAIT OF A WOMAN'S FACE WITH FLOWERS
PUBLICATION: N/A
ART DIRECTION: N/A
DIMENSIONS: 11 ¾ X 14 ¼ IN 297 X 363 MM
MEDIA: GOUACHE AND COLLAGE ON PAPER
ARTIST REPRESENTATION: FRIEND AND JOHNSON
CONTACT: BJOHNSON@FRIENDANDJOHNSON.COM
URL: WWW.FRIENDANDJOHNSON.COM

SARAJO FRIEDEN (USA) *facing page*
TITLE: BATHING BEAUTY
BRIEF: SELF-PROMOTIONAL PORTRAIT OF A SWIMMER
PUBLICATION: N/A
ART DIRECTION: N/A
DIMENSIONS: N/A
MEDIA: GOUACHE ON PAPER
ARTIST REPRESENTATION: LILLA ROGERS
CONTACT: LILLA@LILLAROGERS.COM
URL: WWW.LILLAROGERS.COM

JITESH PATEL (UK) *right*
TITLE: UNDISCOVERED
BRIEF: AN ILLUSTRATION FOR A RANGE OF BEAUTY PRODUCTS, BEAUTIFUL
CREATIONS THAT ARE HIDDEN IN A LOST WORLD WAITING TO BE DISCOVERED
PUBLICATION: N/A
ART DIRECTION: SUPERDRUG
DIMENSIONS: N/A
MEDIA: DIGITAL (ADOBE ILLUSTRATOR 10 VECTOR GRAPHIC)
ARTIST REPRESENTATION: CENTRAL ILLUSTRATION AGENCY (CIA)
CONTACT: INFO@CENTRALILLUSTRATION.COM
URL: WWW.CENTRALILLUSTRATION.COM

ALEXANDRA COMPAIN-TISSIER (FRANCE) *right*
TITLE: FANTASTIC ARMADA
BRIEF: FASHION ILLUSTRATION, PORTRAIT OF A DANCER
FROM THE FANTASTIC ARMADA
PUBLICATION: MAX MAGAZINE, FRANCE, 2005
ART DIRECTION: WILLIAM SNIEG, MAX MAGAZINE
DIMENSIONS: 8 ¼ X 11 ¼ IN 210 X 285 MM
MEDIA: WATERCOLOR ON PAPER
ARTIST REPRESENTATION: ART DEPARTMENT
CONTACT: STEPHANIEP@ART-DEPT.COM
URL: WWW.ART-DEPT.COM

PAULA SANZ CABALLERO (SPAIN) *below left*
TITLE: KENZO ELEGANCE
BRIEF: MAGAZINE ILLUSTRATION
PUBLICATION: ELEGANCE MAGAZINE, THE NETHERLANDS, 2007
ART DIRECTION: ELEGANCE MAGAZINE
DIMENSIONS: N/A
MEDIA: PENCIL, WATERCOLOR, FABRIC
ARTIST REPRESENTATION: TRAFFIC NYC
CONTACT: INFO@TRAFFICNYC.COM
URL: WWW.TRAFFICNYC.COM

LOUISE WALLACE (UK) *center*
TITLE: STANDING GIRL
BRIEF: A CANVAS SHOWING CONTEMPORARY INTERIORS CREATED FOR
A LARGE FURNITURE STORE IN MANCHESTER, UK
PUBLICATION: N/A
ART DIRECTION: HEALS AND SON, LTD.
DIMENSIONS: 25 ⅝ X 25 ⅝ IN 650 X 650 MM
MEDIA: DIGITAL, PRINTED ONTO CANVAS
ARTIST REPRESENTATION: THE INKSHED
CONTACT: ABBY@INKSHED.CO.UK
URL: WWW.INKSHED.CO.UK

AIMEE LEVY (USA) *above right*
TITLE: N/A
BRIEF: SELF-PROMOTIONAL PIECE
PUBLICATION: N/A
ART DIRECTION: N/A
DIMENSIONS: 8 ½ X 13 IN 216 X 330 MM
MEDIA: ACRYLIC ON PAPER
ARTIST REPRESENTATION: ART DEPARTMENT
CONTACT: STEPHANIEP@ART-DEPT.COM
URL: WWW.ART-DEPT.COM

TA-
RA-N-T-
U-L-A

MARTINA WITTE (GERMANY) *left*
TITLE: CHAN MARSHALL
BRIEF: ILLUSTRATION BASED ON AN ARTICLE ABOUT THE LEAD SINGER OF "CAT POWER"—ALLUDING TO THE SINGER'S LYRICS AND INTERVIEW, WHERE SHE IS "THE HOST OF ORGANIC IDEAS"
PUBLICATION: SWINGSET MAGAZINE
ART DIRECTION: STEVE LOWENTHAL, SWINGSET MAGAZINE
DIMENSIONS: 12 X 17 IN 305 X 432 MM
MEDIA: MIXED MEDIA
ARTIST REPRESENTATION: N/A
CONTACT: MARTINA.WITTE@GMAIL.COM

STEVEN TABBUTT (USA) *below*
TITLE: BJÖRK
BRIEF: SELF-PROMOTIONAL ILLUSTRATION OF THE SINGER BJÖRK IN AN ICONIC POSE
PUBLICATION: N/A
ART DIRECTION: N/A
DIMENSIONS: 7 X 10 IN 178 X 254 MM
MEDIA: PASTEL, GESSO, AND INK ON RAW CANVAS. DIGITALLY COLORED BACKGROUND
ARTIST REPRESENTATION: MORGAN GAYNIN, INC.
CONTACT: INFO@MORGANGAYNIN.COM
URL: WWW.MORGANGAYNIN.COM

GREG STEVENSON (CANADA) *facing page*
TITLE: BOB DYLAN TARANTULA
BRIEF: A PORTRAIT OF A YOUNG BOB DYLAN CIRCA 1966, AROUND THE TIME OF THE PUBLICATION OF HIS BOOK OF POETRY, "TARANTULA"
PUBLICATION: N/A
ART DIRECTION: N/A
DIMENSIONS: 8 ¾ X 12 ⅜ IN 222 X 313 MM
MEDIA: DIGITAL AND TRADITIONAL
ARTIST REPRESENTATION: I2I ART
CONTACT: INFO@I2IART.COM
URL: WWW.I2IART.COM

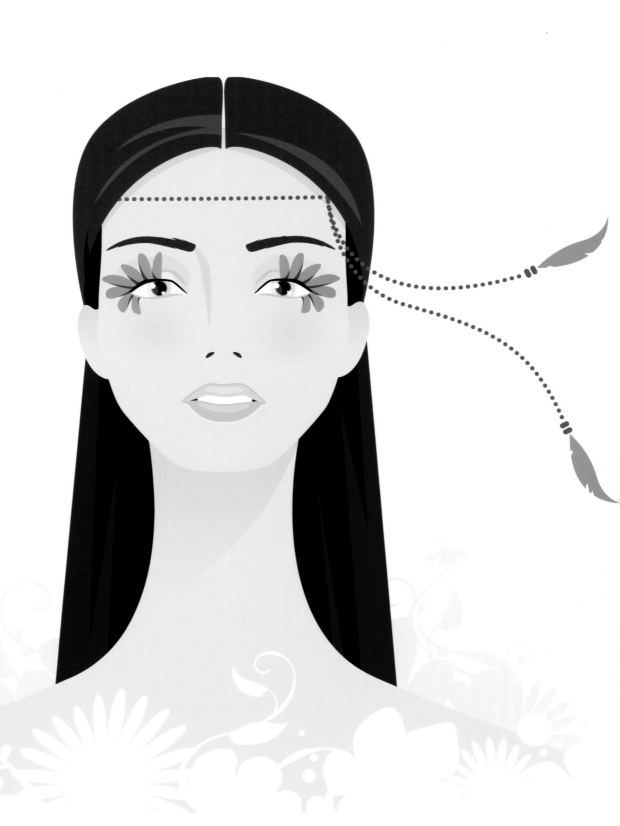

MAYUMI FUJIMOTO (JAPAN) *left*
TITLE: SUNSHINE PLAYS WITH LEAVES
BRIEF: PERSONAL WORK
PUBLICATION: N/A
ART DIRECTION: N/A
DIMENSIONS: 7 ¾ X 8 ⅞ IN 197 X 226 MM
MEDIA: N/A
ARTIST REPRESENTATION: CWC INTERNATIONAL
CONTACT: AGENT@CWC-I.COM
URL: WWW.CWC-I.COM

ROBERT CLYDE ANDERSON (USA) *left*
TITLE: JOSEPH
BRIEF: PORTRAIT USED FOR SELF-PROMOTIONAL MAILER
ENTITLED "GOOD-BYE SUMMER"
PUBLICATION: N/A
ART DIRECTION: N/A
DIMENSIONS: N/A
MEDIA: 3-COLOR OFFSET PRINTING FROM LINE ART
AND CUT OVERLAYS
ARTIST REPRESENTATION: ART DEPARTMENT
CONTACT: STEPHANIEP@ART-DEPT.COM
URL: WWW.ART-DEPT.COM

MONIKA ROE (USA) *facing page*
TITLE: FLOWER CHILD
BRIEF: TO ILLUSTRATE THE CONCEPT OF CLEAN, FRESH,
NATURAL BEAUTY
PUBLICATION: N/A
ART DIRECTION: N/A
DIMENSIONS: 8 ¼ X 8 ½ IN 208 X 216 MM
MEDIA: ADOBE ILLUSTRATOR
ARTIST REPRESENTATION: SHANNON ASSOCIATES
CONTACT: INFORMATION@SHANNONASSOCIATES.COM
URL: WWW.SHANNONASSOCIATES.COM

MARGUERITE SAUVAGE (FRANCE)
TITLE: TANGUY UKULELE ORCHESTRA
BRIEF: CD COVER ART FOR A YOUNG POP MUSICIAN
WHO MIXES UKULELE WITH VIDEO GAME TUNES
PUBLICATION: N/A
ART DIRECTION: N/A
DIMENSIONS: 9 ½ X 4 ¾ IN 240 X 120 MM
MEDIA: PENCIL ON PAPER, ADOBE PHOTOSHOP
ARTIST REPRESENTATION: N/A
CONTACT: MARGUERITESAUVAGE@GMAIL.COM
URL: WWW.MARGUERITESAUVAGE.COM

KALANI LEE (USA) *right*
TITLE: PSYCHEDELIC SKATERS
BRIEF: T-SHIRT ILLUSTRATION FOR INTERNATIONAL FASHION DESIGNER
PUBLICATION: N/A
ART DIRECTION: THOMAS MILLER, ANNA SUI
DIMENSIONS: 7 X 7 IN 178 X 178 MM
MEDIA: ADOBE PHOTOSHOP
ARTIST REPRESENTATION: KATE LARKWORTHY
CONTACT: KATE@LARKWORTHY.COM
URL: WWW.LARKWORTHY.COM

STANLEY CHOW (UK) *right*

TITLE: TWIGGY

BRIEF: SELF-PROMOTIONAL PIECE, PORTAIT OF THE 1960'S ICON

PUBLICATION: N/A

ART DIRECTION: N/A

DIMENSIONS: 11 ¼ X 8 IN 286 X 202 MM

MEDIA: ADOBE ILLUSTRATOR

ARTIST REPRESENTATION: CENTRAL ILLUSTRATION AGENCY (CIA)

CONTACT: INFO@CENTRALILLUSTRATION.COM

URL: WWW.CENTRALILLUSTRATION.COM

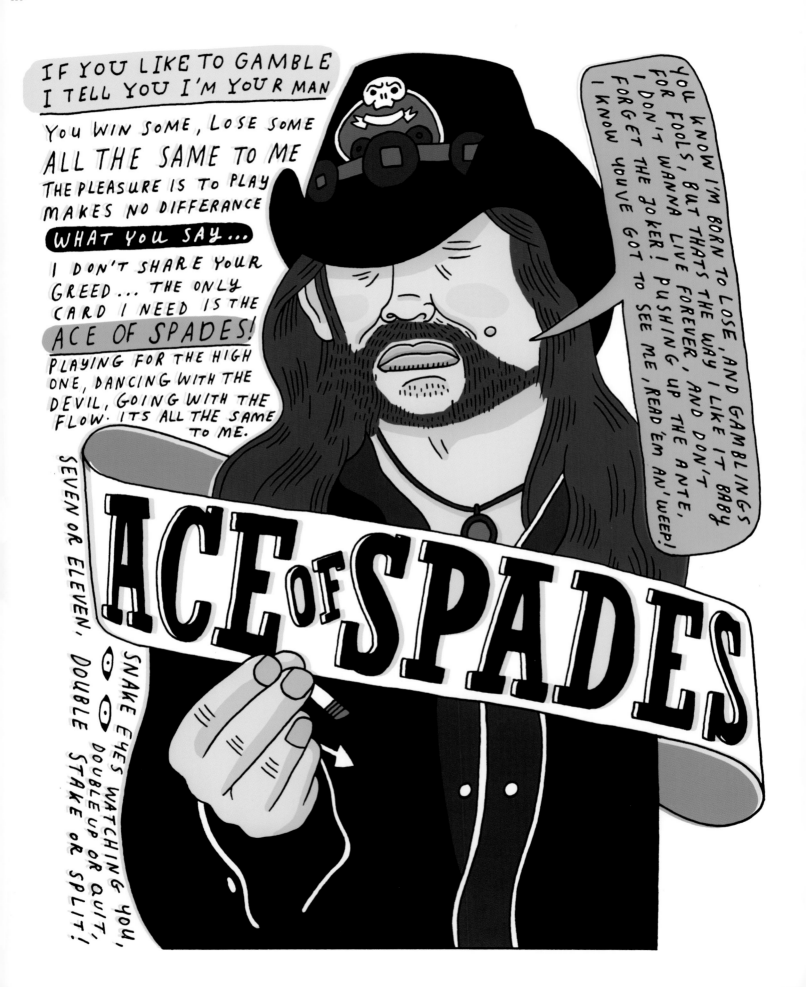

DAN TAYLOR (UK) *left*
TITLE: IAN BROWN, "THE STONE ROSES"
BRIEF: UNPUBLISHED PIECE
PUBLICATION: N/A
ART DIRECTION: N/A
DIMENSIONS: 4 ¾ X 4 ¾ IN 120 X 120 MM
MEDIA: MIXED ACRYLIC, SPRAY PAINT, COLLAGE
ARTIST REPRESENTATION: NB ILLUSTRATION
CONTACT: INFO@NBILLUSTRATION.CO.UK
URL: WWW.NBILLUSTRATION.CO.UK

ROMAN KLONEK (POLAND) *right*
TITLE: JUNGLE GIRL
BRIEF: SELF-PROMOTIONAL WORK
PUBLICATION: N/A
ART DIRECTION: N/A
DIMENSIONS: 19 ¼ X 27 ⅛ IN 490 X 690 MM
MEDIA: WOODCUT PRINT
ARTIST REPRESENTATION: FRANK STURGES REPS
CONTACT: FRANK@STURGESREPS.COM
URL: WWW.STURGESREPS.COM

SERGE SEIDLITZ (UK/GERMANY) *facing page*
TITLE: THE ACE OF SPADES
BRIEF: A PORTRAIT OF LENNY FROM "MOTORHEAD,"
TO ACCOMPANY AN ARTICLE ABOUT THE SINGER
PUBLICATION: FUSED MAGAZINE
ART DIRECTION: FUSED MAGAZINE
DIMENSIONS: N/A
MEDIA: PEN AND INK, DIGITAL
ARTIST REPRESENTATION: DÉBUT ART
CONTACT: INFO@DEBUTART.COM
URL: WWW.DEBUTART.COM

CASSANDRE MONTORIOL (FRANCE) *above*
TITLE: "LE TONE EN INDE"
BRIEF: N/A
PUBLICATION: N/A
ART DIRECTION: N/A
DIMENSIONS: 4 ¾ X 4 ¾ IN 120 X 120 MM
MEDIA: N/A
ARTIST REPRESENTATION: ART DEPARTMENT
CONTACT: STEPHANIEP@ART-DEPT.COM
URL: WWW.ART-DEPT.COM

BONNIE DAIN (USA) *left*
TITLE: PINK WOMAN
BRIEF: PERSONAL PROJECT
PUBLICATION: N/A
ART DIRECTION: N/A
DIMENSIONS: N/A
MEDIA: INK AND PAINT
ARTIST REPRESENTATION: LILLA ROGERS
CONTACT: LILLA@LILLAROGERS.COM
URL: WWW.LILLAROGERS.COM

TRACY WALKER (CANADA) *facing page*
TITLE: MEDITATION
BRIEF: ILLUSTRATION FOR AN ARTICLE ABOUT MEDITATION AS MEDICINE,
DEPICTING THE BENEFITS OF THIS PRACTICE IN THE HEALING PROCESS
PUBLICATION: YOGA JOURNAL, MARCH 2007
ART DIRECTION: RON ESCOBAR, YOGA JOURNAL MAGAZINE
DIMENSIONS: 8 X 10 IN 203 X 254 MM
MEDIA: ACRYLIC
ARTIST REPRESENTATION: I2I ART
CONTACT: INFO@I2IART.COM
URL: WWW.I2IART.COM

TIM TOMKINSON (USA)
TITLE: TERRY RICHARDSON
BRIEF: PERSONAL PIECE
PUBLICATION: N/A
ART DIRECTION: N/A
DIMENSIONS: 10 X 6 ¼ IN 254 X 159 MM
MEDIA: PENCIL, GOUACHE, AND COLLAGE ON PAPER
ARTIST REPRESENTATION: FRIEND AND JOHNSON
CONTACT: SFRIEND@FRIENDANDJOHNSON.COM
URL: WWW.FRIENDANDJOHNSON.COM

MARGARET LEE (CANADA)
TITLE: WARHOL
BRIEF: SELF-PROMOTIONAL PORTRAIT OF ANDY WARHOL
PUBLICATION: N/A
ART DIRECTION: N/A
DIMENSIONS: 8 X 10 IN 203 X254 MM
MEDIA: PENCIL, PAINT, AND DIGITAL
ARTIST REPRESENTATION: I2I ART
CONTACT: INFO@I2IART.COM
URL: WWW.I2IART.COM

JASON STAVROU (UK)
TITLE: BRUCE WILLIS
BRIEF: EDITORIAL PORTRAIT
PUBLICATION: TIMES EYE MAGAZINE
ART DIRECTION: TIMES EYE MAGAZINE
DIMENSIONS: 8 ¼ X 11 ⅝ IN 210 X 296 MM
MEDIA: MIXED MEDIA, DIGITAL
ARTIST REPRESENTATION: EYE CANDY ILLUSTRATION AGENCY
CONTACT: INFO@EYECANDY.CO.UK
URL: WWW.EYECANDY.CO.UK

BO LUNDBERG (SWEDEN)
TITLE: AGENT DOUBLE
BRIEF: GREETING CARD FOR THE ARTIST'S JAPANESE AGENCY
PUBLICATION: N/A
ART DIRECTION: MAI YOSHINO, AGENT DOUBLE
DIMENSIONS: 4 X 5 7/8 IN 100 X 148 MM
MEDIA: ADOBE ILLUSTRATOR
ARTIST REPRESENTATION: ART DEPARTMENT
CONTACT: STEPHANIEP@ART-DEPT.COM
URL: WWW.ART-DEPT.COM

REILLY (UK)
TITLE: TOKYO 1
BRIEF: EXHIBITION PIECE, PART OF A COLLECTION
OF LIMITED EDITION WORKS FOR A ONE-MAN SHOW
AT THE EXPOSURE GALLERY, LONDON
PUBLICATION: N/A
ART DIRECTION: N/A
DIMENSIONS: N/A
MEDIA: DIGITAL
ARTIST REPRESENTATION: ART DEPARTMENT
CONTACT: STEPHANIEP@ART-DEPT.COM
URL: WWW.ART-DEPT.COM

DAVID NAVASCUES (SPAIN)
TITLE: SOUTH BRONX 1
BRIEF: UNPUBLISHED PIECE
PUBLICATION: N/A
ART DIRECTION: N/A
DIMENSIONS: 5 7/8 X 8 1/4 IN 148 X 210 MM
MEDIA: MIXED MEDIA
ARTIST REPRESENTATION: KATE LARKWORTHY
CONTACT: KATE@LARKWORTHY.COM
URL: WWW.LARKWORTHY.COM

DANIEL HASKETT (UK) *facing page, left*
TITLE: CAPOTE
BRIEF: SELF-PROMOTIONAL ILLUSTRATION
OF TRUMAN CAPOTE
PUBLICATION: N/A
ART DIRECTION: N/A
DIMENSIONS: 9 7/8 X 5 5/8 IN 250 X 144 MM
MEDIA: MIXED MEDIA
ARTIST REPRESENTATION: N/A
CONTACT: DANIELHASKETT@GMAIL.COM
URL: WWW.DANIELHASKETT.CO.UK

ADAM OSGOOD (USA) *facing page, below left*
TITLE: KT TUNSTALL
BRIEF: UNPUBLISHED ILLUSTRATION FOR
A PROMOTIONAL POSTER
PUBLICATION: N/A
ART DIRECTION: N/A
DIMENSIONS: 16 X 12 IN 407 X 305 MM
MEDIA: PENCIL, ADOBE PHOTOSHOP
ARTIST REPRESENTATION: N/A
CONTACT: ADAMOSGOOD@GMAIL.COM
URL: WWW.ADAMOSGOOD.COM

LUKE WILSON (UK) *above*
TITLE: DAN TOBIN SMITH
BRIEF: EDITORIAL ILLUSTRATION OF PHOTOGRAPHER
DAN TOBIN SMITH FOR THE CONTRIBUTORS PAGE
PUBLICATION: WALLPAPER* MAGAZINE
ART DIRECTION: DOMINIC BELL, WALLPAPER* MAGAZINE
DIMENSIONS: 2 X 4 IN 50 X 100 MM
MEDIA: MIXED MEDIA
ARTIST REPRESENTATION: SYNERGY
CONTACT: INFO@SYNERGYART.CO.UK
URL: WWW.SYNERGYART.CO.UK

SHAWN BARBER (USA) *left*
TITLE: LOUIS JORDAN
BRIEF: EDITORIAL ILLUSTRATION
PUBLICATION: ROLLING STONE MAGAZINE, "IMMORTALS" ISSUE
ART DIRECTION: MATT COOLEY, ROLLING STONE
DIMENSIONS: 16 X 20 IN 406 X 508 MM
MEDIA: OIL ON PANEL
ARTIST REPRESENTATION: MAGNET REPS
CONTACT: ART@MAGNETREPS.COM
URL: WWW.MAGNETREPS.COM

RINA DONNERSMARCK (GERMANY)
TITLE: N/A
BRIEF: PERSONAL WORK
PUBLICATION: N/A
ART DIRECTION: N/A
DIMENSIONS: 8 ¼ X 12 ½ IN 210 X 318 MM
MEDIA: FELT-TIP PEN ON PAPER
ARTIST REPRESENTATION: N/A
CONTACT: RINAHD@ANOTHER.COM
URL: WWW.RINADONNERSMARCK.CO.UK

food, still life, animals and miscellaneous

WHO'S HUNGRY? Coq au vin? Cat and mouse? Squirrel on a bike? Fish? Fish on a dress? Milk? Polaroid camera, chandelier, stilletto shoes? OK, OK ... Cakes, lots of cakes. How's that? Chairs, a piano and more fish, one looking very surprised. Birds, cats, and an elephant. Really anything you want. Why don't you wash that down with a nice martini (page 151)?

AARON LEIGHTON (CANADA) *left*
TITLE: SQUIRREL RIDER
BRIEF: UNPUBLISHED SKETCHBOOK PIECE
PUBLICATION: N/A
ART DIRECTION: N/A
DIMENSIONS: 5 ¼ X 3 ¾ IN 132 X 96 MM
MEDIA: INK, DIGITAL COLOR
ARTIST REPRESENTATION: LINDGREN & SMITH
CONTACT: INFO@LSILLUSTRATION.COM
URL: WWW.LINDGRENSMITH.COM

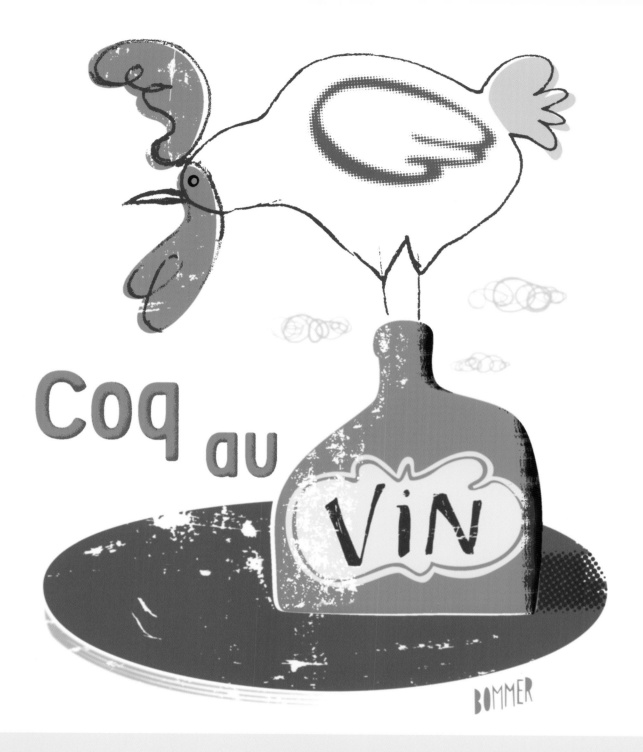

Coq au Vin

BOMMER

RICH LILLASH (USA) *facing page, top*
TITLE: TIME BOMB
BRIEF: ILLUSTRATION INSPIRED BY OLD CARTOONS
WHERE THE CHARACTERS PASS OFF BOMBS TO
BLOW EACH OTHER UP
PUBLICATION: PROMOTIONAL CALENDAR, WITH THE
THEME "PERCEPTIONS OF TIME"
ART DIRECTION: STEVE GABOR, SALVATO, JOE &
GABOR DESIGN
DIMENSIONS: 10 X 10 IN 254 X 254 MM
MEDIA: CUT PAPER COLLAGE
ARTIST REPRESENTATION: FRANK STURGES REPS
CONTACT: FRANK@STURGESREPS.COM
URL: WWW.STURGESREPS.COM

PAUL BOMMER (UK) *above*
TITLE: COQ AU VIN
BRIEF: ONE IN A SERIES OF SELF-INITIATED PIECES
CELEBRATING FRENCH CUISINE
PUBLICATION: N/A
ART DIRECTION: N/A
DIMENSIONS: 6 3/8 X 7 3/4 IN 162 X 198 MM
MEDIA: MIXED MEDIA, ADOBE PHOTOSHOP
ARTIST REPRESENTATION: N/A
CONTACT: PAUL@PAULBOMMER.COM
URL: WWW.PAULBOMMER.COM

IAN PHILLIPS (CANADA) *right*
TITLE: GOLDFISH AND DRAGONFLY
BRIEF: SELF-PROMOTIONAL PIECE, EXPLORING
DIFFERENT CONCEPTS
PUBLICATION: N/A
ART DIRECTION: N/A
DIMENSIONS: 8 ¾ X 11 ¼ IN 222 X 286 MM
MEDIA: DIGITAL
ARTIST REPRESENTATION: I2I ART
CONTACT: INFO@I2IART.COM
URL: WWW.I2IART.COM

CECILY LANG (USA) *left*
TITLE: DINNER
BRIEF: UNPUBLISHED PIECE
PUBLICATION: N/A
ART DIRECTION: N/A
DIMENSIONS: 8 X 10 IN 203 X 254 MM
MEDIA: CUT PAPER, WATERCOLORS,
COLORED PENCIL, GOUACHE
ARTIST REPRESENTATION: N/A
CONTACT: CLANG@NYC.RR.COM
URL: WWW.CECILYLANG.COM

OWEN SHERWOOD (USA) *above*
TITLE: N/A
BRIEF: VOODOO MCDONALDS
PUBLICATION: WAITROSE FOOD MONTHLY MAGAZINE, UK
ART DIRECTION: WAITROSE FOOD MONTHLY, UK
DIMENSIONS: 6 X 4 7/8 IN 153 X 124 MM
MEDIA: PENCIL, ADOBE PHOTOSHOP
ARTIST REPRESENTATION: NB ILLUSTRATION
CONTACT: INFO@NBILLUSTRATION.CO.UK
URL: WWW.NBILLUSTRATION.CO.UK

SCOTT CHAMBERS (UK) *above*
TITLE: KILLERS VS. BRAVERY
BRIEF: TO ILLUSTRATE HOW A MUSIC FAN USED A MILK
CARTON TO SHOW HIS DISLIKE OF THE BAND "THE BRAVERY"
PUBLICATION: THE TIMES, T2 SUPPLEMENT, UK
ART DIRECTION: PHOEBE GREENWOOD
DIMENSIONS: 9 X 9 IN 230 X 230 MM
MEDIA: MIXED MEDIA
ARTIST REPRESENTATION: SYNERGY
CONTACT: INFO@SYNERGYART.CO.UK
URL: WWW.SYNERGYART.CO.UK

GAVIN REECE (UK) *facing page, top*
TITLE: THE UNDOMESTIC GODDESS
BRIEF: BOOK COVER
PUBLICATION: "THE UNDOMESTIC GODDESS"
BY SOPHIE KINSELLA
ART DIRECTION: BANTAM PRESS
DIMENSIONS: N/A
MEDIA: DIGITAL
ARTIST REPRESENTATION: NEW DIVISION
CONTACT: INFO@NEWDIVISION.COM
URL: WWW.NEWDIVISION.COM

HOLLY WALES (UK) *right*
TITLE: POLAROID CAMERA
BRIEF: PERSONAL PIECE FROM A SERIES
ILLUSTRATING HOUSEHOLD OBJECTS
PUBLICATION: N/A
ART DIRECTION: N/A
DIMENSIONS: 16 ½ X 11 ¾ IN 420 X 297 MM
MEDIA: FELT-TIP PENS, DIGITAL
ARTIST REPRESENTATION: N/A
CONTACT: HOLLY@EATJAPANESEFOOD.CO.UK
URL: WWW.EATJAPANESEFOOD.CO.UK

BRITTA STENHOUSE (GERMANY/UK) *above left*

TITLE: FLORAL

BRIEF: SELF-INITIATED PROJECT

PUBLICATION: N/A

ART DIRECTION: N/A

DIMENSIONS: N/A

MEDIA: DIGITAL

ARTIST REPRESENTATION: FOLIO

CONTACT: ALL@FOLIOART.CO.UK

URL: WWW.FOLIOART.CO.UK

JENNY WREN (CANADA) *above right*

TITLE: GRACEFUL GLASS

BRIEF: GREETING CARD DESIGN

PUBLICATION: N/A

ART DIRECTION: N/A

DIMENSIONS: 8 X 11 IN 203 X 279 MM

MEDIA: DIGITAL

ARTIST REPRESENTATION: MAGNET REPS

CONTACT: ART@MAGNETREPS.COM

URL: WWW.MAGNETREPS.COM

TRACY WALKER (CANADA) *above*
TITLE: FIRST-PRESSED VIRGIN
BRIEF: SELF-PROMOTIONAL PIECE
PUBLICATION: N/A
ART DIRECTION: N/A
DIMENSIONS: 10 X 7 IN 254 X 178 MM
MEDIA: ACRYLIC
ARTIST REPRESENTATION: I2I ART
CONTACT: INFO@I2IART.COM
URL: WWW.I2IART.COM

BRITTA STENHOUSE (GERMANY/UK) *left*
TITLE: KITCHEN
BRIEF: FOOD IMAGERY
PUBLICATION: N/A
ART DIRECTION: THE ART GROUP
DIMENSIONS: N/A
MEDIA: DIGITAL
ARTIST REPRESENTATION: FOLIO
CONTACT: ALL@FOLIOART.CO.UK
URL: WWW.FOLIOART.CO.UK

136

ANSON LIAW (USA)
TITLE: RECIPES FOR THE GOOD TIME GIRL
BRIEF: SELF-PROMOTIONAL PIECE, TARGETTED AT MEN
TRYING TO IMPRESS THEIR GIRLFRIEND BY COOKING UP
A SPECIAL VALENTINE'S DAY DINNER
PUBLICATION: N/A
ART DIRECTION: N/A
DIMENSIONS: 17 X 19 IN 432 X 483 MM
MEDIA: CHALK PASTELS AND INK ON PRINT-MAKING PAPER
ARTIST REPRESENTATION: MORGAN GAYNIN, INC.
CONTACT: INFO@MORGANGAYNIN.COM
URL: WWW.MORGANGAYNIN.COM

MASAKI RYO (JAPAN) *right*
TITLE: DIAMOND SHOE
BRIEF: BOOK JACKET ILLUSTRATION OF A SEXY SHOE
PUBLICATION: "PERSONAL SHOPPER" BY CARMEN REID
ART DIRECTION: TRANSWORLD
DIMENSIONS: N/A
MEDIA: ACRYLIC PAINT
ARTIST REPRESENTATION: CWC INTERNATIONAL
CONTACT: AGENT@CWC-I.COM
URL: WWW.CWC-I.COM

ANNIKA WESTER (FRANCE) *left*
TITLE: CUVÉE STILETTO
BRIEF: LABEL ARTWORK TO BE USED ON A LIMITED
EDITION OF CHAMPAGNE BOTTLES
PUBLICATION: N/A
ART DIRECTION: SHEENO
DIMENSIONS: 3 1/8 X 3 1/8 IN 80 X 80 MM
MEDIA: PEN AND INK
ARTIST REPRESENTATION: CWC INTERNATIONAL
CONTACT: AGENT@CWC-I.COM
URL: WWW.CWC-I.COM

ANSON LIAW (USA) *right*
TITLE: CHRYSLER PUMP
BRIEF: UNPUBLISHED ILLUSTRATION INTENDED
TO CAPTURE THE FASHION OF NEW YORK CITY
PUBLICATION: N/A
ART DIRECTION: N/A
DIMENSIONS: 14 X 17 IN 356 X 432 MM
MEDIA: PEN AND INK, CHALK PASTELS, CHARCOAL ON
PAPER, AND ADOBE PHOTOSHOP
ARTIST REPRESENTATION: MORGAN GAYNIN, INC.
CONTACT: INFO@MORGANGAYNIN.COM
URL: WWW.MORGANGAYNIN.COM

SEAN SIMS (UK) *above*
TITLE: G.I. FOODS (BLACK VERSION)
BRIEF: TO ILLUSTRATE A MAGAZINE ARTICLE ON GI DIETS
(THIS VERSION OF THE ILLUSTRATION WAS NOT USED)
PUBLICATION: N/A
ART DIRECTION: N/A
DIMENSIONS: 10 ¾ X 4 ¾ IN 273 X 122 MM
MEDIA: DIGITAL (FREEHAND MX)
ARTIST REPRESENTATION: NEW DIVISION
CONTACT: INFO@NEWDIVISION.COM
URL: WWW.NEWDIVISION.COM

JOANNA WALSH (UK) *facing page, top*
TITLE: WHITE FOOD
BRIEF: PERSONAL PIECE
PUBLICATION: N/A
ART DIRECTION: N/A
DIMENSIONS: 4 X 5 ⅞ IN 103 X 149 MM
MEDIA: ADOBE ILLUSTRATOR
ARTIST REPRESENTATION: EASTWING
CONTACT: ANDREA@EASTWING.CO.UK
URL: WWW.EASTWING.CO.UK

TRINA DALZIEL (UK) *facing page, bottom*
TITLE: A VERY PINK WEDDING
BRIEF: COVER FOR A BOOK ON ORGANIZING
A GAY WEDDING
PUBLICATION: "A VERY PINK WEDDING"
ART DIRECTION: MARK THOMSON,
HARPER COLLINS PUBLISHERS
DIMENSIONS: 6 ⅝ X 6 ⅝ IN 169 X 169 MM
MEDIA: HAND-DRAWN, COLORED IN ADOBE ILLUSTRATOR
ARTIST REPRESENTATION: LILLA ROGERS
CONTACT: LILLA@LILLAROGERS.COM

MARY KILVERT (UK) *facing page, top*
TITLE: THE PROFESSIONAL PORCH-SITTERS CONVENE
FOR NOTHING IN PARTICULAR
BRIEF: ILLUSTRATION TO ACCOMPANY A SHORT
STORY IN A MAGAZINE
PUBLICATION: UTNE MAGAZINE
ART DIRECTION: STEPHANIE GLAROS, UTNE MAGAZINE
DIMENSIONS: 5 7/8 X 4 IN 150 X 103 MM
MEDIA: PEN AND INK, DIGITAL COLOR, COLLAGE
ARTIST REPRESENTATION: NEW DIVISION (UK) /
LINDGREN & SMITH (USA)
CONTACT: INFO@NEWDIVISION.COM /
INFO@LSILLUSTRATION.COM
URL: WWW.NEWDIVISION.COM /
WWW.LINDGRENSMITH.COM

CLEMENTINE HOPE (UK) *facing page, bottom*
TITLE: ROOM, UNDER THE SAME ROOF
BRIEF: EDITORIAL ILLUSTRATION OF A ROOM
WITH A SPIDER AND PIANO
PUBLICATION: SPACE MAGAZINE
ART DIRECTION: JOHN BROWN PUBLISHING
DIMENSIONS: 16 7/8 X 8 5/8 IN 430 X 220 MM
MEDIA: PEN AND INK, ADOBE PHOTOSHOP
ARTIST REPRESENTATION: NB ILLUSTRATION
CONTACT: INFO@NBILLUSTRATION.CO.UK
URL: WWW.NBILLUSTRATION.CO.UK

AGNES DECOURCHELLE (FRANCE) *below*
TITLE: STILL LIFE
BRIEF: SELF-PROMOTIONAL PIECE
PUBLICATION: N/A
ART DIRECTION: N/A
DIMENSIONS: 17 3/8 X 11 1/4 IN 442 X 286 MM
MEDIA: COLOR PENCIL
ARTIST REPRESENTATION: EYE CANDY
ILLUSTRATION AGENCY
CONTACT: INFO@EYECANDY.CO.UK
URL: WWW.EYECANDY.CO.UK

MARY KILVERT (UK) *above*
TITLE: MOROCCAN FOOD
BRIEF: UNPUBLISHED PIECE
PUBLICATION: N/A
ART DIRECTION: N/A
DIMENSIONS: 5 7/8 X 4 IN 150 X 103 MM
MEDIA: PEN AND INK, DIGITAL COLOR
ARTIST REPRESENTATION: NEW DIVISION (UK) / LINDGREN & SMITH (USA)
CONTACT: INFO@NEWDIVISION.COM / INFO@LSILLUSTRATION.COM
URL: WWW.NEWDIVISION.COM / WWW.LINDGRENSMITH.COM

GEORGINA HOUNSOME (UK) *left*
TITLE: FISH AND CHIPS
BRIEF: SELF-PROMOTIONAL PIECE
PUBLICATION: N/A
ART DIRECTION: N/A
DIMENSIONS: 7 3/4 X 11 IN 198 X 280 MM
MEDIA: CUT PAPER AND PLASTIC COLLAGE, DRAWING
ARTIST REPRESENTATION: EYE CANDY ILLUSTRATION AGENCY
CONTACT: INFO@EYECANDY.CO.UK
URL: WWW.EYECANDY.CO.UK

MELVYN EVANS (UK) *above*
TITLE: BEACH OBJECTS
BRIEF: SELF-PROMOTIONAL PIECE
PUBLICATION: N/A
ART DIRECTION: N/A
DIMENSIONS: 17 3/8 X 11 1/4 IN 442 X 286 MM
MEDIA: DIGITAL (ADOBE ILLUSTRATOR)
ARTIST REPRESENTATION: NEW DIVISION
CONTACT: INFO@NEWDIVISION.COM
URL: WWW.NEWDIVISION.COM

SAM WILSON (UK) *left*
TITLE: ROAST HADDOCK AND CREAM
BRIEF: TO ILLUSTRATE THE INGREDIENTS FOR THE RECIPE OF THE MONTH
PUBLICATION: HOUSE & GARDEN MAGAZINE
ART DIRECTION: FIONA HAYES, HOUSE & GARDEN MAGAZINE
DIMENSIONS: 9 X 11 5/8 IN 230 X 295 MM
MEDIA: MIXED MEDIA
ARTIST REPRESENTATION: EYE CANDY ILLUSTRATION AGENCY
CONTACT: INFO@EYECANDY.CO.UK
URL: WWW.EYECANDY.CO.UK

YEE TING KUIT (UK) *previous page*
TITLE: DING DING!
BRIEF: AN IMAGE BASED ON THE THEME OF "ALTERNATIVE
TRANSPORT"—AN OPEN SUBMISSION FOR "AMELIA'S MAGAZINE"
PUBLICATION: N/A
ART DIRECTION: N/A
DIMENSIONS: 16 X 9 7/8 IN 406 X 251 MM
MEDIA: DIGITAL
ARTIST REPRESENTATION: THE ORGANISATION
CONTACT: INFO@ORGANISART.CO.UK
URL: WWW.ORGANISART.CO.UK

ILOVEDUST (UK) *facing page*
TITLE: N/A
BRIEF: PERSONAL WORK
PUBLICATION: N/A
ART DIRECTION: N/A
DIMENSIONS: 7 7/8 X 11 1/4 IN 200 X 287 MM
MEDIA: DIGITAL
ARTIST REPRESENTATION: JELLY LONDON
CONTACT: INFO@JELLYLONDON.COM
URL: WWW.JELLYLONDON.COM

MARIKO JESSE (UK/JAPAN) *above*
TITLE: RICE BOWL
BRIEF: SELF-PROMOTIONAL POSTCARD SHOWING
TRADITIONAL ENGLISH PATTERNS ON AN ASIAN PIECE
OF HOMEWARE—REFLECTING THE ARTIST'S CULTURAL
BACKGROUND
PUBLICATION: N/A
ART DIRECTION: N/A
DIMENSIONS: 4 3/4 X 5 3/4 IN 120 X 145 MM
MEDIA: ETCHING
ARTIST REPRESENTATION: MONSTERS
CONTACT: MARIKO.JESSE@USA.NET
URL: WWW.MONSTERS.CO.UK

JUDY STEVENS (UK) *above*
TITLE: FISH ON ICE
BRIEF: PERSONAL PIECE
PUBLICATION: N/A
ART DIRECTION: N/A
DIMENSIONS: 10 1/4 X 7 1/2 IN 260 X 190 MM
MEDIA: THREE-COLOR LINOCUT PRINT
ARTIST REPRESENTATION: NB ILLUSTRATION
CONTACT: INFO@NBILLUSTRATION.CO.UK
URL: WWW.NBILLUSTRATION.CO.UK

KARINE FAOU (FRANCE) *facing page*
TITLE: CAT WORLD
BRIEF: TO CREATE A WRAPPING PAPER DESIGN FOR SHEBA
PUBLICATION: N/A
ART DIRECTION: SHEBA
DIMENSIONS: 8 1/4 X 11 5/8 IN 210 X 297 MM
MEDIA: DIGITAL
ARTIST REPRESENTATION: EYE CANDY
ILLUSTRATION AGENCY
CONTACT: INFO@EYECANDY.CO.UK
URL: WWW.EYECANDY.CO.UK

FRÉDÉRIC PÉAULT (FRANCE) *right*
TITLE: N/A
BRIEF: SELF-PROMOTIONAL WORK
PUBLICATION: N/A
ART DIRECTION: N/A
DIMENSIONS: N/A
MEDIA: N/A
ARTIST REPRESENTATION: VIRGINIE
CONTACT: VIRGINIE@VIRGINIE.FR
URL: WWW.VIRGINIE.FR

JOSEF GAST (USA) *left*
TITLE: SAFE MIGRATIONS
BRIEF: EDITORIAL ILLUSTRATION OF GEESE FLYING
THROUGH A DARK CITY
PUBLICATION: SIERRA MAGAZINE
ART DIRECTION: SIERRA MAGAZINE
DIMENSIONS: 6 1/4 X 7 3/4 IN 160 X 195 MM
MEDIA: DIGITAL
ARTIST REPRESENTATION: FRANK STURGES REPS
CONTACT: FRANK@STURGESREPS.COM
URL: WWW.STURGESREPS.COM

1 Cornflake 2. Oat 3. Linseed
4. Cranberry 5. Raisin

TRISHA KRAUSS (USA) *facing page, far left*
TITLE: PEONIES
BRIEF: ILLUSTRATION USED ON BAGS AND HANG-TAGS FOR THE
CLOTHES AND ACCESSORIES CHAIN, MONSOON ACCESSORIZE
PUBLICATION: N/A
ART DIRECTION: SONJA FRICK, MONSOON
DIMENSIONS: 13 X 17 IN 330 X 432 MM
MEDIA: ACRYLIC ON PLYWOOD
ARTIST REPRESENTATION: LINDGREN & SMITH
CONTACT: INFO@LSILLUSTRATION.COM
URL: WWW.LINDGRENSMITH.COM

AGNESE BICOCCHI (ITALY) *facing page, right*
TITLE: A BOWL OF MUESLI
BRIEF: SELF-PROMOTIONAL PIECE ILLUSTRATING
EVERYDAY FOOD
PUBLICATION: N/A
ART DIRECTION: N/A
DIMENSIONS: 5 1/8 X 6 1/2 IN 130 X 165 MM
MEDIA: MIXED MEDIA
ARTIST REPRESENTATION: EYE CANDY ILLUSTRATION
AGENCY
CONTACT: INFO@EYECANDY.CO.UK
URL: WWW.EYECANDY.CO.UK

JANELL GENOVESE (USA) *facing page, bottom*
TITLE: N/A
BRIEF: MAGAZINE ILLUSTRATION OF "SPOTS OF FOOD"
PUBLICATION: GOOD HOUSEKEEPING MAGAZINE
ART DIRECTION: GOOD HOUSEKEEPING MAGAZINE
DIMENSIONS: 10 X 7 IN 254 X 178 MM
MEDIA: GOUACHE
ARTIST REPRESENTATION: LILLA ROGERS
CONTACT: LILLA@LILLAROGERS.COM
URL: WWW.LILLAROGERS.COM

BELLA PILAR (USA) *below right*
TITLE: BEJEWELLED MARTINI
BRIEF: ADVERTISING ILLUSTRATION FOR A COCKTAIL
RING EVENT INVITATION
PUBLICATION: N/A
ART DIRECTION: HEATHER DAVIS, TIFFANY & CO.
DIMENSIONS: 8 X 11 IN 203 X 279 MM
MEDIA: GOUACHE
ARTIST REPRESENTATION: MAGNET REPS
CONTACT: ART@MAGNETREPS.COM
URL: WWW.MAGNETREPS.COM

REBECCA BRADLEY (UK) *below left*
TITLE: PROSCIUTTO
BRIEF: EDITORIAL ILLUSTRATION OF PARMA HAM
PUBLICATION: CHATELAINE MAGAZINE, QUEBEC
ART DIRECTION: ILANA SHAMIR, CHATELAINE MAGAZINE
DIMENSIONS: 3 3/4 X 3 1/2 IN 98 X 89 MM
MEDIA: WATERCOLOR AND INK
ARTIST REPRESENTATION: LILLA ROGERS
CONTACT: LILLA@LILLAROGERS.COM
URL: WWW.LILLAROGERS.COM

LA POULE AU POT

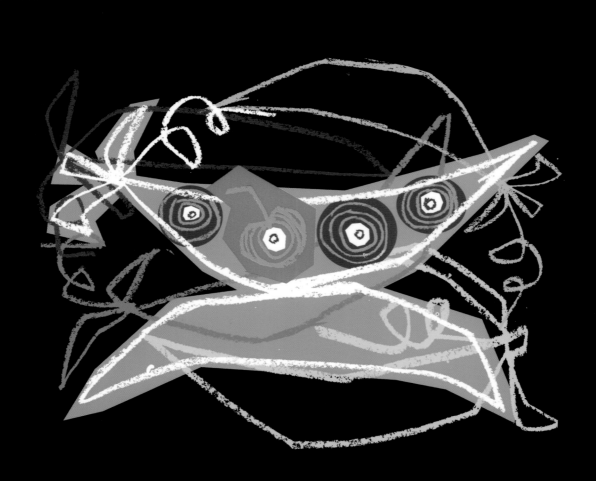

PAUL BOMMER (UK) *facing page, top*
TITLE: LA POULE AU POT
BRIEF: ONE IN A SERIES OF SELF-INITIATED PIECES
CELEBRATING FRENCH CUISINE
PUBLICATION: N/A
ART DIRECTION: N/A
DIMENSIONS: 6 ⅜ X 7 ¾ IN 308 X 286 MM
MEDIA: MIXED MEDIA, ADOBE PHOTOSHOP
ARTIST REPRESENTATION: N/A
CONTACT: PAUL@PAULBOMMER.COM
URL: WWW.PAULBOMMER.COM

WALSHWORKS (UK) *facing page, bottom*
TITLE: PEAS IN A POD
BRIEF: EDITORIAL ILLUSTRATION TO ACCOMPANY AN ARTICLE
ABOUT GENETIC MODIFICATION—SHOWING A CHERRY GROWING
IN A PEA-POD.
PUBLICATION: THE TIMES NEWSPAPER, UK
ART DIRECTION: THE TIMES NEWSPAPER, UK
DIMENSIONS: 6 ⅝ X 5 ⅛ IN 169 X 129 MM
MEDIA: HAND-DRAWN, ADOBE PHOTOSHOP
ARTIST REPRESENTATION: EASTWING
CONTACT: ANDREA@EASTWING.CO.UK
URL: WWW.EASTWING.CO.UK

ANNE SMITH (USA) *left*
TITLE: APRIL
BRIEF: ONE OF A SERIES OF TWELVE IMAGES FOR A KITCHEN
AND GARDEN CALENDAR
PUBLICATION: CALENDAR
ART DIRECTION: LINDA COCHRANE, JARROLD PUBLISHING, UK
DIMENSIONS: 8 ½ X 11 IN 216 X 279 MM
MEDIA: GOUACHE
ARTIST REPRESENTATION: N/A
CONTACT: ANNE@ANNESMITH.NET
URL: WWW.ANNESMITH.NET

GUNNLAUG MOEN HEMBERY (NORWAY/UK)
facing page, top
TITLE: BIRD FLU
BRIEF: NEWSPAPER ILLUSTRATION TO ACCOMPANY AN
ARTICLE ABOUT THE HYSTERIA SURROUNDING BIRD FLU
PUBLICATION: DAGBLADET, NORWAY
ART DIRECTION: DAGBLADET
DIMENSIONS: N/A
MEDIA: PEN AND INK AND DIGITAL
ARTIST REPRESENTATION: EYE CANDY
ILLUSTRATION AGENCY
CONTACT: INFO@EYECANDY.CO.UK
URL: WWW.EYECANDY.CO.UK

JOJO ENSSLIN (GERMANY) *below*
TITLE: BAD GUYS
BRIEF: SELF-PROMOTIONAL PIECE DEPICTING A BIRD
AND BULL SMOKING CIGARETTES
PUBLICATION: N/A
ART DIRECTION: N/A
DIMENSIONS: 12 1/4 X 16 7/8 IN 310 X 430 MM
MEDIA: SERIGRAPH ON WOOD
ARTIST REPRESENTATION: KOMBINATROTWEISS
CONTACT: INFO@KOMBINATROTWEISS.DE
URL: WWW.KOMBINATROTWEISS.DE

NADIA BERKANE (FRANCE) *facing page, bottom*
TITLE: MON PETIT LUTIN
BRIEF: GREETING CARD ILLUSTRATION
PUBLICATION: LES EDITIONS DU DESASTRE
ART DIRECTION: FLORENT
DIMENSIONS: 5 7/8 X 5 7/8 IN 150 X 150 MM
MEDIA: DIGITAL (ADOBE ILLUSTRATOR)
ARTIST REPRESENTATION: CHEZ ANTOINE
CONTACT: INFO@CHEZANTOINE.COM
URL: WWW.CHEZANTOINE.COM

HOLLY WALES (UK)
TITLE: RADIO
BRIEF: PERSONAL WORK FROM A SERIES OF ILLUSTRATIONS
OF ANTIQUE RADIOS
PUBLICATION: N/A
ART DIRECTION: N/A
DIMENSIONS: 8 ¼ X 11 ¾ IN 210 X 297 MM
MEDIA: FELT-TIP PENS, DIGITAL
ARTIST REPRESENTATION: ZEEGENRUSH
CONTACT: INFO@ZEEGENRUSH.COM
URL: WWW.ZEEGENRUSH.COM

LEE WOODGATE (UK) *facing page*
TITLE: ICONS
BRIEF: SELF-PROMOTIONAL PIECE
PUBLICATION: N/A
ART DIRECTION: N/A
DIMENSIONS: 11 X 11 IN 280 X 280 MM
MEDIA: ADOBE PHOTOSHOP
ARTIST REPRESENTATION: EYE CANDY
ILLUSTRATION AGENCY
CONTACT: INFO@EYECANDY.CO.UK
URL: WWW.EYECANDY.CO.UK

158

EYEPORT (UK) *left*
TITLE: SALARY SURVEY
BRIEF: EDITORIAL ILLUSTRATION
PUBLICATION: DESIGN WEEK
ART DIRECTION: IVAN COTTRELL, DESIGN WEEK
DIMENSIONS: 9 X 10 ¼ IN 230 X 260 MM
MEDIA: DIGITAL
ARTIST REPRESENTATION: CHEZ ANTOINE
CONTACT: INFO@CHEZANTOINE.COM
URL: WWW.CHEZANTOINE.COM

HELEN DARDIK (CANADA) *right*
TITLE: JUST A CRAVING!
BRIEF: TO DEPICT A PREGNANT WOMAN
DREAMING UP DELICIOUS FOODS
PUBLICATION: N/A
ART DIRECTION: N/A
DIMENSIONS: 6 ½ X 8 ¼ IN 165 X 208 MM
MEDIA: ADOBE ILLUSTRATOR
ARTIST REPRESENTATION: LILLA ROGERS
CONTACT: LILLA@LILLAROGERS.COM
URL: WWW.LILLAROGERS.COM

BELINDA PEARCE (AUSTRALIA) *above*
TITLE: ICE CREAM DREAM
BRIEF: UNPUBLISHED PIECE
PUBLICATION: N/A
ART DIRECTION: N/A
DIMENSIONS: 9 ½ X 9 ½ IN 240 X 240 MM
MEDIA: ACRYLIC, DIGITAL
ARTIST REPRESENTATION: NEW DIVISION
CONTACT: INFO@NEWDIVISION.COM
URL: WWW.NEWDIVISION.COM

GINA TRIPLETT & MATT CURTIUS (USA) *above*
TITLE: 1, 2, 3, 4, 5, 6, 7 … ALL GOOD PAINTERS GO
TO HEAVEN
BRIEF: SELF-PROMOTIONAL PIECE
PUBLICATION: N/A
ART DIRECTION: N/A
DIMENSIONS: 16 X 12 IN 406 X 305 MM
MEDIA: ACRYLIC PAINT
ARTIST REPRESENTATION: FRANK STURGES REPS
CONTACT: FRANK@STURGESREPS.COM
URL: WWW.STURGESREPS.COM

CHARLES WILKIN (USA) *facing page*
TITLE: URBAN FOREST
BRIEF: OUTDOOR BANNER ILLUSTRATION FOR THE AIGA
URBAN FOREST PROJECT; HUNG IN TIMES SQUARE, NEW YORK
PUBLICATION: N/A
ART DIRECTION: AIGA, NEW YORK
DIMENSIONS: 8 X 11 IN 203 X 279 MM
MEDIA: MIXED MEDIA, DIGITAL
ARTIST REPRESENTATION: MAGNET REPS
CONTACT: ART@MAGNETREPS.COM
URL: WWW.MAGNETREPS.COM

D 25

MARTINA WITTE (GERMANY)
TITLE: TEXTILE SPRING/SUMMER 2006
BRIEF: AN ILLUSTRATION CREATED TO SUMMARIZE THE
TRENDS IN SEASONAL TEXTILES
PUBLICATION: N/A
ART DIRECTION: JEN UNER, CALIFORNIA MARKET CENTER
DIMENSIONS: 11 X 16 IN 279 X 406 MM
MEDIA: MIXED MEDIA
ARTIST REPRESENTATION: N/A
CONTACT: MARTINA.WITTE@GMAIL.COM

4

*landscaped&
architecture*

THEY'RE BEAUTIFUL, AREN'T THEY? Mountains, stadiums (or should that be stadia?), office blocks, houses, houses for pigeons, sheds, a moonscape, parks, a herbaceous border, a bath on wheels, a table on a terrace, a sky full of flowers, a volcano erupting with butterflies, flowers and bugs, that guy with the bull horn—what's he doing here? Well, this section certainly is surprising ... and what about the cat looking at the little girl in the tree, and the lovebirds on the park bench ...?

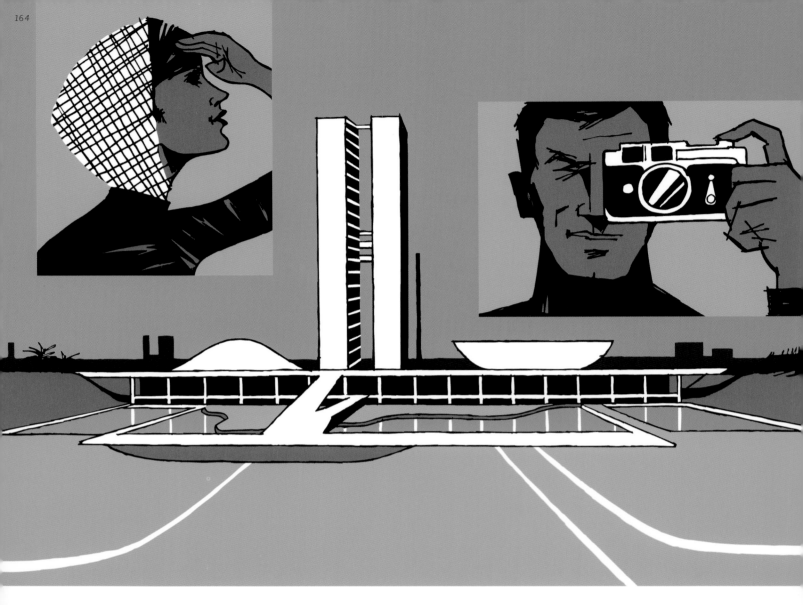

DAVID NAVASCUES (SPAIN) *above*
TITLE: BRASILIA
BRIEF: UNPUBLISHED WORK
PUBLICATION: N/A
ART DIRECTION: N/A
DIMENSIONS: 7 ⅞ X 5 ⅞ IN 200 X 150 MM
MEDIA: MIXED MEDIA
ARTIST REPRESENTATION: KATE LARKWORTHY
CONTACT: KATE@LARKWORTHY.COM
URL: WWW.LARKWORTHY.COM

FRÉDÉRIC PÉAULT (FRANCE) *facing page, top*
TITLE: UNTITLED
BRIEF: SELF-PROMOTIONAL PIECE
PUBLICATION: N/A
ART DIRECTION: N/A
DIMENSIONS: N/A
MEDIA: N/A
ARTIST REPRESENTATION: VIRGINIE
CONTACT: VIRGINIE@VIRGINIE.FR
URL: WWW.VIRGINIE.FR

LIZZIE GARDINER (UK) *facing page, bottom*
TITLE: CANARY WHARF
BRIEF: MAGAZINE ILLUSTRATION
PUBLICATION: CANARY WHARF MAGAZINE
ART DIRECTION: CANARY WHARF MAGAZINE
DIMENSIONS: N/A
MEDIA: PEN, ADOBE PHOTOSHOP
ARTIST REPRESENTATION: THE INKSHED
CONTACT: ABBY@INKSHED.CO.UK
URL: WWW.INKSHED.CO.UK

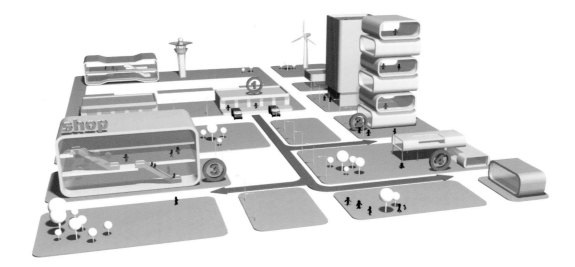

ANN BOYAJIAN (USA) *facing page*
TITLE: LES PIGEONNIERS
BRIEF: PERSONAL PIECE, A DEPICTION OF ASSORTED
DOVECOTES IN THE FRENCH COUNTRYSIDE
PUBLICATION: N/A
ART DIRECTION: N/A
DIMENSIONS: 7 X 11 ¼ IN 190 X 286 MM
MEDIA: PASTEL
ARTIST REPRESENTATION: LILLA ROGERS
CONTACT: LILLA@LILLAROGERS.COM
URL: WWW.LILLAROGERS.COM

les pigeonniers

TIM TOMKINSON (USA) *below*
TITLE: DECONSTRUCTIVISM
BRIEF: ONE OF NINE ILLUSTRATIONS COVERING THE
HISTORY OF 20TH CENTURY DESIGN MOVEMENTS,
AND THE MANIFESTOS THAT ACCOMPANIED THEM
PUBLICATION: DWELL MAGAZINE
ART DIRECTION: BRENDAN CALLAHAN, DWELL MAGAZINE
DIMENSIONS: 7 X 6 IN 178 X 152 MM
MEDIA: PENCIL, INK, GOUACHE, COLLAGE ON BOARD
ARTIST REPRESENTATION: FRIEND AND JOHNSON
CONTACT: SFRIEND@FRIENDANDJOHNSON.COM
URL: WWW.FRIENDANDJOHNSON.COM

CAROLINE TOMLINSON (UK) *facing page*
TITLE: VISIT LONDON'S NEW ARCHITECTURE
BRIEF: POSTER FOR TRANSPORT FOR LONDON (TFL)
PUBLICATION: N/A
ART DIRECTION: TRANSPORT FOR LONDON /
JELLY LONDON
DIMENSIONS: 8 X 11 IN 216 X 279 MM
MEDIA: COLLAGE
ARTIST REPRESENTATION: JELLY LONDON
CONTACT: INFO@JELLYLONDON.COM
URL: WWW.JELLYLONDON.COM

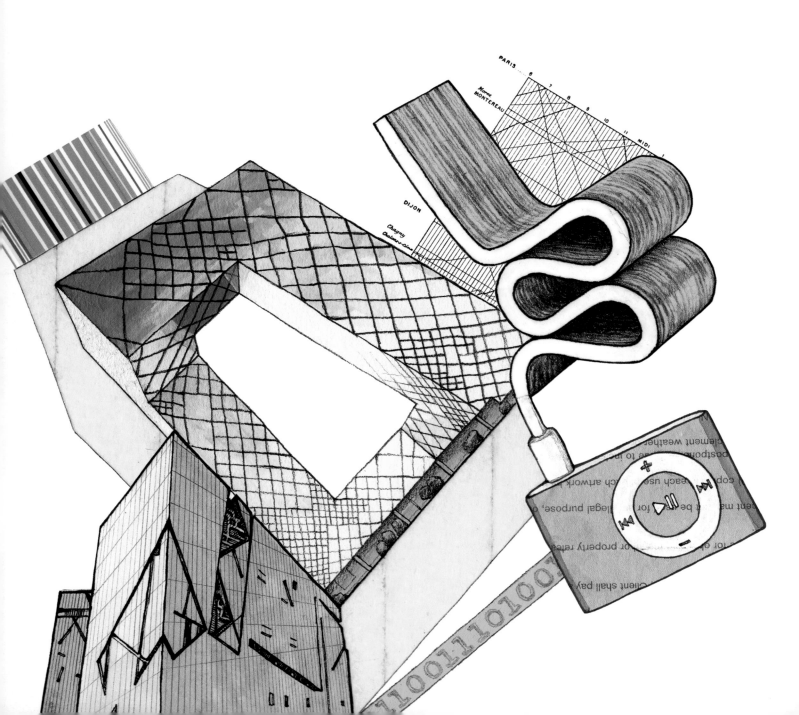

VISIT LONDONS NEW ARCHITECTURE

JOHN SPENCER (UK) *above left*
TITLE: REIGATE OLD TOWN HALL
BRIEF: PRIVATE COMMISSION
PUBLICATION: N/A
ART DIRECTION: N/A
DIMENSIONS: N/A
MEDIA: PRINT
ARTIST REPRESENTATION:
CENTRAL ILLUSTRATION AGENCY (CIA)
CONTACT: INFO@CENTRALILLUSTRATION.COM
URL: WWW.CENTRALILLUSTRATION.COM

ALEXANDRA HIGLETT (UK) *right*
TITLE: SHED
BRIEF: PERSONAL WORK
PUBLICATION: N/A
ART DIRECTION: N/A
DIMENSIONS: 11 ¼ X 17 ⅜ IN 286 X 442 MM
MEDIA: PAINTING ON ENDPAPER
ARTIST REPRESENTATION: N/A
CONTACT: ALEXHIGLETT@HOTMAIL.COM
URL: WWW.ALEXANDGEORGE.CO.UK

JUDY STEVENS (UK) *facing page, left*
TITLE: PINOT GRIGIO
BRIEF: WINE LABEL FOR PINOT GRIGIO WINE
PUBLICATION: N/A
ART DIRECTION: ABI CHESHIRE, ASDA
DIMENSIONS: 8 ¼ X 6 ¼ IN 210 X 160 MM
MEDIA: COMPUTER-COLORED LINOCUT PRINT
ARTIST REPRESENTATION: NB ILLUSTRATION
CONTACT: INFO@NBILLUSTRATION.CO.UK
URL: WWW.NBILLUSTRATION.CO.UK

LISA DEJOHN (USA) *below, left*
TITLE: PLACES AND SPACES
BRIEF: COLLAGES OF BUILDINGS
SHOWN AT THE GRASS HUT GALLERY
IN PORTLAND, OREGON
PUBLICATION: N/A
ART DIRECTION: N/A
DIMENSIONS: 10 X 12 IN 254 X 305 MM
MEDIA: MIXED MEDIA WITH
VINTAGE EPHEMERA
ARTIST REPRESENTATION: LILLA ROGERS
CONTACT: LILLA@LILLAROGERS.COM
URL: WWW.LILLAROGERS.COM

WALSHWORKS (UK) *below, right*
TITLE: SEEDBED
BRIEF: EDITORIAL ILLUSTRATION TO
ACCOMPANY AN ARTICLE ABOUT THE
REGENERATION OF OXBRIDGE UNIVERSITIES
PUBLICATION: THE GUARDIAN, UK
ART DIRECTION: THE GUARDIAN, UK
DIMENSIONS: 4 ⅝ X 6 ¼ IN 117 X 159 MM
MEDIA: MIXED MEDIA, ADOBE PHOTOSHOP
ARTIST REPRESENTATION: EASTWING
CONTACT: ANDREA@EASTWING.CO.UK
URL: WWW.EASTWING.CO.UK

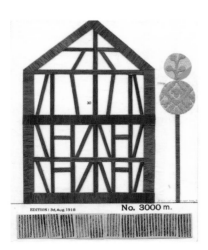

SYLVIE PINSONNEAUX (FRANCE) *above*

TITLE: KITCHEN 70
BRIEF: MAGAZINE ILLUSTRATION OF A KITCHEN IN 1970'S STYLE
PUBLICATION: LUX DECO
ART DIRECTION: N/A
DIMENSIONS: 18 ⅛ X 11 ⅝ IN 460 X 297 MM
MEDIA: N/A
ARTIST REPRESENTATION: EYE CANDY ILLUSTRATION AGENCY
CONTACT: INFO@EYECANDY.CO.UK
URL: WWW.EYECANDY.CO.UK

LINDA KETELHUT (USA) *above and right*
BRIEF: PERSONAL WORK
PUBLICATION: N/A
ART DIRECTION: N/A
MEDIA: DIGITAL
ARTIST REPRESENTATION: LILLA ROGERS
CONTACT: LILLA@LILLAROGERS.COM
URL: WWW.LILLAROGERS.COM

TITLE: UNTITLED *above*
DIMENSIONS: 8 X 6 7/8 IN 203 X 175 MM

TITLE: HUMMINGBIRDS *right*
DIMENSIONS: 5 x 7 1/4 IN 140 X 184 MM

STÉPHANE GAMAIN (FRANCE) *top right*
TITLE: PARIS
BRIEF: ADVERTISEMENT FOR PARIS CONVENTION
AND VISITORS' BUREAU
PUBLICATION: POSTERS, GUIDEBOOKS
ART DIRECTION: PASCALE BOUMENDIL, PUBLICIS
DIMENSIONS: 11 X 13 3/8 IN 280 X 340 MM
MEDIA: TRADITIONAL AND DIGITAL
ARTIST REPRESENTATION: NB ILLUSTRATION
CONTACT: INFO@NBILLUSTRATION.CO.UK
URL: WWW.NBILLUSTRATION.CO.UK

174

LINDA KETELHUT (USA) *below*
TITLE: UNTITLED
BRIEF: PERSONAL WORK
PUBLICATION: N/A
ART DIRECTION: N/A
DIMENSIONS: 5 X 7 1/4 IN 140 X 184 MM
MEDIA: DIGITAL
ARTIST REPRESENTATION: LILLA ROGERS
CONTACT: LILLA@LILLAROGERS.COM
URL: WWW.LILLAROGERS.COM

JONATHAN CROFT (UK) *below*
TITLE: AUTUMN PARK
BRIEF: SELF-PROMOTIONAL PIECE
PUBLICATION: N/A
ART DIRECTION: N/A
DIMENSIONS: 9 7/8 X 9 7/8 IN 250 X 250 MM
MEDIA: DIGITAL
ARTIST REPRESENTATION: N/A
CONTACT: JONATHAN.CROFT@BTINTERNET.COM
URL: WWW.JONATHANCROFT.COM

JOANNA WALSH (UK) *facing page, top*
TITLE: BORDER
BRIEF: A BOTANICALLY ACCURATE PICTURE OF A GARDEN BORDER
TO ACCOMPANY A GARDENING ARTICLE
PUBLICATION: THE GUARDIAN WEEKEND MAGAZINE, UK
ART DIRECTION: THE GUARDIAN, UK
DIMENSIONS: 17 3/8 X 9 1/8 IN 440 X 233 MM
MEDIA: ADOBE ILLUSTRATOR
ARTIST REPRESENTATION: EASTWING
CONTACT: ANDREA@EASTWING.CO.UK
URL: WWW.EASTWING.CO.UK

STEFAN G. BUCHER (USA) *facing page, bottom*
TITLE: 344 FLOWERS
BRIEF: SELF-PROMOTIONAL PIECE, A DRAWING OF 344 "VERY
PERSONABLE" FLOWERS WITH A ROOT SYSTEM OF CLEAR VARNISH
PUBLICATION: N/A
ART DIRECTION: N/A
DIMENSIONS: 24 X 18 IN 610 X 457 MM
MEDIA: PEN AND INK, DIGITAL ASSEMBLY AND COLOR
ARTIST REPRESENTATION: N/A
CONTACT: STEFAN@344DESIGN.COM
URL: WWW.DAILYMONSTER.COM

ALLAN DEAS (UK) *below*
TITLE: TRAVEL GUIDES
BRIEF: TRAVEL GUIDES AIMED AT WOMEN
(SELF-PROMOTIONAL PIECE)
PUBLICATION: N/A
ART DIRECTION: N/A
DIMENSIONS: 4 X 7 3/8 IN 100 X 188 MM
MEDIA: PEN AND INK, DIGITAL
ARTIST REPRESENTATION: N/A
CONTACT: ALLAN.DEAS@MAC.COM
URL: WWW.ALLANDEAS.COM

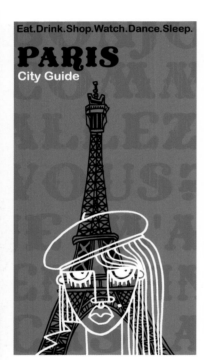   

BO LUNDBERG (SWEDEN) *facing page*
TITLE: DOCUMENTARIES ON DVD
BRIEF: EDITORIAL ILLUSTRATION FOR AN ARTICLE ABOUT
THE POPULARITY OF DOCUMENTARIES ON DVD FOR
PEOPLE TO WATCH FROM THE COMFORT OF HOME
PUBLICATION: RESIDENCE MAGAZINE, SWEDEN
ART DIRECTION: STAFFAN FRID, RESIDENCE
DIMENSIONS: 8 7/8 X 11 3/8 IN 225 X 290 MM
MEDIA: ADOBE ILLUSTRATOR
ARTIST REPRESENTATION: ART DEPARTMENT
CONTACT: STEPHANIEP@ART-DEPT.COM
URL: WWW.ART-DEPT.COM

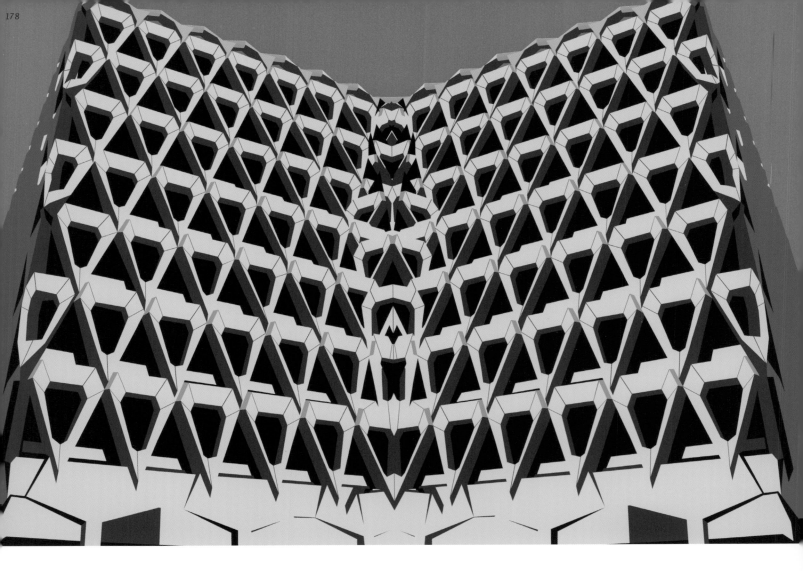

REILLY (UK) *above*
TITLE: NCP CAR PARK
BRIEF: PART OF A COLLECTION OF LIMITED-EDITION WORKS
FOR A ONE-MAN SHOW AT THE EXPOSURE GALLERY, LONDON
PUBLICATION: N/A
ART DIRECTION: N/A
DIMENSIONS: N/A
MEDIA: DIGITAL
ARTIST REPRESENTATION: ART DEPARTMENT
CONTACT: STEPHANIEP@ART-DEPT.COM
URL: WWW.ART-DEPT.COM

DAN TAYLOR (UK) *right*
TITLE: FIREPLACE
BRIEF: SELF-PROMOTIONAL PIECE
PUBLICATION: N/A
ART DIRECTION: N/A
DIMENSIONS: 4 ³/₈ X 5 ½ IN 112 X 141 MM
MEDIA: MIXED ACRYLIC, SPRAY-PAINT, COLLAGE
ARTIST REPRESENTATION: NB ILLUSTRATION
CONTACT: INFO@NBILLUSTRATION.CO.UK
URL: WWW.NBILLUSTRATION.CO.UK

PAUL JACKSON (UK) *left*
TITLE: THE BIG GAME
BRIEF: ILLUSTRATION FOR A SHORT STORY
PUBLICATION: N/A
ART DIRECTION: N/A
DIMENSIONS: 5 3/4 X 8 IN 146 X 202 MM
MEDIA: DRAWING, XEROX, OMNICROM
ARTIST REPRESENTATION: JELLY LONDON
CONTACT: INFO@JELLYLONDON.COM
URL: WWW.JELLYLONDON.COM

REILLY (UK) *above*
TITLE: LA MAISON DU FADA
BRIEF: PART OF A COLLECTION OF LIMITED-EDITION WORKS
FOR A ONE-MAN SHOW AT THE EXPOSURE GALLERY, LONDON
PUBLICATION: N/A
ART DIRECTION: N/A
DIMENSIONS: N/A
MEDIA: DIGITAL
ARTIST REPRESENTATION: ART DEPARTMENT
CONTACT: STEPHANIEP@ART-DEPT.COM
URL: WWW.ART-DEPT.COM

PHILIPPE LECHIEN (FRANCE) *facing page, top*
TITLE: GARE D'AUSTERLITZ
BRIEF: SELF-PROMOTIONAL PIECE, NIGHT VIEW
OF A TRAIN STATION AND SUBWAY TRAIN
PUBLICATION: N/A
ART DIRECTION: N/A
DIMENSIONS: 14 ⅝ X 11 ¼ IN 373 X 286 MM
MEDIA: WATERCOLOR PENCIL, INK
ARTIST REPRESENTATION: MORGAN GAYNIN, INC.
CONTACT: INFO@MORGANGAYNIN.COM
URL: WWW.MORGANGAYNIN.COM

OWEN SHERWOOD (USA) *above right*
TITLE: N/A
BRIEF: N/A
PUBLICATION: ANOTHER LATE NIGHT MAGAZINE
ART DIRECTION: ANOTHER LATE NIGHT MAGAZINE
DIMENSIONS: 14 ⅛ X 5 3/4 IN 360 X 147 MM
MEDIA: PENCIL, ADOBE PHOTOSHOP
ARTIST REPRESENTATION: NB ILLUSTRATION
CONTACT: INFO@NBILLUSTRATION.CO.UK
URL: WWW.NBILLUSTRATION.CO.UK

PABLO BERNASCONI (ARGENTINA) *facing page, bottom*
TITLE: UNROOT
BRIEF: BOOK ILLUSTRATION ON THE THEME
OF DEMOLITION OF OLD CLASSIC HOUSES
PUBLICATION: ALMANAQUE BARILOCHE
ART DIRECTION: N/A
DIMENSIONS: 23 ⅝ X 11 3/4 IN 600 X 300 MM
MEDIA: COLLAGE
ARTIST REPRESENTATION: SHANNON ASSOCIATES (USA) /
DÉBUT ART (UK)
CONTACT: INFORMATION@SHANNONASSOCIATES.COM /
INFO@DEBUTART.COM
URL: WWW.SHANNONASSOCIATES.COM /
WWW.DEBUTART.COM

CAROLE HÉNAFF (FRANCE) *facing page*
TITLE: SMARA
BRIEF: BOOK ILLUSTRATION, PRESENTING THE MUSLIM
VILLAGE OF SMARA, WITH ITS MOSQUE AND MARKET
PUBLICATION: SMARA, KALANDRAKA EDITION
ART DIRECTION: OLALLA GONZALES
DIMENSIONS: 11 ¾ X 15 ¾ IN 300 X 400 MM
MEDIA: ACRYLIC ON WOOD
ARTIST REPRESENTATION: MARLENA AGENCY
CONTACT: MARLENA@MARLENAAGENCY.COM
URL: WWW.MARLENAAGENCY.COM

KEVIN MCBRIDE (CANADA) *right*
TITLE: SHUTER ST. (yellow houses)
TITLE: KING ST. (red building)

BRIEF: SELF-PROMOTIONAL WORK
PUBLICATION: N/A
ART DIRECTION: N/A
DIMENSIONS: 20 X 16 IN 508 X 406 MM
MEDIA: INK, ACRYLIC, WATERCOLOR ON PAPER
ARTIST REPRESENTATION: N/A
CONTACT: KMCBRIDE@SYMPATICO.CA
URL: WWW.KEVMCBRIDE.COM

JASON STAVROU (UK) *below*
TITLE: DANNY WALLACE IN PRAGUE
BRIEF: EDITORIAL ILLUSTRATION FOR A SHORT STORY
PUBLICATION: THE GUARDIAN, UK
ART DIRECTION: ROGER BROWNING, THE GUARDIAN, UK
DIMENSIONS: 14 ¾ X 6 ¾ IN 375 X 170 MM
MEDIA: MIXED MEDIA, DIGITAL
ARTIST REPRESENTATION: EYE CANDY ILLUSTRATION AGENCY
CONTACT: INFO@EYECANDY.CO.UK
URL: WWW.EYECANDY.CO.UK

CHLOÉ POIZAT (FRANCE) *left, top*
TITLE: SEPTEMBER
BRIEF: CALENDAR ILLUSTRATION
PUBLICATION: (CALENDAR)
ART DIRECTION: ALAIN LACHARTRE, VUE SUR LA VILLE
DIMENSIONS: 12 1/8 X 15 1/4 IN 308 X 388 MM
MEDIA: ACRYLIC AND TRANSFER ON PAPER
ARTIST REPRESENTATION: N/A
CONTACT: CHLOEPOIZAT@FREE.FR
URL: WWW.CHLOEPOIZAT.COM

GINA TRIPLETT & MATT CURTIUS (USA) *left, center*
TITLE: BUMBERSHOOT POSTER
BRIEF: POSTER PROMOTING THE BUMBERSHOOT FESTIVAL IN SEATTLE
PUBLICATION: N/A
ART DIRECTION: KAREN HITE AND LEAH JACOBSON,
WIEDEN + KENNEDY FOR STARBUCKS
DIMENSIONS: 10 X 14 IN 254 X 356 MM
MEDIA: ACRYLIC PAINT
ARTIST REPRESENTATION: FRANK STURGES REPS
CONTACT: FRANK@STURGESREPS.COM
URL: WWW.STURGESREPS.COM

SARAH PERKINS (UK) *left, bottom*
TITLE: NIGHT OF RAIN AND STARS
BRIEF: BOOK ILLUSTRATION INTENDED TO TRANSPORT THE READER
TO A GREEK TAVERN SCENE, WITH AZURE WATERS AND BLUE SKIES
PUBLICATION: NIGHT OF RAIN AND STARS
ART DIRECTION: RABAB ADAMS, ORION PUBLISHING
DIMENSIONS: 4 5/8 X 7 7/8 IN 117 X 200 MM
MEDIA: MIXED MEDIA
ARTIST REPRESENTATION: THE INKSHED
CONTACT: ABBY@INKSHED.CO.UK
URL: WWW.INKSHED.CO.UK

MANDY PRITTY (UK) *facing page, top*
TITLE: DREAM RACER
BRIEF: SELF-PROMOTIONAL PIECE DEPICTING TWO GIRLS PULLING
A VICTORIAN BATHTUB ON WHEELS IN A MOONLIT LANDSCAPE
PUBLICATION: N/A
ART DIRECTION: N/A
DIMENSIONS: 11 X 6 IN 291 X 165 MM
MEDIA: OIL ON CANVAS
ARTIST REPRESENTATION: N/A
CONTACT: ART@MANDYPRITTY.COM
URL: WWW.MANDYPRITTY.COM

CHLOÉ POIZAT (FRANCE) *facing page, bottom*
TITLE: N/A
BRIEF: SELF-PROMOTIONAL ILLUSTRATION
PUBLICATION: N/A
ART DIRECTION: N/A
DIMENSIONS: 17 X 12 5/8 IN 444 X 322 MM
MEDIA: ACRYLIC AND TRANSFER ON PAPER
ARTIST REPRESENTATION: N/A
CONTACT: CHLOEPOIZAT@FREE.FR
URL: WWW.CHLOEPOIZAT.COM

OLAF HAJEK (GERMANY) *below*
TITLE: VOLCANO
BRIEF: PERSONAL PIECE FOR "ILLUSTRATIVE 2007" EXHIBITION
PUBLICATION: N/A
ART DIRECTION: N/A
DIMENSIONS: N/A
MEDIA: ACRYLIC ON CARDBOARD
ARTIST REPRESENTATION: BERNSTEIN & ANDRIULLI (USA)
CONTACT: LOUISA@BA-REPS.COM
URL: WWW.BA-REPS.COM

GINA TRIPLETT & MATT CURTIUS (USA) *above*
TITLE: THE WORLD IS NEVER ENOUGH
BRIEF: ILLUSTRATION FOR A CALENDAR BASED ON
JAMES BOND MOVIE TITLES
PUBLICATION: (CALENDAR)
ART DIRECTION: SALVATO COE AND GABOR
DIMENSIONS: 24 X 24 IN 610 X 610 MM
MEDIA: ACRYLIC PAINT
ARTIST REPRESENTATION: FRANK STURGES REPS
CONTACT: FRANK@STURGESREPS.COM
URL: WWW.STURGESREPS.COM

GIANPAOLO PAGNI (FRANCE) *facing page*
TITLE: N/A
BRIEF: ILLUSTRATION FOR "VUE SUR LA VILLE" AGENCY CALENDAR
PUBLICATION: (CALENDAR)
ART DIRECTION: ALAIN LACHARTRE, VUE SUR LA VILLE
DIMENSIONS: 11 X 14 1/8 IN 280 X 360 MM
MEDIA: ACRYLIC ON PAPER
ARTIST REPRESENTATION: COSTUME 3 PIÈCES (UK, FRANCE) /
MARLENA AGENCY (USA)
CONTACT: CONTACT@COSTUME3PIECES.COM /
MARLENA@MARLENAAGENCY.COM
URL: WWW.COSTUME3PIECES.COM /
WWW.MARLENAAGENCY.COM

CHRIS ANDREWS (UK) *above, left*
TITLE: SKATER
BRIEF: SELF-PROMOTIONAL POSTCARD IMAGE
TO PROMOTE AN EXHIBITION FROM THE GUMBO
ILLUSTRATION COLLECTIVE
PUBLICATION: N/A
ART DIRECTION: N/A
DIMENSIONS: 10 ⅜ X 11 ¼ IN 262 X 286 MM
MEDIA: PAINT, DIGITAL
ARTIST REPRESENTATION: EASTWING
CONTACT: ANDREA@EASTWING.CO.UK
URL: WWW.EASTWING.CO.UK

GARY EMBURY (UK) *above, right*
TITLE: SNOW
BRIEF: SELF-INITIATED PROJECT ON SURVEILLANCE
PUBLICATION: N/A
ART DIRECTION: N/A
DIMENSIONS: 5 ⅛ X 4 ¾ IN 129 X 121 MM
MEDIA: MIXED MEDIA, DIGITAL
ARTIST REPRESENTATION: THE INKSHED
CONTACT: ABBY@INKSHED.CO.UK
URL: WWW.INKSHED.CO.UK

YEE TING KUIT (UK) *facing page*
TITLE: BIRDWIRE
BRIEF: SELF-PROMOTIONAL PIECE
PUBLICATION: N/A
ART DIRECTION: N/A
DIMENSIONS: 8 ¼ X 11 ¾ IN 210 X 297 MM
MEDIA: DIGITAL
ARTIST REPRESENTATION: THE ORGANISATION
CONTACT: INFO@ORGANISART.CO.UK
URL: WWW.ORGANISART.CO.UK

190

ROMAN KLONEK (POLAND) *facing page*
TITLE: HELLO MOSKVA
BRIEF: SELF-PROMOTIONAL PIECE
PUBLICATION: N/A
ART DIRECTION: N/A
DIMENSIONS: 19 1/4 X 27 1/8 IN 490 X 690 MM
MEDIA: WOODCUT PRINT
ARTIST REPRESENTATION: FRANK STURGES REPS
CONTACT: FRANK@STURGESREPS.COM
URL: WWW.STURGESREPS.COM

JONATHAN CROFT (UK) *left*
TITLE: SEEDY CAR PARK
BRIEF: ILLUSTRATION OF AN URBAN SCENE
FOR A WEBSITE DESIGN
PUBLICATION: N/A
ART DIRECTION: N/A
DIMENSIONS: 7 7/8 X 5 7/8 IN 200 X 150 MM
MEDIA: DIGITAL
ARTIST REPRESENTATION: N/A
CONTACT: JONATHAN.CROFT@BTINTERNET.COM
URL: WWW.JONATHANCROFT.COM

MARY KILVERT (UK) *right*
TITLE: MAGICAL LANDS
BRIEF: SELF-PROMOTIONAL PIECE
PUBLICATION: N/A
ART DIRECTION: N/A
DIMENSIONS: 10 1/8 X 13 3/8 IN 257 X 340 MM
MEDIA: PEN AND INK, DIGITAL COLOR
ARTIST REPRESENTATION: NEW DIVISION (UK) /
LINDGREN & SMITH (USA)
CONTACT: INFO@NEWDIVISION.COM /
INFO@LSILLUSTRATION.COM
URL: WWW.NEWDIVISION.COM /
WWW.LINDGRENSMITH.COM

RINA DONNERSMARCK (GERMANY) *facing page*
TITLE: I TELL YOU
BRIEF: EXHIBITION PIECE
PUBLICATION: N/A
ART DIRECTION: N/A
DIMENSIONS: 9 ³⁄₈ X 12 ¹⁄₂ IN 238 X 319 MM
MEDIA: PEN ON PAPER
ARTIST REPRESENTATION: N/A
CONTACT: RINAHD@ANOTHER.COM
URL: WWW.RINADONNERSMARCK.CO.UK

NADIA BERKANE (FRANCE) *right*
TITLE: NEIGE BLANCHE
BRIEF: EDITORIAL ILLUSTRATION
PUBLICATION: TOBOGAN MAGAZINE, MILAN PRESS GROUP
ART DIRECTION: TOBOGAN MAGAZINE
DIMENSIONS: 5 ⁷⁄₈ X 5 ⁷⁄₈ IN 150 X 150 MM
MEDIA: DIGITAL (ADOBE ILLUSTRATOR)
ARTIST REPRESENTATION: CHEZ ANTOINE
CONTACT: INFO@CHEZANTOINE.COM
URL: WWW.CHEZANTOINE.COM

YEE TING KUIT (UK) *below*
TITLE: PANORAMA
BRIEF: ARTWORK BASED ON THE THEME OF "ENVIRONMENT,"
CREATED FOR ORANGE OPTIMISM YCN AWARDS 07/08
PUBLICATION: N/A
ART DIRECTION: N/A
DIMENSIONS: 8 ¹⁄₄ X 11 ³⁄₄ IN 210 X 297 MM
MEDIA: DIGITAL
ARTIST REPRESENTATION: THE ORGANISATION
CONTACT: INFO@ORGANISART.CO.UK
URL: WWW.ORGANISART.CO.UK

JUDY STEVENS (UK) *right*
TITLE: PARC GUELL
BRIEF: PERSONAL PIECE
PUBLICATION: N/A
ART DIRECTION: N/A
DIMENSIONS: 16 ½ X 15 IN 420 X 380 MM
MEDIA: FOUR-COLOR LINOCUT PRINT
ARTIST REPRESENTATION: NB ILLUSTRATION
CONTACT: INFO@NBILLUSTRATION.CO.UK
URL: WWW.NBILLUSTRATION.CO.UK

CHRIS RUBINO (USA) *left*
TITLE: PARENTS' VACATION
BRIEF: ILLUSTRATION PROMOTING A NEW GERMAN
LIFESTYLE MAGAZINE
PUBLICATION: N/A
ART DIRECTION: KIRCHER BURKHARDT
DIMENSIONS: 8 X 10 IN 203 X 254 MM
MEDIA: PEN AND INK, DIGITAL COLOR
ARTIST REPRESENTATION: ART DEPARTMENT
CONTACT: STEPHANIEP@ART-DEPT.COM
URL: WWW.ART-DEPT.COM

GEORGINA HOUNSOME (UK) *facing page*
TITLE: RED BENCH
BRIEF: WEDDING INVITATION DESIGN
PUBLICATION: N/A
ART DIRECTION: N/A
DIMENSIONS: 7 X 11 IN 189 X 280 MM
MEDIA: DIGITAL IMAGE PRINTED ON TEXTURED PAPER
ARTIST REPRESENTATION: EYE CANDY ILLUSTRATION AGENCY
CONTACT: INFO@EYECANDY.CO.UK
URL: WWW.EYECANDY.CO.UK

KEITH HERBERT (UK) *above*

TITLE: AA

BRIEF: WEB BANNER ILLUSTRATION

PUBLICATION: AUTOMOBILE ASSOCIATION WEBSITE

ART DIRECTION: DLKW

DIMENSIONS: 29 ⅝ X 7 ½ IN 751 X 191 MM

MEDIA: DIGITAL

ARTIST REPRESENTATION: JELLY LONDON

CONTACT: INFO@JELLYLONDON.COM

URL: WWW.JELLYLONDON.COM

CHRIS KEEGAN (UK) *facing page, bottom*

TITLE: GRASS

BRIEF: TO ILLUSTRATE CLEAN AIR SKIES

PUBLICATION: AIRLINES INTERNATIONAL MAGAZINE

ART DIRECTION: AIRLINES INTERNATIONAL MAGAZINE

DIMENSIONS: 10 X 11 ¼ IN 253 X 287 MM

MEDIA: PHOTOMONTAGE

ARTIST REPRESENTATION: SYNERGY

CONTACT: INFO@SYNERGYART.CO.UK

URL: WWW.SYNERGYART.CO.UK

BARBARA SPOETTEL (GERMANY) *above*
TITLE: HAMBURG
BRIEF: ILLUSTRATION FOR A CALENDAR ON HAMBURG CITY
PUBLICATION: CALENDAR FOR RESET PRINT HOUSE, HAMBURG
ART DIRECTION: MARIUS FAHRNER, MARIUS FAHRNER DESIGN
DIMENSIONS: 5 7/8 X 4 3/8 IN 150 X 110 MM
MEDIA: DIGITAL
ARTIST REPRESENTATION: NEW DIVISION
CONTACT: INFO@NEWDIVISION.COM
URL: WWW.NEWDIVISION.COM

ROBIN CHEVALIER (UK) *above, left*
TITLE: PARIS
BRIEF: SELF-PROMOTIONAL WORK
PUBLICATION: N/A
ART DIRECTION: N/A
DIMENSIONS: N/A
MEDIA: HAND-DRAWN AND DIGITAL
ARTIST REPRESENTATION: EASTWING
CONTACT: ANDREA@EASTWING.CO.UK
URL: WWW.EASTWING.CO.UK

MELVYN EVANS (UK) *facing page, top*
TITLE: BIRDLAND
BRIEF: SELF-PROMOTIONAL PIECE
PUBLICATION: N/A
ART DIRECTION: N/A
DIMENSIONS: 17 3/8 X 11 1/4 MM 442 X 286 MM
MEDIA: ADOBE ILLUSTRATOR
ARTIST REPRESENTATION: NEW DIVISION
CONTACT: INFO@NEWDIVISION.COM
URL: WWW.NEWDIVISION.COM

JOSH COCHRAN (USA) *above, right*
TITLE: THE YEAR THAT WAS
BRIEF: EDITORIAL ILLUSTRATION FOR A SPECIAL
END-OF-YEAR ISSUE, FEATURING THE
DECONSTRUCTION OF A GIANT CLOCK TOWER
PUBLICATION: THE YEAR THAT WAS,
ENTERTAINMENT WEEKLY
ART DIRECTION: BRIAN ANSTEY,
ENTERTAINMENT WEEKLY
DIMENSIONS: 16 X 14 7/8 IN 406 X 379 MM
MEDIA: MIXED MEDIA, DIGITAL
ARTIST REPRESENTATION: BOUTIQUE
CONTACT: LOUISA@BA-REPS.COM
URL: WWW.BOUTIQUE-ART.COM

SIMON SPILSBURY (UK) *facing page, bottom*
TITLE: US SCAPE
BRIEF: OPEN BRIEF TO DECORATE A 15-FOOT PILLAR IN
BBH'S NEW YORK OFFICE
PUBLICATION: N/A
ART DIRECTION: KEVIN RODDY, BBH
DIMENSIONS: 15 X 3 FT 4.54 X 0.97 M
MEDIA: BRUSH AND INK
ARTIST REPRESENTATION: CENTRAL ILLUSTRATION
AGENCY (CIA)
CONTACT: INFO@CENTRALILLUSTRATION.COM
URL: WWW.CENTRALILLUSTRATION.COM

ALEXANDRA HIGLETT (UK) *left*
TITLE: POLLUTION
BRIEF: PERSONAL WORK
PUBLICATION: N/A
ART DIRECTION: N/A
DIMENSIONS: 11 ¼ X 17 ⅜ IN 286 X 442 MM
MEDIA: PAINTING AND COLLAGE/CUT PAPER ON ENDPAPER
ARTIST REPRESENTATION: N/A
CONTACT: ALEXHIGLETT@HOTMAIL.COM
URL: WWW.ALEXANDGEORGE.CO.UK

GINA TRIPLETT & MATT CURTIUS (USA) *below*
TITLE: THE ZEN OF SURFING
BRIEF: ILLUSTRATION FOR AN ARTICLE ABOUT
BUDDHISM AND SURFING
PUBLICATION: N/A
ART DIRECTION: STEPHANIE GLAROS, UTNE READER
DIMENSIONS: 6 ½ X 4 ½ IN 165 X 114 MM
MEDIA: ACRYLIC PAINT
ARTIST REPRESENTATION: FRANK STURGES REPS
CONTACT: FRANK@STURGESREPS.COM
URL: WWW.STURGESREPS.COM

CHRISTOPHER HADJINICOLA (UK)
TITLE: LONDON'S PARKS
BRIEF: UNIVERSITY PROSPECTUS ILLUSTRATION
PUBLICATION: MIDDLESEX UNIVERSITY PROSPECTUS
ART DIRECTION: MIDDLESEX UNIVERSITY
DIMENSIONS: 10 5/8 X 15 3/4 IN 270 X 400 MM
MEDIA: DIGITAL
ARTIST REPRESENTATION: JELLY LONDON
CONTACT: INFO@JELLYLONDON.COM
URL: WWW.JELLYLONDON.COM

VINCENT BALAS (FRANCE) *right, top*
TITLE: WOOD CREATURE
BRIEF: SELF-PROMOTIONAL PIECE
PUBLICATION: N/A
ART DIRECTION: N/A
DIMENSIONS: 7 7/8 X 4 3/8 IN 200 X 110 MM
MEDIA: INK AND DIGITAL
ARTIST REPRESENTATION: COSTUME 3 PIÈCES
CONTACT: CONTACT@COSTUME3PIECES.COM
URL: WWW.COSTUME3PIECES.COM

SERGE SEIDLITZ (UK/GERMANY) *right, bottom*
TITLE: MANCHESTER INTERNATIONAL FAIR 2007,
THE GREAT INDOORS
BRIEF: PROMOTION FOR MANCHESTER INTERNATIONAL FAIR
PUBLICATION: N/A
ART DIRECTION: LOVE CREATIVE
DIMENSIONS: N/A
MEDIA: PEN AND INK, DIGITAL
ARTIST REPRESENTATION: DÉBUT ART
CONTACT: INFO@DEBUTART.COM
URL: WWW.DEBUTART.COM

TRINA DALZIEL (UK) *below*
TITLE: LIST-BUYING
BRIEF: TO ILLUSTRATE OVERUSE OF MARKETING DATABASES
PUBLICATION: N/A
ART DIRECTION: DINAH LONE, DIRECT MARKETING
DIMENSIONS: 7 1/2 X 8 1/4 IN 190 X 211 MM
MEDIA: HAND-DRAWN, COLORED IN ADOBE ILLUSTRATOR
ARTIST REPRESENTATION: LILLA ROGERS
CONTACT: LILLA@LILLAROGERS.COM
URL: WWW.LILLAROGERS.COM

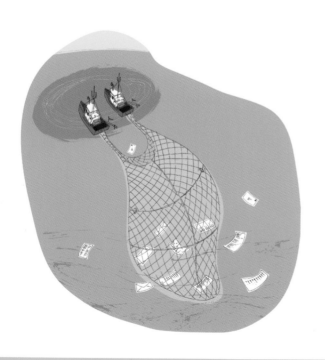

MIKAEL KANGAS (SWEDEN)
TITLE: FAIRYTALE IDEALS
BRIEF: EDITORIAL ILLUSTRATION, PART
OF A SERIES EXPLORING THE WORLD
OF FAIRY TALES
PUBLICATION: +ROSEBUD MAGAZINE,
NO.6
ART DIRECTION: RALF HERMS,
+ROSEBUD MAGAZINE
DIMENSIONS: 16 7/8 X 11 3/4 IN
430 X 300 MM
MEDIA: N/A
ARTIST REPRESENTATION: SYNERGY
CONTACT: INFO@SYNERGYART.CO.UK
URL: WWW.SYNERGYART.CO.UK

STEVEN TABUTT (USA)
TITLE: THE ORACLES
BRIEF: COMPETITION PIECE TO CREATE A FUTURISTIC IDEA OF THE ORACLE,
DRAWING ON THEMES (SUCH AS THE YARN CONNECTING PAST IMAGES
TO FUTURE INTERPRETATIONS) FROM GREEK AND ROMAN MYTHOLOGY
PUBLICATION: N/A
ART DIRECTION: N/A
DIMENSIONS: 11 X 14 IN 279 X 356 MM
MEDIA: MIXED MEDIA
ARTIST REPRESENTATION: MORGAN GAYNIN, INC.
CONTACT: INFO@MORGANGAYNIN.COM
URL: WWW.MORGANGAYNIN.COM

5

conceptual & abstract

WHOA... LONG HAIR STUFF, OR WHAT? Is that a pencil that's crying? Why is it raining bubbles on the guy with the umbrella? What is happening to that girl's eye with the cotton reel things? Who thinks this stuff up? Are those robots in love? What's that DNA strip doing with a police tag round it's neck? Oh, I get it. That's very clever, actually. But, what's the girl with no clothes on lying on the sheep that's standing on the banana all about? And the fully-clothed guy in the bath? Weird, weird, weird, weird, weird, weird, weird. I like it, though. And you should really check out Aunty Gloria, page 229.

NOBBY SPROUTS (UK) *left*
TITLE: OLD FLAME
BRIEF: SELF-PROMOTIONAL PIECE
PUBLICATION: N/A
ART DIRECTION: N/A
DIMENSIONS: 7 1/8 X 12 5/8 IN 180 X 320 MM
MEDIA: MIXED MEDIA
ARTIST REPRESENTATION: N/A
CONTACT: AJPOTTER@PLYMOUTH.AC.UK
URL: WWW.THEDAIRYSTUDIOS.CO.UK

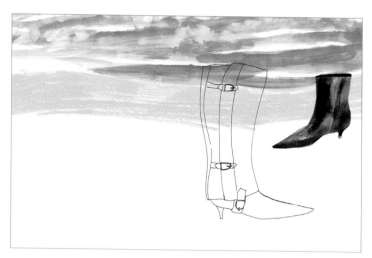

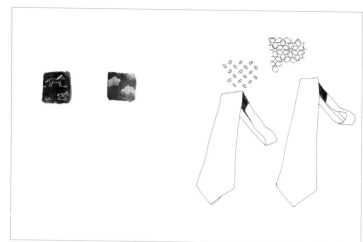

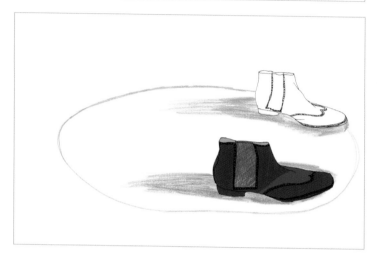

MATTHEW LEBARON (USA) *facing page, bottom*
TITLE: FAKING IT!
BRIEF: COLOR ILLUSTRATION FOR AN ARTICLE ON HOW
HETEROSEXUAL MEN CAN "FAKE" ALMOST EVERYTHING
IN LIFE, FROM DATES TO INTELLIGENCE TO CLASS
PUBLICATION: N/A
ART DIRECTION: HENRY OBASI, PPAINT
DIMENSIONS: 9 ½ X 4 ⅜ IN 241 X 111 MM
MEDIA: PEN AND INK, FOUND TEXTURES, ADOBE
ILLUSTRATOR AND ADOBE PHOTOSHOP
ARTIST REPRESENTATION: N/A
CONTACT: MATTHEWTLEBARON@GMAIL.COM
URL: WWW.MATTHEWLEBARON.BLOGSPOT.COM

CASSANDRE MONTORIOL (FRANCE) *above*
TITLE: HERMÈS CATALOG FALL–WINTER 2003
BRIEF: CATALOG ARTWORK
PUBLICATION: HERMÈS CATALOG FALL–WINTER 2003
ART DIRECTION: ERIC JOUZEAU, HERMÈS EDITIONS
DIMENSIONS: 9 ½ X 6 ⅞ IN 240 X 175 MM
MEDIA: ACRYLIC ON PAPER
ARTIST REPRESENTATION: ART DEPARTMENT
CONTACT: STEPHANIEP@ART-DEPT.COM
URL: WWW.ART-DEPT.COM

OLIVER BARRETT (USA) *left*
TITLE: UMBRELLA MAN
BRIEF: SELF-PROMOTIONAL
CONCEPTUAL ILLUSTRATION
PUBLICATION: N/A
ART DIRECTION: N/A
DIMENSIONS: 4 3/8 X 6 1/8 IN 110 X 155 MM
MEDIA: DIGITAL VECTOR ILLUSTRATION
ARTIST REPRESENTATION: BERNSTEIN &
ANDRIULLI (USA)
CONTACT: LOUISA@BA-REPS.COM
URL: WWW.BA-REPS.COM

DAVE BAIN (UK) *facing page*
TITLE: CREATIVE BRISTOL POSTER
BRIEF: A POSTER IMAGE EXPRESSING
THE DIVERSE RANGE OF ARTISTIC
CREATIVITY IN BRISTOL, ENGLAND
PUBLICATION: (POSTER)
ART DIRECTION: BRISTOL CREATIVES
DIMENSIONS: 11 1/8 X 15 3/4 IN
283 X 400 MM
MEDIA: ACRYLIC ON WOOD
ARTIST REPRESENTATION:
THE ORGANISATION
CONTACT: INFO@ORGANISART.CO.UK
URL: WWW.ORGANISART.CO.UK

SÉVERINE SCAGLIA (FRANCE) *below*
TITLE: BLUE EYE AND BIRD
BRIEF: UNPUBLISHED PERSONAL PIECE
PUBLICATION: N/A
ART DIRECTION: N/A
DIMENSIONS: 11 3/4 X 8 3/8 IN 300 X 212 MM
MEDIA: N/A
ARTIST REPRESENTATION: COSTUME 3 PIÈCES
CONTACT: CONTACT@COSTUME3PIECES.COM
URL: WWW.COSTUME3PIECES.COM

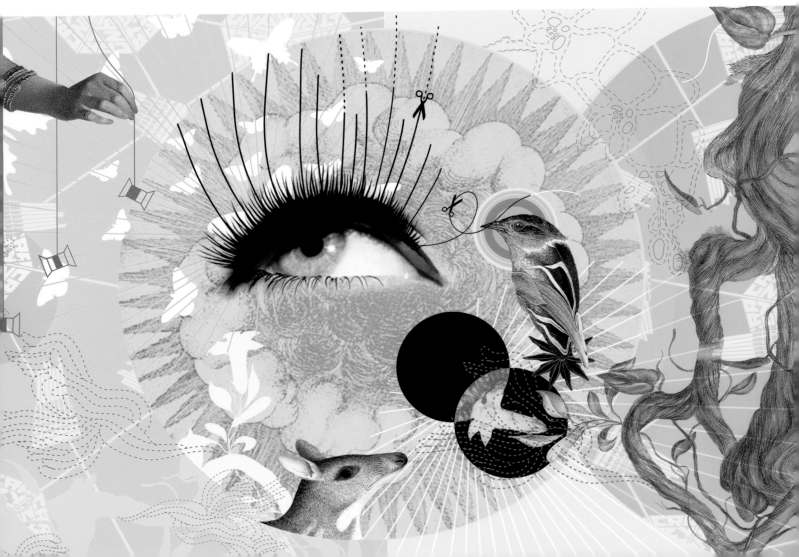

JESSICA HISCHE (USA) *above, left*
TITLE: DESIGNER'S DIET
BRIEF: SELF-PROMOTIONAL WORK, PART OF A SERIES
ENTITLED "JESSICA HISCHE'S BODY OF WORK"
PUBLICATION: N/A
ART DIRECTION: N/A
DIMENSIONS: 5 ½ X 9 IN 140 X 229 MM
MEDIA: DIGITAL VECTOR ARTWORK, TEXTURE
ARTIST REPRESENTATION: FRANK STURGES REPS
CONTACT: FRANK@STURGESREPS.COM
URL: WWW.STURGESREPS.COM

SUSANNE SAENGER (GERMANY) *above, center*
TITLE: CANDY
BRIEF: SELF-PROMOTIONAL WORK; VISUALIZATION
OF THE TERM "CANDY" ON A POSTCARD
PUBLICATION: N/A
ART DIRECTION: N/A
DIMENSIONS: 5 ¾ X 8 ⅛ IN 146 X 207 MM
MEDIA: PEN AND INK, DIGITAL
ARTIST REPRESENTATION: KATE LARKWORTHY
CONTACT: KATE@LARKWORTHY.COM
URL: WWW.LARKWORTHY.COM

STEPHAN BRITT (USA) *above, right*
TITLE: DNA MUG SHOT
BRIEF: MAGAZINE ILLUSTRATION, TO SHOW HOW
WE ARE "CONDEMNED BY OUR GENETIC MAKEUP"
PUBLICATION: POZ MAGAZINE
ART DIRECTION: POZ MAGAZINE
DIMENSIONS: 8 X 11 IN 203 X 279 MM
MEDIA: DIGITAL
ARTIST REPRESENTATION: MAGNET REPS
CONTACT: ART@MAGNETREPS.COM
URL: WWW.MAGNETREPS.COM

MARK BLADE (UK) *right*
TITLE: ROBOT LOVE IS AUTOMATIC
BRIEF: AGENCY ADVERTISING PIECE FOR VALENTINE'S DAY, FOR WEB AND PRINT
PUBLICATION: NEW DIVISION AGENCY HOME PAGE
ART DIRECTION: NEW DIVISION
DIMENSIONS: 4 X 4 IN 100 X 100 MM
MEDIA: DIGITAL
ARTIST REPRESENTATION: NEW DIVISION
CONTACT: INFO@NEWDIVISION.COM
URL: WWW.NEWDIVISION.COM

REILLY (UK) *left*
TITLE: EXQUISITE CORPSE
BRIEF: ADVERTISEMENT ARTWORK SHOWING A GAME OF "EXQUISITE CORPSE" PROMOTING ADOBE CS3 IN CONJUNCTION WITH SURFACE MAGAZINE
PUBLICATION: N/A
ART DIRECTION: N/A
DIMENSIONS: N/A
MEDIA: DIGITAL
ARTIST REPRESENTATION: ART DEPARTMENT
CONTACT: STEPHANIEP@ART-DEPT.COM
URL: WWW.ART-DEPT.COM

KONNICHIWA

KRISTIAN RUSSELL (UK/SWEDEN) *right*
TITLE: BALLERS (TONY PARKER)
BRIEF: ADVERTISING IMAGE FOR NIKE ASIA
PUBLICATION: N/A
ART DIRECTION: WIEDEN KENNEDY, TOKYO
DIMENSIONS: N/A
MEDIA: PEN AND INK, DIGITAL
ARTIST REPRESENTATION: BIG ACTIVE
CONTACT: TIM@BIGACTIVE.COM
URL: WWW.BIGACTIVE.COM

BEN HASLER (UK) *right*
TITLE: GOD OF DRIVING
BRIEF: CAR ADVERTISEMENT
PUBLICATION: N/A
ART DIRECTION: HONDA / MAX POWER
DIMENSIONS: 11 ¾ X 8 ¼ IN 297 X 210 MM
MEDIA: ADOBE ILLUSTRATOR
ARTIST REPRESENTATION: NB ILLUSTRATION
CONTACT: INFO@NBILLUSTRATION.CO.UK
URL: WWW.NBILLUSTRATION.CO.UK

KERRY ROPER (UK) *right*
TITLE: JORDAN
BRIEF: T-SHIRT DESIGN WITH AN ILLUSTRATION
CELEBRATING JORDAN
PUBLICATION: N/A
ART DIRECTION: NIKE
DIMENSIONS: N/A
MEDIA: N/A
ARTIST REPRESENTATION: DÉBUT ART
CONTACT: INFO@DEBUTART.COM
URL: WWW.DEBUTART.COM

SILJA GÖTZ (GERMANY) *above*
TITLE: LASHES
BRIEF: MAGAZINE ILLUSTRATION TO ACCOMPANY AN
ARTICLE COVERING EXTENSIONS FOR EYELASHES
PUBLICATION: NYLON MAGAZINE
ART DIRECTION: NYLON MAGAZINE
DIMENSIONS: 8 ¼ X 5 ⅞ IN 210 X 150 MM
MEDIA: COLLAGE, INK DRAWING
ARTIST REPRESENTATION: ART DEPARTMENT
CONTACT: STEPHANIEP@ART-DEPT.COM
URL: WWW.ART-DEPT.COM

JONATHAN BURTON (UK) *facing page, top left*
TITLE: BUNNY
BRIEF: MAGAZINE ILLUSTRATION FOR AN ARTICLE ABOUT
UNUSUAL EXPENSES CLAIMED BY EMPLOYEES
PUBLICATION: GQ MAGAZINE
ART DIRECTION: HELEN WHITLEY-NILAND, GQ MAGAZINE
DIMENSIONS: 6 ¼ X 6 ¾ IN 160 X 170 MM
MEDIA: MIXED MEDIA
ARTIST REPRESENTATION: NB ILLUSTRATION
CONTACT: INFO@NBILLUSTRATION.CO.UK
URL: WWW.NBILLUSTRATION.CO.UK

VALERIA PETRONE (ITALY) *above right*
TITLE: HORNS
BRIEF: PROMOTIONAL BROCHURE ILLUSTRATION
PUBLICATION: N/A
ART DIRECTION: MORGAN GAYNIN
DIMENSIONS: N/A
MEDIA: DIGITAL
ARTIST REPRESENTATION:
MORGAN GAYNIN, INC.
CONTACT: INFO@MORGANGAYNIN.COM
URL: WWW.MORGANGAYNIN.COM

GÉRARD DUBOIS (FRANCE) *left*
TITLE: COGNITIVE THERAPY
BRIEF: MAGAZINE COVER ILLUSTRATION FOR
AN ISSUE ABOUT DIFFERENT THERAPIES
PUBLICATION: THE SAN FRANCISCO
CHRONICLE
ART DIRECTION: DOROTHY YULE,
THE SAN FRANCISCO CHRONICLE
DIMENSIONS: 9 5/8 X 11 1/4 IN 245 X 285 MM
MEDIA: ACRYLIC ON PAPER
ARTIST REPRESENTATION:
MARLENA AGENCY (N.AMERICA)
/ COSTUME 3 PIÈCES (EUROPE)
CONTACT: MARLENA@MARLENAAGENCY.COM
/ CONTACT@COSTUME3PIECES.COM
URL: WWW.MARLENAAGENCY.COM
/ WWW.COSTUME3PIECES.COM

PABLO PICYK (ARGENTINA) *right*
TITLE: MUSICWORLD
BRIEF: SELF-PROMOTIONAL PIECE
PUBLICATION: N/A
ART DIRECTION: N/A
DIMENSIONS: 5 ³⁄₈ X 5 ³⁄₈ IN 135 X 135 MM
MEDIA: COLLAGE
ARTIST REPRESENTATION: N/A
CONTACT: CAVOLT@YAHOO.COM.AR

NATE WILLIAMS (USA) *left*
TITLE: FESTIVAL DE L'OH!
BRIEF: POSTER FOR A SERIES OF OUTDOOR SIGNS FOR
THE ANNUAL WATER FESTIVAL IN VAL-DE-MARNE, FRANCE
PUBLICATION: N/A
ART DIRECTION: SOPHIE ESCALMEL, CONSEIL GENERAL DU
VAL-DE-MARNE
DIMENSIONS: 16 X 20 IN 406 X 508 MM
MEDIA: MIXED MEDIA, DIGITAL
ARTIST REPRESENTATION: MAGNET REPS
CONTACT: ART@MAGNETREPS.COM
URL: WWW.MAGNETREPS.COM

BEN CHALLENOR (UK) *right*
TITLE: DROOPY PROBLEM
BRIEF: TO ILLUSTRATE AN ELDERLY MAN'S PROBLEM OF
LOW-HANGING GENITALS
PUBLICATION: THE TIMES, BODY AND SOUL SUPPLEMENT
ART DIRECTION: THE TIMES, UK
DIMENSIONS: 5 1/8 X 8 1/4 IN 130 X 210 MM
MEDIA: MIXED MEDIA
ARTIST REPRESENTATION: EYE CANDY ILLUSTRATION AGENCY
CONTACT: INFO@EYECANDY.CO.UK
URL: WWW.EYECANDY.CO.UK

NATE WILLIAMS (USA) *left*
TITLE: REVISION
BRIEF: ADVERTISEMENT ILLUSTRATION CREATED FOR
A COMPETITION FOR VISIONARY ARCHITECTS ENTITLED
"CHANGING THE WORLD ONE BLOCK AT A TIME"
PUBLICATION: N/A
ART DIRECTION: TYLER YOUNG, YOUNG NOMAD
DIMENSIONS: 16 X 20 IN 406 X 508 MM
MEDIA: MIXED MEDIA, DIGITAL
ARTIST REPRESENTATION: MAGNET REPS
CONTACT: ART@MAGNETREPS.COM
URL: WWW.MAGNETREPS.COM

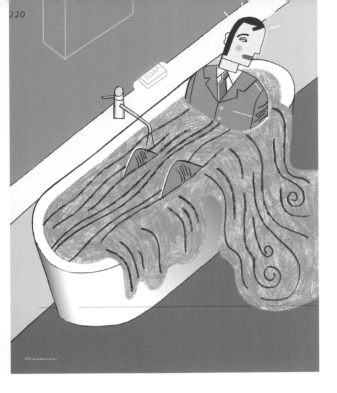

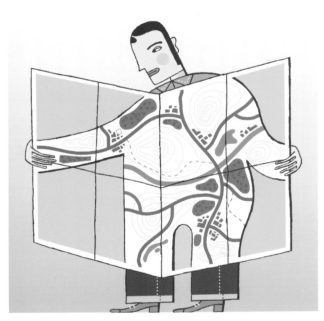

ROBIN CHEVALIER (UK) *left, top*
TITLE: BATH
BRIEF: MAGAZINE ILLUSTRATION FOR A FEATURE ABOUT
OVERAMBITIOUS BUSINESS EXPANSION
PUBLICATION: DIRECTOR MAGAZINE
ART DIRECTION: DIRECTOR MAGAZINE
DIMENSIONS: N/A
MEDIA: HAND-DRAWN, DIGITAL
ARTIST REPRESENTATION: EASTWING
CONTACT: ANDREA@EASTWING.CO.UK
URL: WWW.EASTWING.CO.UK

ROBIN CHEVALIER (UK) *left, center*
TITLE: HUMAN MAP
BRIEF: MAGAZINE ILLUSTRATION FOR A FEATURE ABOUT
UNDERSTANDING HOW YOUR BODY WORKS
PUBLICATION: THE GUARDIAN WEEKEND MAGAZINE, UK
ART DIRECTION: THE GUARDIAN, UK
DIMENSIONS: N/A
MEDIA: HAND-DRAWN, DIGITAL
ARTIST REPRESENTATION: EASTWING
CONTACT: ANDREA@EASTWING.CO.UK
URL: WWW.EASTWING.CO.UK

EMILIANO PONZI (ITALY) *left, bottom*
TITLE: NO EMISSIONS
BRIEF: MAGAZINE ILLUSTRATION, A COMMENTARY ON
NEW EMISSION LAWS
PUBLICATION: IO DONNA MAGAZINE, ITALY
ART DIRECTION: GLORIA GHISI, IO DONNA MAGAZINE
DIMENSIONS: 8 X 11 IN 203 X 279 MM
MEDIA: DIGITAL
ARTIST REPRESENTATION: MAGNET REPS
CONTACT: ART@MAGNETREPS.COM
URL: WWW.MAGNETREPS.COM

COLE GERST (USA) *facing page*
TITLE: SURGE PROTECTOR
BRIEF: SELF-PROMOTIONAL PIECE FOR
OPTION-G STUDIOS
PUBLICATION: N/A
ART DIRECTION: OPTION-G STUDIOS
DIMENSIONS: 13 X 19 IN 330 X 483 MM
MEDIA: ARCHIVAL GICLÉE PRINT
ARTIST REPRESENTATION: ART DEPARTMENT
CONTACT: STEPHANIEP@ART-DEPT.COM
URL: WWW.ART-DEPT.COM

STEPHEN LEDWIDGE (IRELAND) *facing page*
TITLE: DON'T BUY INTO THE LIE
BRIEF: TO ILLUSTRATE AN ARTICLE ABOUT SPORTS SPECIALIZATION
IN SCHOOLS AND HOW IT CAN AFFECT STUDENTS' WORK
PUBLICATION: INDEPENDENT SCHOOLS MAGAZINE
ART DIRECTION: GLENN PIERCE, INDEPENDENT SCHOOLS MAGAZINE
DIMENSIONS: N/A
MEDIA: ACRYLIC AND PENCIL
ARTIST REPRESENTATION: ANNA GOODSON MANAGEMENT
CONTACT: ANNA@AGOODSON.COM
URL: WWW.AGOODSON.COM

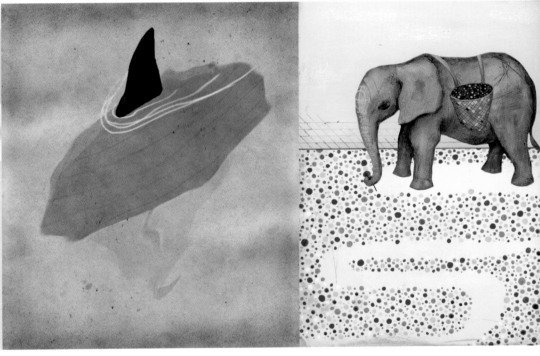

THOMAS KUHLENBECK (GERMANY)
above, left
TITLE: TOO BIG TO GROW
BRIEF: MAGAZINE ILLUSTRATION ABOUT
THE LARGE BLUE-CHIP COMPANIES THAT
DOMINATE THE MARKETS AND MAY HAVE
BECOME TOO BIG TO GROW
PUBLICATION: NEWSWEEK
ART DIRECTION: LEAH PURCELL,
NEWSWEEK
DIMENSIONS: 8 5/8 X 11 1/4 IN
218 X 286 MM
MEDIA: DIGITAL
ARTIST REPRESENTATION:
KATE LARKWORTHY
CONTACT: KATE@LARKWORTHY.COM
URL: WWW.LARKWORTHY.COM

DAVID HUMPHRIES (UK) *above, center*
TITLE: HELP!
BRIEF: DEPICTION OF A VISUAL CONUNDRUM,
FOR A SELF-PROMOTIONAL MAILER
PUBLICATION: N/A
ART DIRECTION: N/A
DIMENSIONS: 8 1/4 X 9 1/8 IN 210 X 231 MM
MEDIA: DIGITAL
ARTIST REPRESENTATION: MONSTERS
CONTACT: DAVID@MONSTERS.CO.UK
URL: WWW.MONSTERS.CO.UK

DANIEL CHANG (USA) *above, right*
TITLE: COLLECTOR
BRIEF: FULL-PAGE MAGAZINE ILLUSTRATION
FOR AN ARTICLE ABOUT TAPE LIBRARIES
BECOMING THE MEDIUM OF CHOICE
FOR LONG-TERM ARCHIVING
PUBLICATION: STORAGE MAGAZINE
ART DIRECTION: MARY BETH CADWELL,
STORAGE MAGAZINE
DIMENSIONS: 8 1/4 X 11 1/4 IN 208 X 286 MM
MEDIA: MIXED MEDIA
ARTIST REPRESENTATION:
FRANK STURGES REPS
CONTACT: FRANK@STURGESREPS.COM
URL: WWW.STURGESREPS.COM

KERASCOËT (FRANCE) *above*
TITLE: LIFE TREE
BRIEF: SELF-PROMOTIONAL POSTER
PUBLICATION: N/A
ART DIRECTION: N/A
DIMENSIONS: N/A
MEDIA: N/A
ARTIST REPRESENTATION: COSTUME 3 PIÈCES
CONTACT: CONTACT@COSTUME3PIECES.COM
URL: WWW.COSTUME3PIECES.COM

COLE GERST (USA) *right, top*
TITLE: BURDEN
BRIEF: SELF-PROMOTIONAL PIECE FOR OPTION-G STUDIOS
PUBLICATION: N/A
ART DIRECTION: OPTION-G STUDIOS
DIMENSIONS: 18 X 24 IN 457 X 610 MM
MEDIA: SCREEN PRINT
ARTIST REPRESENTATION: ART DEPARTMENT
CONTACT: STEPHANIEP@ART-DEPT.COM
URL: WWW.ART-DEPT.COM

GEORGINA HOUNSOME (UK) *above*
TITLE: POST
BRIEF: ILLUSTRATION FOR AN ARTICLE ABOUT POST-PRODUCTION
PUBLICATION: SHOTS MAGAZINE
ART DIRECTION: SHOTS MAGAZINE
DIMENSIONS: 8 ¾ X 11 IN 222 X 280 MM
MEDIA: SCANNED AND MANIPULATED DRAWINGS
ARTIST REPRESENTATION: EYE CANDY ILLUSTRATION AGENCY
CONTACT: INFO@EYECANDY.CO.UK
URL: WWW.EYECANDY.CO.UK

LUCY DAVEY (UK) *above, right*
TITLE: TAX HAVEN
BRIEF: TO ILLUSTRATE AN ARTICLE ABOUT THE CONTROVERSY
SURROUNDING OFFSHORE TAX HAVENS
PUBLICATION: FINANCIAL MANAGEMENT MAGAZINE
ART DIRECTION: GARY HILL, CASPIAN PUBLISHING
DIMENSIONS: 8 ⅞ X 11 ¼ IN 225 X 285 MM
MEDIA: MIXED MEDIA (COLLAGE, PAINT, PEN, DIGITAL, PRINT)
ARTIST REPRESENTATION: THE ARTWORKS
CONTACT: STEPH@THEARTWORKSINC.COM
URL: WWW.THEARTWORKSINC.COM

OLAF HAJEK (GERMANY) *facing page*
TITLE: TIFFANY
BRIEF: A JEWELRY SERIES SPREAD FOR A MAGAZINE
PUBLICATION: QUEST MAGAZINE, GERMANY
ART DIRECTION: N/A
DIMENSIONS: N/A
MEDIA: ACRYLIC ON CARDBOARD
ARTIST REPRESENTATION: BERNSTEIN & ANDRIULLI (USA)
CONTACT: LOUISA@BA-REPS.COM
URL: WWW.BA-REPS.COM

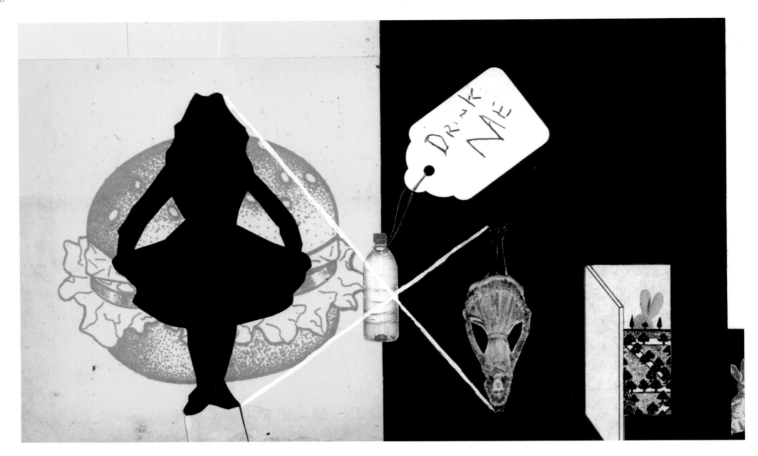

MARK LAZENBY (UK) *above*
TITLE: DRINK ME
BRIEF: MAGAZINE PIECE ON THE THEME OF NEW
DIET PILLS AND DRINKS
PUBLICATION: NYLON MAGAZINE
ART DIRECTION: NYLON MAGAZINE
DIMENSIONS: 6 X 9 7/8 IN 151 X 250 MM
MEDIA: MIXED MEDIA (COLLAGE)
ARTIST REPRESENTATION: EYE CANDY
ILLUSTRATION AGENCY
CONTACT: INFO@EYECANDY.CO.UK
URL: WWW.EYECANDY.CO.UK

CAROLE HENAFF (FRANCE) *right*
TITLE: HOW BEST TO COMMUNICATE THE
HORROR OF DARFUR?
BRIEF: MAGAZINE ILLUSTRATION ABOUT THE
SANITATION WORK OF THE INTERNATIONAL
RESCUE COMMITTEE IN DARFUR
PUBLICATION: PRINCETON ALUMNI WEEKLY
ART DIRECTION: MARIANNE NELSON
DIMENSIONS: 8 1/4 X 11 3/4 IN 210 X 300 MM
MEDIA: ACRYLIC ON WOOD
ARTIST REPRESENTATION: MARLENA AGENCY
CONTACT: MARLENA@MARLENAAGENCY.COM
URL: WWW.MARLENAAGENCY.COM

LIZZIE COLLCUTT (UK) *facing page*
TITLE: FLIGHT PATTERN
BRIEF: FRONT-COVER IMAGE FOR AN ARTICLE ENTITLED "THE JET SET," ABOUT
UPGRADING AVIATION REGULATIONS WITH A NEW EUROPEAN SAFETY AGENCY
PUBLICATION: QUALITY WORLD MAGAZINE
ART DIRECTION: QUALITY WORLD MAGAZINE
DIMENSIONS: 8 ¼ X 11 ¾ IN 210 X 297 MM
MEDIA: PEN AND INK, PAINT, MIXED MEDIA
ARTIST REPRESENTATION: NB ILLUSTRATION
CONTACT: INFO@NBILLUSTRATION.CO.UK
URL: WWW.NBILLUSTRATION.CO.UK

MARK LAZENBY (UK) *top right*
TITLE: IDEAS TAKING FLIGHT
BRIEF: CHRISTMAS CARD ILLUSTRATION ABOUT THE MOMENT WHEN
INSPIRATION STRIKES
PUBLICATION: WPP CHRISTMAS CARD
ART DIRECTION: WPP
DIMENSIONS: 6 ⅛ X 7 ⅞ IN 156 X 199 MM
MEDIA: MIXED MEDIA (COLLAGE)
ARTIST REPRESENTATION: EYE CANDY ILLUSTRATION AGENCY
CONTACT: INFO@EYECANDY.CO.UK
URL: WWW.EYECANDY.CO.UK

JOSEPH DANIEL FIEDLER (USA) *center right*
TITLE: GENDER SELECTION
BRIEF: MAGAZINE ILLUSTRATION ABOUT THE POTENTIAL FOR PARENTS
TO CHOOSE THE GENDER OF THEIR UNBORN CHILDREN
PUBLICATION: THE SAN FRANCISCO CHRONICLE
ART DIRECTION: DOROTHY YULE, THE SAN FRANCISCO CHRONICLE
DIMENSIONS: 11 X 14 IN 279 X 356 MM
MEDIA: MIXED MEDIA
ARTIST REPRESENTATION: MAGNET REPS
CONTACT: ART@MAGNETREPS.COM
URL: WWW.MAGNETREPS.COM

GÉRARD DUBOIS (FRANCE) *bottom right*
TITLE: THE WELSH GIRL
BRIEF: BOOK REVIEW ILLUSTRATION ABOUT A JEWISH WELSH GIRL LIVING
BY A POW CAMP WITH GERMAN PRISONERS
PUBLICATION: THE BOSTON GLOBE / THE BOOK REVIEW
ART DIRECTION: SUSAN LEVIN, THE BOSTON GLOBE
DIMENSIONS: 7 ¼ X 7 ¼ IN 184 X 184 MM
MEDIA: ACRYLIC ON PAPER
ARTIST REPRESENTATION: MARLENA AGENCY / COSTUME 3 PIÈCES
CONTACT: MARLENA@MARLENAAGENCY.COM / CONTACT@COSTUME3PIECES.COM
URL: WWW.MARLENAAGENCY.COM / WWW.COSTUME3PIECES.COM

AKA (UK) *facing page*
TITLE: AUDI SELF-PROMOTION
BRIEF: IMAGERY FOR PROSPECTIVE CLIENTS
PUBLICATION: N/A
ART DIRECTION: N/A
DIMENSIONS: 11 ³/₈ X 18 ¹/₂ IN 290 X 471 MM
MEDIA: MIXED MEDIA (3-D SOFTWARE, PAINT, SCANNED
IMAGES, ADOBE PHOTOSHOP)
ARTIST REPRESENTATION: SHANNON ASSOCIATES
CONTACT: INFORMATION@SHANNONASSOCIATES.COM
URL: WWW.SHANNONASSOCIATES.COM

KUMKUM NOODLES (FRANCE) *above left*
TITLE: EVERY DAY COME OUT TO PLAY
BRIEF: EXPERIMENTAL COLLAGE WORK
PUBLICATION: N/A
ART DIRECTION: N/A
DIMENSIONS: 8 ¹/₂ X 11 ¹/₄ IN 215 X 286 MM
MEDIA: MIXED MEDIA (3-D SOFTWARE, PHOTOGRAPHS,
PENCIL, DIGITAL VECTOR ART)
ARTIST REPRESENTATION: COSTUME 3 PIÈCES
CONTACT: CONTACT@COSTUME3PIECES.COM
URL: WWW.COSTUME3PIECES.COM

ALEXANDER BLUE (USA) *above right*
TITLE: SEA MONSTER
BRIEF: PERSONAL WORK
PUBLICATION: N/A
ART DIRECTION: N/A
DIMENSIONS: 8 X 11 IN 203 X 279 MM
MEDIA: DIGITAL
ARTIST REPRESENTATION: MAGNET REPS
CONTACT: ART@MAGNETREPS.COM
URL: WWW.MAGNETREPS.COM

GORDON WIEBE (CANADA) *above*
TITLE: UNDER THE RAINBOW
BRIEF: PERSONAL PIECE
PUBLICATION: N/A
ART DIRECTION: N/A
DIMENSIONS: 8 X 11 IN 203 X 279 MM
MEDIA: COLLAGE
ARTIST REPRESENTATION: MAGNET REPS
CONTACT: ART@MAGNETREPS.COM
URL: WWW.MAGNETREPS.COM

FRAZER HUDSON (UK) *above*
TITLE: UNDER ATTACK
BRIEF: MAGAZINE ILLUSTRATION ABOUT THE BENEFITS OF A HEALTHY DIET
PUBLICATION: NORWICH UNION MAGAZINE
ART DIRECTION: IAN DUTNALL, ATOM PUBLISHING
DIMENSIONS: 8 ¼ X 6 ¾ IN 210 X 170 MM
MEDIA: DIGITAL
ARTIST REPRESENTATION: N/A
CONTACT: FRAZER@HUDSONFAMILY.DEMON.CO.UK
URL: WWW.FRAZERHUDSON.COM

TOMASZ WALENTA (POLAND) *facing page*
TITLE: LOVE
BRIEF: TO CREATE A POSTER ON THE SUBJECT OF LOVE
PUBLICATION: FUTU MAGAZINE
ART DIRECTION: MICHAŁ ŁOJEWSKI AND TOMASZ WALENTA
DIMENSIONS: 26 ⅜ X 33 ½ IN 670 X 850 MM
MEDIA: N/A
ARTIST REPRESENTATION: MARLENA AGENCY
CONTACT: MARLENA@MARLENAAGENCY.COM
URL: WWW.MARLENAAGENCY.COM

F₂

SELF
PEOPLE
SURROUND

Love

Love

T. Walenta

MARIE LAFRANCE (CANADA) *above left*
TITLE: ROMANCE OF THE 20TH CENTURY
BRIEF: BOOK ILLUSTRATION OF A SONG
PUBLICATION: "TRACES DANS LE SABLE," BY PIERRE FLYN
ART DIRECTION: 400 COUPS EDITEUR
DIMENSIONS: 7 3/8 X 10 3/8 IN 187 X 264 MM
MEDIA: ACRYLICS
ARTIST REPRESENTATION: WANDA NOWAK CREATIVE
ILLUSTRATORS' AGENCY
CONTACT: WANDA@WANDANOW.COM
URL: WWW.WANDANOW.COM

BEPPE GIACOBBE (ITALY) *above right*
TITLE: FURNITURE DESIGNER
BRIEF: CATALOG COVER
PUBLICATION: CATALOG FOR A FURNITURE DESIGN COMPANY
ART DIRECTION: TARGAITALIA
DIMENSIONS: 9 3/8 X 11 3/8 IN 239 X 289 MM
MEDIA: DIGITAL
ARTIST REPRESENTATION: MORGAN GAYNIN, INC.
CONTACT: INFO@MORGANGAYNIN.COM
URL: WWW.MORGANGAYNIN.COM

LAURENCE WHITELEY (UK) *above left*

TITLE: N/A

BRIEF: MAGAZINE ILLUSTRATION

PUBLICATION: MEN'S HEALTH MAGAZINE

ART DIRECTION: MEN'S HEALTH MAGAZINE

DIMENSIONS: 8 ½ X 11 IN 215 X 280 MM

MEDIA: ADOBE PHOTOSHOP

ARTIST REPRESENTATION: NB ILLUSTRATION

CONTACT: INFO@NBILLUSTRATION.CO.UK

URL: WWW.NBILLUSTRATION.CO.UK

A. RICHARD ALLEN (UK) *above right*

TITLE: CARDS

BRIEF: ILLUSTRATION FOR AN ARTICLE ABOUT YOUNG PEOPLE'S ATTITUDES TO SHOPPING ON CREDIT

PUBLICATION: NEW STATESMAN MAGAZINE, UK

ART DIRECTION: DAVID GIBBONS, NEW STATESMAN MAGAZINE

DIMENSIONS: 7 ³/₈ X 7 ³/₄ IN 187 X 197 MM

MEDIA: INK, ACRYLIC, DIGITAL

ARTIST REPRESENTATION: EYE CANDY ILLUSTRATION AGENCY

CONTACT: INFO@EYECANDY.CO.UK

URL: WWW.EYECANDY.CO.UK

ALEXANDRA HIGLETT (UK) right
TITLE: DEPRESSION
BRIEF: SELF-PROMOTIONAL PORTRAYAL OF A MAN
SUFFERING FROM DEPRESSION
PUBLICATION: N/A
ART DIRECTION: N/A
DIMENSIONS: 11 ¼ X 17 ⅜ IN 286 X 442 MM
MEDIA: PAINTING ON ENDPAPER
ARTIST REPRESENTATION: N/A
CONTACT: ALEXHIGLETT@HOTMAIL.COM
URL: WWW.ALEXANDGEORGE.CO.UK

MARIE LAFRANCE (CANADA) above
TITLE: BORI, DANS CE MONDE POUTT POUTT
BRIEF: CD COVER FOR AN ENIGMATIC SINGER
PUBLICATION: BORI, DANS CE MONDE POUTT POUTT
ART DIRECTION: STEPHAN LORTI
DIMENSIONS: 6 ⅛ X 6 ⅜ IN 155 X 160 MM
MEDIA: ACRYLICS
ARTIST REPRESENTATION: WANDA NOWAK CREATIVE
ILLUSTRATORS' AGENCY
CONTACT: WANDA@WANDANOW.COM
URL: WWW.WANDANOW.COM

ANNE HORST (GERMANY) facing page
TITLE: HOPE
BRIEF: SELF-PROMOTIONAL PIECE
PUBLICATION: N/A
ART DIRECTION: N/A
DIMENSIONS: 6 ¾ X 9 ¼ IN 170 X 235 MM
MEDIA: MIXED MEDIA
ARTIST REPRESENTATION: I2I ART
CONTACT: INFO@I2IART.COM
URL: WWW.I2IART.COM

STEPHEN LEDWIDGE (IRELAND) above
TITLE: CONFESSIONS OF A CUTTER
BRIEF: ARTWORK BASED ON AN ARTICLE ABOUT SELF-HARM
PUBLICATION: GLOW MAGAZINE
ART DIRECTION: NATHALIE CUSSONS, GLOW MAGAZINE
DIMENSIONS: N/A
MEDIA: ACRYLIC AND PENCIL
ARTIST REPRESENTATION: ANNA GOODSON MANAGEMENT
CONTACT: ANNA@AGOODSON.COM
URL: WWW.AGOODSON.COM

VIKTORIA FOMINA (RUSSIA) *above, left*
TITLE: ALICE IN WONDERLAND
BRIEF: BOOK ILLUSTRATION
PUBLICATION: ALICE IN WONDERLAND
ART DIRECTION: N/A
DIMENSIONS: 9 7/8 X 15 3/8 IN 250 X 390 MM
MEDIA: MIXED MEDIA
ARTIST REPRESENTATION: PIART ART &
DESIGN AGENCY
CONTACT: PIART2000@PIART.ORG
URL: WWW.PIART.ORG

ROB HARE (UK) *above, center*
TITLE: SITTING IN THE PARK
BRIEF: PERSONAL PIECE
PUBLICATION: N/A
ART DIRECTION: N/A
DIMENSIONS: 8 1/4 X 11 3/4 IN 210 X 297 MM
MEDIA: N/A
ARTIST REPRESENTATION: JELLY LONDON
CONTACT: INFO@JELLYLONDON.COM
URL: WWW.JELLYLONDON.COM

MARK TODD (USA) *above, right*
TITLE: FLOWERS
BRIEF: EXHIBITION PIECE
PUBLICATION: N/A
ART DIRECTION: N/A
DIMENSIONS: 10 X 13 IN 254 X 330 MM
MEDIA: MIXED MEDIA
ARTIST REPRESENTATION: BERNSTEIN &
ANDRIULLI (USA)
CONTACT: LOUISA@BA-REPS.COM
URL: WWW.BA-REPS.COM

MARK TODD (USA) *facing page*
TITLE: EYE OF THE TIGER
BRIEF: EXHIBITION PIECE
PUBLICATION: N/A
ART DIRECTION: N/A
DIMENSIONS: 10 X 13 IN 254 X 330 MM
MEDIA: MIXED MEDIA
ARTIST REPRESENTATION: BERNSTEIN &
ANDRIULLI (USA)
CONTACT: LOUISA@BA-REPS.COM
URL: WWW.BA-REPS.COM

FRANCK OMER (FRANCE) *above*
TITLE: PROCESSION EPILEPTIQUE
BRIEF: A SURREALISTIC SCENE SHOWING ANIMAL AND
CHILD CHARACTERS GATHERING AROUND LETTERS
AND NUMBERS
PUBLICATION: N/A
ART DIRECTION: N/A
DIMENSIONS: 17 ³/₈ X 5 ¹/₂ IN 442 X 141 MM
MEDIA: PAINTING, DIGITAL
ARTIST REPRESENTATION: COSTUME 3 PIÈCES
CONTACT: CONTACT@COSTUME3PIECES.COM
URL: WWW.COSTUME3PIECES.COM

NICKY ACKLAND-SNOW (USA) *below*
TITLE: CONSERVATION
BRIEF: UNPUBLISHED PIECE, ILLUSTRATING AN ARTICLE
ABOUT VOLUNTEERING FOR CONSERVATION
PUBLICATION: DOMINO MAGAZINE
ART DIRECTION: DOMINO MAGAZINE
DIMENSIONS: N/A
MEDIA: COLLAGE
ARTIST REPRESENTATION: WANDA NOWAK CREATIVE
ILLUSTRATORS' AGENCY
CONTACT: WANDA@WANDANOW.COM
URL: WWW.WANDANOW.COM

FRAZER HUDSON (UK) *below*

TITLE: G8: TIGHTENING THE GRIP

BRIEF: TO ILLUSTRATE AN ARTICLE ABOUT THE G8
COUNTRIES' SUMMIT AND THE WAR IN IRAQ

PUBLICATION: THE GUARDIAN, UK

ART DIRECTION: MIKE TOPP AND GINA CROSS,
THE GUARDIAN, UK

DIMENSIONS: 5 7/8 X 5 7/8 IN 150 X 150 MM

MEDIA: DIGITAL

ARTIST REPRESENTATION: N/A

CONTACT: FRAZER@HUDSONFAMILY.DEMON.CO.UK

URL: WWW.FRAZERHUDSON.COM

HOLLY WALES (UK) *below*

TITLE: NESTBUILDING

BRIEF: TEATOWEL DESIGN, BASED ON THE WAY PEOPLE
HOLD TEATOWELS WHEN DRYING MUGS

PUBLICATION: 8 1/4 X 11 3/4 IN 210 X 297 MM

ART DIRECTION: THIRD DRAWER DOWN, AUSTRALIA

DIMENSIONS: 8 1/4 X 11 3/4 IN 210 X 297 MM

MEDIA: FELT-TIP PEN AND DIGITAL DESIGN FOR A
2-COLOR SCREENPRINT

ARTIST REPRESENTATION: ZEEGENRUSH

CONTACT: INFO@ZEEGENRUSH.COM

URL: WWW.ZEEGENRUSH.COM

PAUL ZWOLAK (CANADA) *top left*
TITLE: "IF YOU HAVE TWO SHIRTS, SELL ONE
AND BUY A ROSE"
BRIEF: SELF-PROMOTIONAL CARD, PART OF THE
AGENCY'S SUFI CARD COLLECTION 2007
PUBLICATION: N/A
ART DIRECTION: LYNN BROFSKY, BROFSKY DESIGN
DIMENSIONS: 9 ½ X 13 IN 241 X 330 MM
MEDIA: ACRYLIC PAINT ON CARD
ARTIST REPRESENTATION: MARLENA AGENCY
CONTACT: MARLENA@MARLENAAGENCY.COM
URL: WWW.MARLENAAGENCY.COM

KERRY ROPER (UK) *top right*
TITLE: OBESITY—CAKE
BRIEF: ONE OF A SERIES OF ILLUSTRATIONS FOR
A MAGAZINE FEATURE ON OBESITY
PUBLICATION: THE BIG ISSUE MAGAZINE
ART DIRECTION: THE BIG ISSUE
DIMENSIONS: 8 ¼ X 11 ¾ IN 210 X 297 MM
MEDIA: N/A
ARTIST REPRESENTATION: DÉBUT ART
CONTACT: INFO@DEBUTART.COM
URL: WWW.DEBUTART.COM

KRISTIAN RUSSELL (UK/SWEDEN) *left*
TITLE: PACK OF LOVE
BRIEF: CONTRACEPTIVE PACKAGING
PUBLICATION: N/A
ART DIRECTION: PACK OF LOVE, SWEDEN
DIMENSIONS: N/A
MEDIA: ADOBE EPS
ARTIST REPRESENTATION: BIG ACTIVE
CONTACT: TIM@BIGACTIVE.COM
URL: WWW.BIGACTIVE.COM

GARY NEILL (UK) *above*
TITLE: STEROIDS IN WEIGHTLIFTING
BRIEF: MAGAZINE ILLUSTRATION
PUBLICATION: THE GUARDIAN, UK
ART DIRECTION: THE GUARDIAN, UK
DIMENSIONS: N/A
MEDIA: MIXED MEDIA
ARTIST REPRESENTATION: N/A
CONTACT: GARY@GARYNEILL.COM
URL: WWW.GARYNEILL.COM

GARY NEILL (UK) *left*
TITLE: OVERLOAD
BRIEF: MAGAZINE ILLUSTRATION SHOWING HOW PEOPLE
ARE "OVERLOADED" WITH MEDIA TECHNOLOGY
PUBLICATION: CONNECTED MAGAZINE
ART DIRECTION: CONNECTED MAGAZINE
DIMENSIONS: N/A
MEDIA: MIXED MEDIA
ARTIST REPRESENTATION: N/A
CONTACT: GARY@GARYNEILL.COM
URL: WWW.GARYNEILL.COM

CHRIS RUBINO (USA) *below*
TITLE: BIRD STACKS
BRIEF: ILLUSTRATION USED TO ADVERTISE
NEW STACKING CONTAINERS
PUBLICATION: N/A
ART DIRECTION: GLAD
DIMENSIONS: 9 X 11 IN 229 X 279 MM
MEDIA: PEN AND INK, DIGITAL
ARTIST REPRESENTATION: ART DEPARTMENT
CONTACT: STEPHANIEP@ART-DEPT.COM
URL: WWW.ART-DEPT.COM

DAVE BAIN (UK) *below*
TITLE: SEARCH FOR A HERO
BRIEF: UNPUBLISHED BOOK ILLUSTRATION—A VISUAL
NARRATIVE BASED ON THE HERO ILLUSION
PUBLICATION: N/A
ART DIRECTION: N/A
DIMENSIONS: 13 5/8 X 9 3/8 IN 346 X 238 MM
MEDIA: ACRYLIC ON WOOD
ARTIST REPRESENTATION: THE ORGANISATION
CONTACT: INFO@ORGANISART.CO.UK
URL: WWW.ORGANISART.CO.UK

JONATHAN BALL (UK) *left*
TITLE: SNIGGER
BRIEF: PERSONAL PROJECT
PUBLICATION: N/A
ART DIRECTION: N/A
DIMENSIONS: PENCIL
MEDIA: 8 ⅛ X 11 ⅝ IN 205 X 296 MM
ARTIST REPRESENTATION: JELLY LONDON
CONTACT: INFO@JELLYLONDON.COM
URL: WWW.JELLYLONDON.COM

ESTHER WATSON (USA) *below*
TITLE: SAVE US, CAPTAIN KIRK!
BRIEF: A PIECE FOR A GALLERY SHOW ABOUT
CAPTAIN KIRK FROM STAR TREK
PUBLICATION: N/A
ART DIRECTION: N/A
DIMENSIONS: 10 X 13 IN 254 X 330 MM
MEDIA: ACRYLIC ON PANEL
ARTIST REPRESENTATION: N/A
CONTACT: FUNCHICKEN@EARTHLINK.NET
URL: WWW.ESTHERWATSON.COM

IAN PHILLIPS (CANADA) *above*
TITLE: RINGS 1
BRIEF: EXHIBITION PIECE, PART OF A SERIES
PUBLICATION: N/A
ART DIRECTION: N/A
DIMENSIONS: 8 ½ X 11 IN 216 X 279 MM
MEDIA: DIGITAL
ARTIST REPRESENTATION: I2I ART
CONTACT: INFO@I2IART.COM
URL: WWW.I2IART.COM

MARK LAZENBY (UK) *above*
TITLE: FEAR FACTOR
BRIEF: MAGAZINE PIECE ILLUSTRATING THE STATE OF
FEAR AND PANIC IN MODERN SOCIETY
PUBLICATION: VOGUE AUSTRALIA
ART DIRECTION: VOGUE AUSTRALIA
DIMENSIONS: 11 X 15 ½ IN 280 X 394 MM
MEDIA: MIXED MEDIA (COLLAGE)
ARTIST REPRESENTATION: EYE CANDY ILLUSTRATION AGENCY
CONTACT: INFO@EYECANDY.CO.UK
URL: WWW.EYECANDY.CO.UK

JULIETTE BORDA (USA) *above*
TITLE: AIDS RESEARCH
BRIEF: TO ILLUSTRATE AN ARTICLE ABOUT UCLA
SCIENTISTS' RESEARCH ON AIDS
PUBLICATION: UCLA MAGAZINE
ART DIRECTION: CHARLES HESS, UCLA
DIMENSIONS: 6 X 4 IN 152 X 102 MM
MEDIA: GOUACHE
ARTIST REPRESENTATION: N/A
CONTACT: JULIETTEB@EARTHLINK.NET
URL: WWW.JULIETTEBORDA.COM

SÉVERINE SCAGLIA (FRANCE) *above*
TITLE: LA MODE PORTE BONHEUR
BRIEF: WALL ILLUSTRATION FOR GALERIES LAFAYETTE
PUBLICATION: N/A
ART DIRECTION: GALERIES LAFAYETTE, FRANCE
DIMENSIONS: 17 5/8 X 8 3/4 IN 448 X 221 MM
MEDIA: N/A
ARTIST REPRESENTATION: COSTUME 3 PIÈCES
CONTACT: CONTACT@COSTUME3PIECES.COM
URL: WWW.COSTUME3PIECES.COM

CARINE ABRAHAM (FRANCE) *below*
TITLE: L'ÉVEIL DES SENS
BRIEF: WALL DECORATION FOR AN EXHIBITION SPACE TOILET (SPRING THEME)
PUBLICATION: N/A
ART DIRECTION: LE TRIPOSTAL EXHIBITION
DIMENSIONS: 15 FT 7 ³/₈ IN X 8 FT 2 ³/₈ IN 4.76 X 2.51 M
MEDIA: N/A
ARTIST REPRESENTATION: ABRAKA DESIGN
CONTACT: CARINE.ABRAHAM@FREE.FR
URL: WWW.ABRAKA.COM

MATT JOHNSTONE (UK)
TITLE: GREEN PEACE MAP
BRIEF: PERSONAL PROJECT
PUBLICATION: D&AD STUDENT AWARDS
ART DIRECTION: N/A
DIMENSIONS: 5 X 7 ⅜ IN 127 X 188 MM
MEDIA: DIGITAL
ARTIST REPRESENTATION: JELLY LONDON
CONTACT: INFO@JELLYLONDON.COM
URL: WWW.JELLYLONDON.COM

6 *maps& diagrams*

FROM A VIEW OF THE WORLD to a view of the intestines—and many places in between, including the United States, London, sign language, the "rapture preparedness" diagram, Easter Island, molecules, Spain, Italy, honey bees, astronauts, the Mitsukoshi Treasure Hunt map, China ... doesn't it just make you dizzy?

ARCTIC OCEAN

NORTH AMERICA

EUROPE

ATLANTIC OCEAN

AFRICA

PACIFIC OCEAN

SOUTH AMERICA

ANTARC

ASIA

INDIAN
OCEAN

OCEANIA

CA

OLIVIER LATYK (FRANCE)
TITLE: WORLD MAP PUZZLE
BRIEF: JIGSAW PUZZLE DESIGN
PUBLICATION: N/A
ART DIRECTION: MUDPUPPY, USA
DIMENSIONS: 17 ¾ X 13 ¾ IN 450 X 350 MM
MEDIA: DIGITAL
ARTIST REPRESENTATION: WANDA NOWAK CREATIVE
ILLUSTRATORS' AGENCY
CONTACT: WANDA@WANDANOW.COM
URL: WWW.WANDANOW.COM

SERGE SEIDLITZ (UK/GERMANY) *above*
TITLE: VODAFONE WORLD MAP
BRIEF: A MAP MADE UP OF ICONIC IMAGES FROM EACH
COUNTRY—USED IN VODAFONE ADVERTISEMENTS AT
EUROPEAN AIRPORTS
PUBLICATION: ADVERTISEMENT
ART DIRECTION: MARK REDDY / BBH
DIMENSIONS: VARIOUS FORMATS, INCLUDING
48-SHEET BILLBOARDS AND BANNERS
MEDIA: MIXED MEDIA, PEN / INK / DIGITAL
ARTIST REPRESENTATION: DEBUT ART
CONTACT: INFO@DEBUTART.COM
URL: WWW.DEBUTART.COM

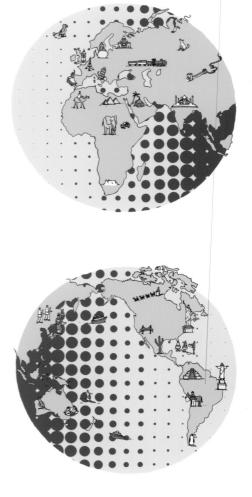

LIZZIE GARDINER (UK) *facing page, bottom*
TITLE: WORLD 1 AND WORLD 2
BRIEF: MAILER FOR AMERICAN EXPRESS
PUBLICATION: N/A
ART DIRECTION: N/A
DIMENSIONS: N/A
MEDIA: PEN / DIGITAL (PHOTOSHOP)
ARTIST REPRESENTATION: THE INKSHED
CONTACT: ABBY@INKSHED.CO.UK
URL: WWW.INKSHED.CO.UK

GEMMA ROBINSON (UK) *above*
TITLE: LONDON MARATHON 2007
BRIEF: ICONOGRAPHIC MAP OF THE 2007 LONDON
MARATHON ROUTE INCLUDING MILE MARKERS,
WATER STOPS, AND FAMOUS LANDMARKS
PUBLICATION: RUNNER'S WORLD
ART DIRECTION: RUSSELL FAIRBROTHER,
THE NATIONAL MAGAZINE COMPANY
DIMENSIONS: 15 ¾ X 6 IN 399 X 153 MM
MEDIA: DIGITAL
ARTIST REPRESENTATION: EYE CANDY
CONTACT: INFO@EYECANDY.CO.UK
WWW.EYECANDY.CO.UK

MATT JOHNSTONE (UK) *right*
TITLE: OBJECT-SWALLOWING SIDESHOW
BRIEF: T-SHIRT DESIGN
PUBLICATION: N/A
ART DIRECTION: N/A
DIMENSIONS: 11 ¾ X 16 ½ IN 297 X 420 MM
MEDIA: LINE DRAWING, DIGITAL
ARTIST REPRESENTATION: JELLY LONDON
CONTACT: INFO@JELLYLONDON.COM
URL: WWW.JELLYLONDON.COM

SERGE SEIDLITZ (UK / GERMANY) *facing page*
MEDIA: DIGITAL
ARTIST REPRESENTATION: DÉBUT ART
CONTACT: INFO@DEBUTART.COM
WEBSITE: WWW.DEBUTART.COM

TITLE: USA MAP *top*
BRIEF: A MAP OF THE STATES OF NORTH AMERICA USING
ICON IMAGES TO REFERENCE ELEMENTS OF THE COUNTRY
(SELF-PROMOTIONAL PIECE).
PUBLICATION: N/A
ART DIRECTION: N/A
DIMENSIONS: N/A

TITLE: LONDON MAP *bottom*
BRIEF: A MAP OF LONDON ILLUSTRATING THE TOP PUBS,
CAFES, CINEMAS, AND GRAFFITI HOTSPOTS
PUBLICATION: LONDON ARCHITECTURE WEEK BROCHURE
ART DIRECTION: LONDON ARTS COUNCIL, LONDON
ARCHITECTURE WEEK 2007
DIMENSIONS: 5 ⅞ X 8 ¼ IN 148 X 210 MM (A5)

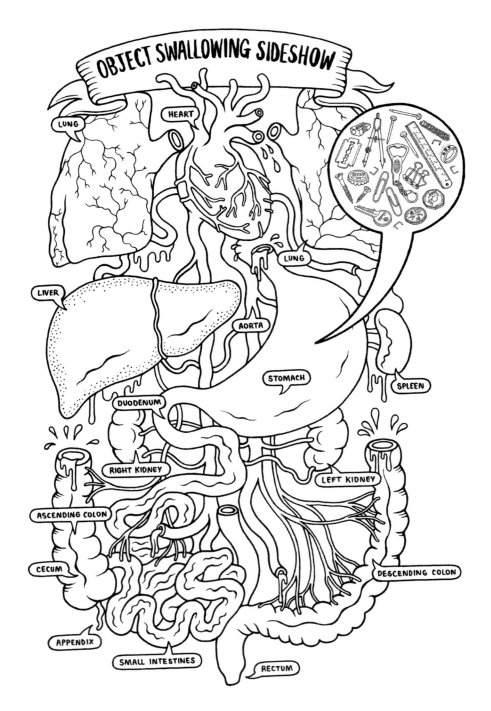

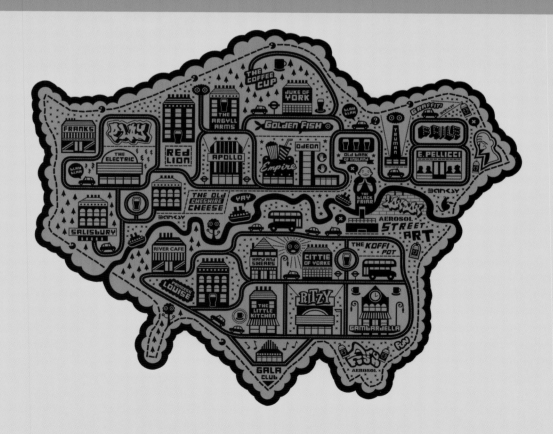

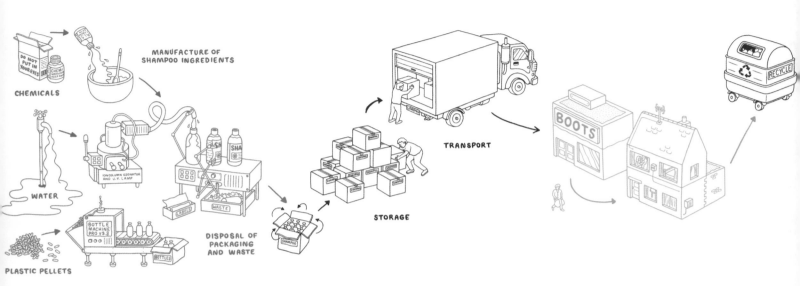

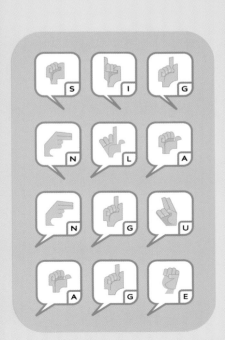

MATT JOHNSTONE (UK) *above*
TITLE: CARBON TRUST
BRIEF: CARBON TRUST ILLUSTRATION
PUBLICATION: N/A
ART DIRECTION: FISHBURN HEDGES
DIMENSIONS: 8 ¼ X 11 ¾ IN 210 X 297 MM
MEDIA: LINE DRAWING, DIGITAL
ARTIST REPRESENTATION: JELLY LONDON
CONTACT: INFO@JELLYLONDON.COM
URL: WWW.JELLYLONDON.COM

LEE WOODGATE (UK) *facing page*
TITLE: RAPTURE PREPAREDNESS
BRIEF: SELF-PROMOTIONAL CRASH-CARD
STYLE ILLUSTRATION
PUBLICATION: N/A
ART DIRECTION: N/A
DIMENSIONS: 10 ⅝ X 10 ⅝ IN 270 X 270 MM
MEDIA: ADOBE PHOTOSHOP
ARTIST REPRESENTATION: EYE CANDY
ILLUSTRATION AGENCY
CONTACT: INFO@EYECANDY.CO.UK
URL: WWW.EYECANDY.CO.UK

ADRIAN D'ALIMONTE (CANADA) *left*
TITLE: SIGN LANGUAGE
BRIEF: SELF-PROMOTIONAL PIECE
PUBLICATION: N/A
ART DIRECTION: N/A
DIMENSIONS: N/A
MEDIA: DIGITAL VECTOR ARTWORK
ARTIST REPRESENTATION: N/A
CONTACT: MAIL@ADRIANDD.COM
URL: WWW.ADRIANDD.COM

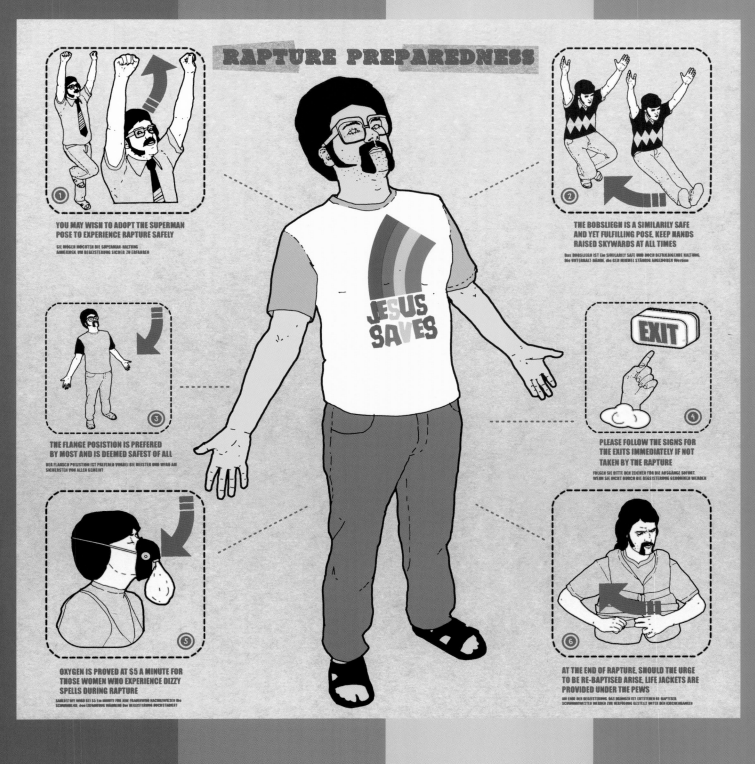

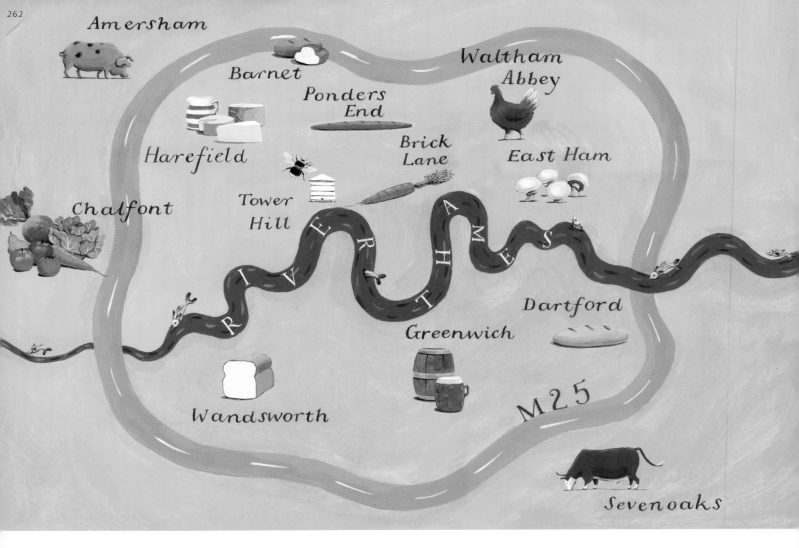

RACHEL ROSS (UK) *facing page, top*
TITLE: M25 FOOD
BRIEF: A MAP ILLUSTRATING THE AREA IN AND AROUND
THE M25 (THE BELTWAY ENCIRCLING GREATER LONDON)
TO SHOW WHERE THE CHEF OLIVER ROWE SOURCES LOCAL
PRODUCE FOR HIS RESTAURANT
PUBLICATION: EVENING STANDARD ES MAGAZINE, UK
ART DIRECTION: CHRISTOPHER WHALE / ES MAGAZINE
DIMENSIONS: 16 X 11 IN 406 X 281 MM
MEDIA: ACRYLIC / DIGITAL
ARTIST REPRESENTATION: THE INKSHED
CONTACT: ABBY@INKSHED.CO.UK /
WWW.INKSHED.CO.UK

MARIKO JESSE (UK/JAPAN) *above*
TITLE: EASTER ISLAND MAP
BRIEF: MAGAZINE ILLUSTRATION SHOWING PARTICULAR
POINTS OF INTEREST ON EASTER ISLAND
PUBLICATION: CONDÉ NAST TRAVELLER, UK
ART DIRECTION: PAULA ELLIS, CONDÉ NAST TRAVELLER
DIMENSIONS: 4 ¾ X 9 ¼ IN 120 X 235 MM
MEDIA: ACRYLIC
ARTIST REPRESENTATION: MONSTERS.CO.UK
CONTACT: MARIKO.JESSE@USA.NET
URL: WWW.MONSTERS.CO.UK

JANELL GENOVESE (USA) *facing page, bottom*
TITLE: N/A
BRIEF: MAGAZINE ILLUSTRATION SHOWING THE NEW
CALIFORNIA SECTION OF DISNEYLAND
PUBLICATION: N/A
ART DIRECTION: N/A
DIMENSIONS: 8 ⅛ X 6 IN 206 X 152 MM
MEDIA: GOUACHE
ARTIST REPRESENTATION: LILLA ROGERS
CONTACT: LILLA@LILLAROGERS.COM
URL: WWW.LILLAROGERS.COM

24+
Vitamins
+
Minerals

15

Amin
ACIDS

11

ANTI

Oxidants

NAME: (PLACE OF ORIGIN ABBREVIATED) *below left*
TITLE:
BRIEF
FULL NATION:
ART DIRECTION:
DESIGNS:
META:
ARTIST REPRESENTATION:
CONTACT:

ANDREW FOSTER (UK) *facing page*
TITLE: KIEHL'S PRODUCTS
BRIEF: SHOP WINDOW POSTERS FOR A GLOBAL COSMETICS
BRAND, HIGHLIGHTING THE PRODUCT'S INGREDIENTS
PUBLICATION: ADVERTISEMENT
ART DIRECTION: VICTORIA MADDOCKS
DIMENSIONS: 7 7/8 X 11 3/4 IN 200 X 300 MM
MEDIA: MIXED MEDIA ON PAPER
ARTIST REPRESENTATION: CENTRAL ILLUSTRATION
AGENCY (CIA)
CONTACT: INFO@CENTRALILLUSTRATION.COM
URL: WWW.CENTRALILLUSTRATION.COM

ROBIN HURSTHOUSE (UK) *below*
TITLE: BUSINESS CONNECTIONS
BRIEF: TO ILLUSTRATE THE IMPORTANCE
AND INTERACTION OF KEY FIGURES IN A
BUSINESS ENVIRONMENT
PUBLICATION: TRUSTED CONNECTIONS, WORLD BUSINESS
ART DIRECTION: ANDREA PEMBERTON, HAYMARKET
BUSINESS PUBLICATIONS
DIMENSIONS: 15 3/4 X 5 1/2 IN 400 X 141 MM
MEDIA: PENCIL, BRUSH, AND INK, AND DIGITAL
(ADOBE PHOTOSHOP)
ARTIST REPRESENTATION: EYE CANDY
ILLUSTRATION AGENCY
CONTACT: INFO@EYECANDY.CO.UK
URL: WWW.EYECANDY.CO.UK

266

PATRICK BATEMAN (USA) *facing page*
TITLE: MAPS
BRIEF: MAGAZINE ILLUSTRATION
PUBLICATION: THE SHOPAHOLIC'S GUIDE 2007
ART DIRECTION: SALLY BEAMES, VALUE RETAIL PLC
DIMENSIONS: 2 ³/₄ X 4 ³/₈ IN 70 X 110 MM
MEDIA: WATERCOLOR WASHES OVER INK DRAWING
ARTIST REPRESENTATION: MAPS ILLUSTRATED
CONTACT: MAIL@MAPSILLUSTRATED.COM
URL: WWW.MAPSILLUSTRATED.COM

GLYN BREWERTON (UK) *above*
TITLE: MAD IN MADRID
BRIEF: A MAP OF PLACES TO VISIT IN MADRID USED
IN A PITCH FOR AN ONLINE LEARNING GAME
PUBLICATION: N/A
ART DIRECTION: JAMES BRUCE, CIMEX LTD.
DIMENSIONS: 4 ¹/₈ X 5 ⁷/₈ IN 105 X 150 MM
MEDIA: ADOBE ILLUSTRATOR
ARTIST REPRESENTATION: NEW DIVISION
CONTACT: INFO@NEWDIVISION.COM
URL: WWW.NEWDIVISION.COM

MARTIN HAAKE (GERMANY) *above*
TITLE: PIEMONT (PIEDMONT)
BRIEF: MAGAZINE ILLUSTRATION
PUBLICATION: GAULT MILLAU MAGAZINE
ART DIRECTION: MICHAEL WEISS,
GAULT MILLAU MAGAZINE
DIMENSIONS: N/A
MEDIA: MIXED MEDIA
ARTIST REPRESENTATION: LINDGREN & SMITH (USA) /
CENTRAL ILLUSTRATION AGENCY (UK)
CONTACT: INFO@LSILLUSTRATION.COM /
INFO@CENTRALILLUSTRATION.COM
URL: WWW.LINDGRENSMITH.COM /
WWW.CENTRALILLUSTRATION.COM

CASTILLA Y LEÓN

SEGOVIA

NIIO

SIERRA DE GUADARRAMA

ALCÁZAR

EL CENADOR DE SALVADOR

MANZANARES EL REAL

SAN LORENZO DE EL ESCORIAL

Museo Thyssen-Bornemisza

A1

Las Rozas Village

Gran Hotel Almenar

LAS ROZAS A6

Barajas airport

Museo del Prado

FINE FOOD

HOTELS

MADRID

Museo Reina Sofía

To TOLEDO (65 Kms)

N

PUERTA DE ALCALÁ

JESSICA HISCHE (USA) *left*
TITLE: CITY WALKS, WASHINGTON, D.C.
BRIEF: SAMPLE ILLUSTRATIONS FOR AN INFORMATIVE
CARD DECK FOR CHILDREN ABOUT WASHINGTON, D.C.
PUBLICATION: N/A
ART DIRECTION: ANNE DONNARD, CHRONICLE BOOKS
DIMENSIONS: 3 ¾ X 4 ½ IN 95 X 115 MM
MEDIA: DIGITAL VECTOR ARTWORK, TEXTURE
ARTIST REPRESENTATION: FRANK STURGES REPS
CONTACT: FRANK@STURGESREPS.COM
URL: WWW.STURGESREPS.COM

A. SKWISH (USA) *facing page*
TITLE: SOUTH CHICAGO MAP
BRIEF: MAP SHOWING SCHOOLS FOR AN URBAN
RENEWAL MAGAZINE
PUBLICATION: CATALYST
ART DIRECTION: CHRISTINE OLIVA, CATALYST
DIMENSIONS: 9 X 11 IN 229 X 279 MM
MEDIA: DIGITAL (ADOBE PHOTOSHOP)
ARTIST REPRESENTATION: N/A
CONTACT: ILLUSTRATION@SKWISH.COM
URL: WWW.SKWISH.COM

SOUTH CHICAGO

EXCHANGE AVE

SOUTH SHORE DRIVE

RAINBOW PARK

Lake Michigan

79TH STREET

HORACE MANN

SOUTH CHICAGO COMMUNITY ELEMENTARY

81ST STREET

ECKERSALL PARK

LAS CASAS OCCUPATIONAL HIGH

USX STEEL CLOSED

83RD STREET

SULLIVAN

COLES

NIÑOS HEROES

ACE

87TH STREET

BOWEN HIGH CAMPUS

JN THORP

OWENS PARK

89TH STREET

THE SKYWAY

STONY ISLAND AVE

SOUTH CHICAGO

BESSEMER PARK

SOUTH CHICAGO LIBRARY

MACKINAW

Calumet River

MIRELES

OUR LADY OF GUADALUPE CATHOLIC CHURCH

91ST STREET

CHICAGO

SOUTH CHICAGO

93RD STREET

SAGINAW

95TH STREET

CALUMET PARK

EWING

MICHAEL A. HILL (UK) *below, left*
TITLE: THE MITSUKOSHI GREAT TREASURE HUNT
BRIEF: FICTITIOUS MAP SHOWING BRITISH "TREASURES"
AVAILABLE IN MITSUKOSHI DEPARTMENT STORE, JAPAN
PUBLICATION: MITSUKOSHI ADVERTISEMENT
ART DIRECTION: HIDEHIRO UENO,
MITSUKOSHI DESIGN DEPT.
DIMENSIONS: 9 7/8 X 9 7/8 IN 250 X 250 MM
MEDIA: WATERCOLOR ON PAPER, BURNT EDGES
ARTIST REPRESENTATION: KATE LARKWORTHY
CONTACT: KATE@LARKWORTHY.COM
URL: WWW.LARKWORTHY.COM

DAVID ATKINSON (UK) *below, right*
TITLE: RUSTY BRITAIN
BRIEF: MAGAZINE ILLUSTRATION, ALLUDING TO
THE USE OF METAL DETECTORS IN THE UK
PUBLICATION: BIZARRE MAGAZINE
ART DIRECTION: TIM HARRISON, JOHN BROWN PUBLISHING
DIMENSIONS: 17 3/4 X 23 5/8 IN 450 X 600 MM
MEDIA: METAL ON BOARD
ARTIST REPRESENTATION: NB ILLUSTRATION
CONTACT: INFO@NBILLUSTRATION.CO.UK
URL: WWW.NBILLUSTRATION.CO.UK

FRED VAN DEELEN (THE NETHERLANDS) *above*
TITLE: LION BOY 3
BRIEF: BOOK ILLUSTRATION SHOWING THE ROUTE TAKEN
BY THE PROTAGONIST
PUBLICATION: LION BOY BY ZIZOU CORDER, PUFFIN BOOKS
ART DIRECTION: TOM SANDERSON, PUFFIN BOOKS
DIMENSIONS: 16 ½ X 11 ¾ IN 420 X 297 MM
MEDIA: PEN AND INK
ARTIST REPRESENTATION: THE ORGANISATION
CONTACT: INFO@ORGANISART.COM
URL: WWW.ORGANISART.CO.UK

ANDY WARD (UK) *right*
TITLE: THE ITALIAN JOB
BRIEF: MAGAZINE ILLUSTRATION SHOWING THE CHEF
JAMIE OLIVER'S GASTRONOMIC TOUR OF ITALY
PUBLICATION: BBC RADIO TIMES
ART DIRECTION: JAMIE TRENDALL, BBC RADIO TIMES
DIMENSIONS: N/A
MEDIA: MIXED MEDIA, DIGITAL
ARTIST REPRESENTATION: NB ILLUSTRATION
CONTACT: INFO@NBILLUSTRATION.CO.UK
URL: WWW.NBILLUSTRATION.CO.UK

SUSAN MCKENNA (UK) *facing page*
TITLE: INDIA
BRIEF: N/A
PUBLICATION: N/A
ART DIRECTION: N/A
DIMENSIONS: N/A
MEDIA: N/A
ARTIST REPRESENTATION: LILLA ROGERS
CONTACT: LILLA@LILLAROGERS.COM
URL: WWW.LILLAROGERS.COM

ANNE SMITH (USA) *left, top*
TITLE: BELLENDEN ROAD
BRIEF: MAGAZINE ILLUSTRATION SHOWING AN AREA OF
REDEVELOPMENT IN PECKHAM, LONDON
PUBLICATION: LIVING SOUTH MAGAZINE
ART DIRECTION: SHARON MUNROE DENNY, ARCHANT LIFE
DIMENSIONS: 10 X 7 IN 254 X 178 MM
MEDIA: GOUACHE
ARTIST REPRESENTATION: N/A
CONTACT: ANNE@ANNESMITH.NET
URL: WWW.ANNESMITH.NET

SUSY PILGRIM-WATERS (UK/USA) *left, center*
TITLE: MAP OF CONCORD
BRIEF: MAGAZINE ILLUSTRATION
PUBLICATION: BRIDES MAGAZINE
ART DIRECTION: CHRISTINA JONES, BRIDES MAGAZINE
DIMENSIONS: 8 X 8 IN 203 X 203 MM
MEDIA: PAINT, COLLAGE, DIGITAL (ADOBE PHOTOSHOP)
ARTIST REPRESENTATION: LILLA ROGERS
CONTACT: LILLA@LILLAROGERS.COM
URL: WWW.LILLAROGERS.COM

JOY GOSNEY (UK) *left, bottom*
TITLE: MADRID
BRIEF: MAP SHOWING TAPAS BARS AND HOTELS IN MADRID
PUBLICATION: CONDÉ NAST TRAVELLER, UK
ART DIRECTION: DANIEL BIASSATI, CONDÉ NAST
DIMENSIONS: 4 ½ X 6 ⅛ IN 115 X 155 MM
MEDIA: HAND-DRAWN, DIGITAL
ARTIST REPRESENTATION: EYE CANDY
ILLUSTRATION AGENCY
CONTACT: INFO@EYECANDY.CO.UK
URL: WWW.EYECANDY.CO.UK

SARAJO FRIEDEN (USA) *overleaf*
TITLE: HEARTLAND MAP
BRIEF: MAGAZINE ILLUSTRATION TO ACCOMPANY AN
ARTICLE DISCUSSING HOW CHANGING ECONOMIC
REALITIES MIGHT AFFECT AMERICAN CITIES
PUBLICATION: THE AMERICAN
ART DIRECTION: TARA BENYEI, ALEXANDER ISLEY DESIGN
DIMENSIONS: N/A
MEDIA: ADOBE ILLUSTRATOR, PHOTOSHOP, SCANNED ART
ARTIST REPRESENTATION: LILLA ROGERS
CONTACT: LILLA@LILLAROGERS.COM
URL: WWW.LILLAROGERS.COM

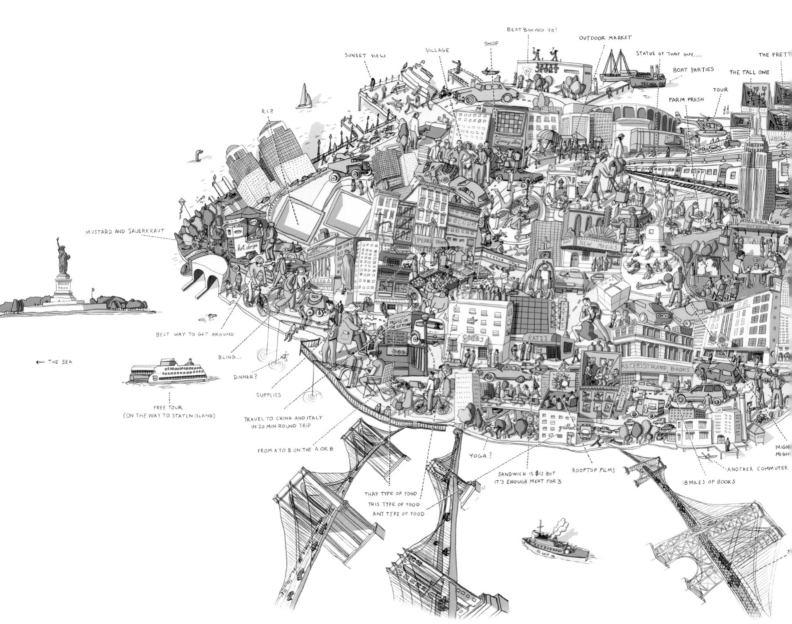

LEIF PARSONS (USA)
TITLE: NYC
BRIEF: MAP FOR SCHOOL OF VISUAL ARTS
PUBLICATION: N/A
ART DIRECTION: MICHAEL WALSH,
SCHOOL OF VISUAL ARTS
DIMENSIONS: 55 X 35 IN 1397 X 889 MM
MEDIA: N/A
ARTIST REPRESENTATION: N/A
CONTACT: LEIF@LEIFPARSONS.COM
URL: WWW.LEIFPARSONS.COM

KATHERINE BAXTER (UK) *above*
TITLE: TIMES POSTER OF NEW YORK
BRIEF: AXONOMETRIC MAP OF MANHATTAN FOR
A NEWSPAPER POSTER
PUBLICATION: THE TIMES, THE KNOWLEDGE SUPPLEMENT
ART DIRECTION: GRUFFYD PRYDERI, THE TIMES, UK
DIMENSIONS: 23 3/8 X 33 1/8 IN 594 X 841 MM
MEDIA: WATERCOLOR, PEN & INK
ARTIST REPRESENTATION: N/A
CONTACT: KATHERINE@BAXILLUSTRATIONS.FSNET.CO.UK
URL: WWW.PORTFOLIOS.COM/KATHERINEBAXTER

LUCY TRUMAN (UK) *facing page*
TITLE: ITALIAN CUISINE
BRIEF: SELF-PROMOTIONAL ILLUSTRATION
PUBLICATION: N/A
ART DIRECTION: N/A
DIMENSIONS: 7 ³/₈ X 11 IN 187 X 280 MM
MEDIA: DIGITAL
ARTIST REPRESENTATION: NEW DIVISION
CONTACT: INFO@NEWDIVISION.COM
URL: WWW.NEWDIVISION.COM

MARY KILVERT (UK) *above*
TITLE: ASIA
BRIEF: ILLUSTRATION OF ASIA TO PROMOTE A RANGE
OF SUPERMARKET READY MEALS
PUBLICATION: N/A
ART DIRECTION: 7 PUBLISHING
DIMENSIONS: 5 ⁷/₈ X 6 ½ IN 148 X 166 MM
MEDIA: PEN AND INK, DIGITAL COLOR, COLLAGE
ARTIST REPRESENTATION: NEW DIVISION (UK) /
LINDGREN & SMITH (USA)
CONTACT: INFO@NEWDIVISION.COM /
INFO@LSILLUSTRATION.COM
URL: WWW.NEWDIVISION.COM /
WWW.LINDGRENSMITH.COM

MARTIN HAAKE (GERMANY) *above*
TITLE: SIZILIEN (SICILY)
BRIEF: MAGAZINE ILLUSTRATION
PUBLICATION: GAULT MILLAU MAGAZINE
ART DIRECTION: MICHAEL WEISS,
GAULT MILLAU MAGAZINE
DIMENSIONS: N/A
MEDIA: MIXED MEDIA
ARTIST REPRESENTATION: LINDGREN & SMITH (USA) /
CENTRAL ILLUSTRATION AGENCY (UK)
CONTACT: INFO@LSILLUSTRATION.COM /
INFO@CENTRALILLUSTRATION.COM
URL: WWW.LINDGRENSMITH.COM /
WWW.CENTRALILLUSTRATION.COM

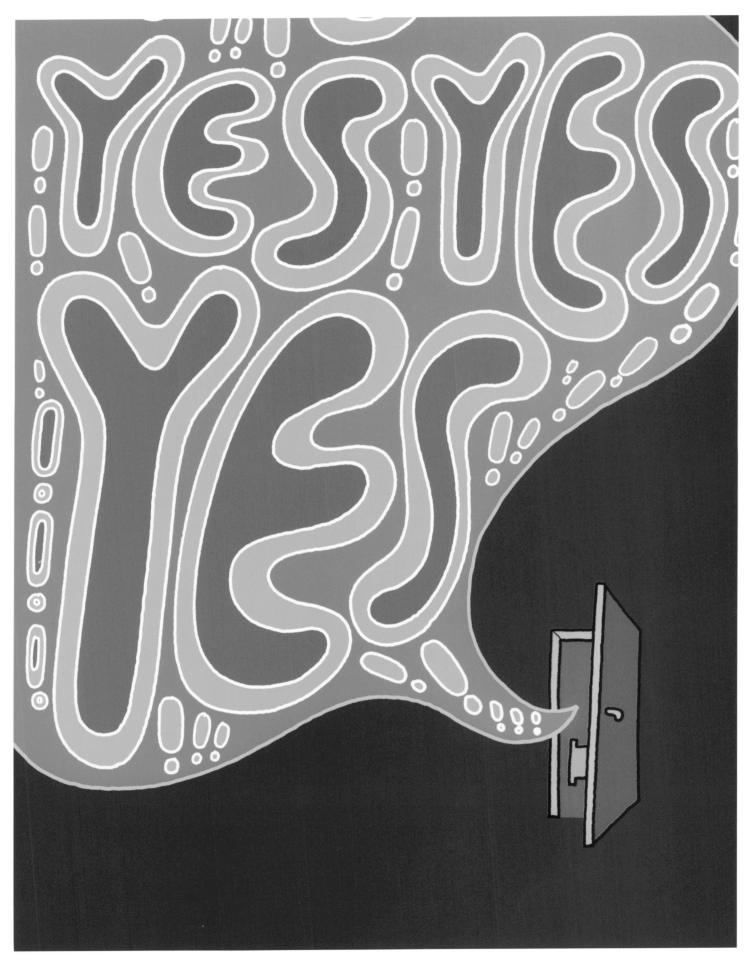

SUSANNE SAENGER (GERMANY)
TITLE: ORGASM
BRIEF: MAGAZINE ILLUSTRATION FOR AN ARTICLE
ABOUT IMPROVING YOUR SEX LIFE
PUBLICATION: THE SUNDAY TELEGRAPH STELLA MAGAZINE, UK
ART DIRECTION: JASON MORRIS, THE SUNDAY TELEGRAPH, UK
DIMENSIONS: 9 ¼ X 11 IN 235 X 280 MM
MEDIA: INK AND DIGITAL
ARTIST REPRESENTATION: KATE LARKWORTHY
CONTACT: KATE@LARKWORTHY.COM
URL: WWW.LARKWORTHY.COM

with text

IF A PICTURE IS WORTH A THOUSAND WORDS, how much is a picture with words worth? Hah! Answer me that.

EMILIANO PONZI (ITALY)
TITLE: ADDICTED TO ADJECTIVES
BRIEF: AN EDITORIAL ILLUSTRATION FOR A SECTION
ON CURRENT TRENDS IN WRITING
PUBLICATION: IO DONNA MAGAZINE, ITALY
ART DIRECTION: GLORIA GHISI, IO DONNA MAGAZINE
DIMENSIONS: 8 X 11 IN 203 X 279 MM
MEDIA: DIGITAL
ARTIST REPRESENTATION: MAGNET REPS
CONTACT: ART@MAGNETREPS.COM
URL: WWW.MAGNETREPS.COM

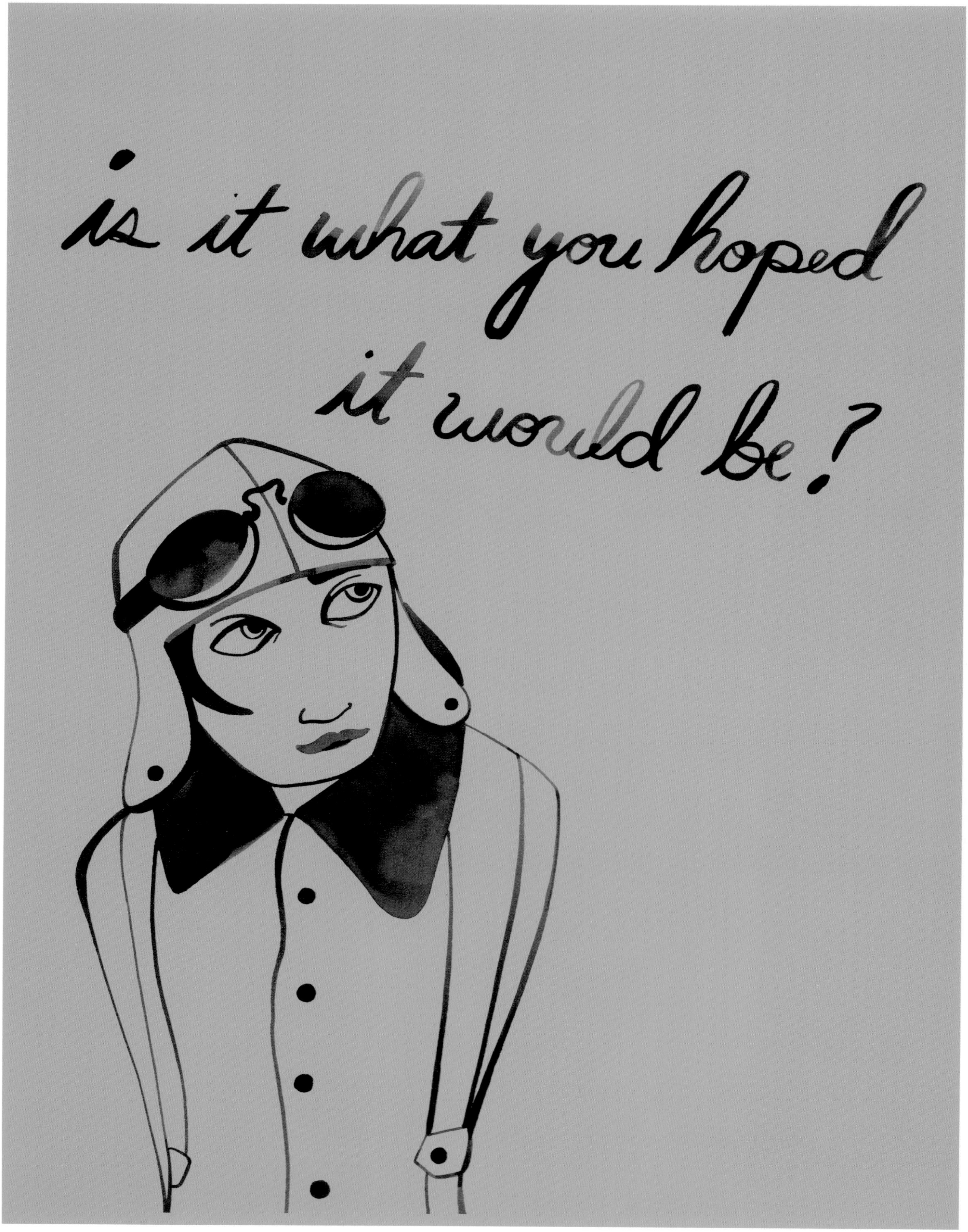
is it what you hoped
it would be?

TRISHA KRAUSS (USA) *facing page*
TITLE: BIG QUESTION
BRIEF: PERSONAL WORK—THE ARTIST ENJOYS SENDING
POSTCARDS WITH SAYINGS TO FRIENDS, AND SOME ARE
ILLUSTRATED FOR EMPHASIS
PUBLICATION: N/A
ART DIRECTION: N/A
DIMENSIONS: 7 X 9 IN 178 X 229 MM
MEDIA: PEN AND INK, ADOBE PHOTOSHOP
ARTIST REPRESENTATION: LINDGREN & SMITH
CONTACT: INFO@LSILLUSTRATION.COM
URL: WWW.LINDGRENSMITH.COM

HANNA MELIN (SWEDEN) *above*
TITLE: I HATE COMEDY
BRIEF: UNPUBLISHED MAGAZINE PIECE DESIGNED
TO ILLUSTRATE HUMOR; HERE, A SUNBATHING LADY
TELLING FUNNY STORIES
PUBLICATION: MAGMA
ART DIRECTION: RICHARD BERETON, MAGMA
DIMENSIONS: 8 5/8 X 5 3/4 IN 220 X 147 MM
MEDIA: PENCIL
ARTIST REPRESENTATION: PRIVATE VIEW, UK
CONTACT: CREATE@PVUK.COM
URL: WWW.PVUK.COM

GIANPAOLO PAGNI (FRANCE)

TITLE: N/A

BRIEF: MAGAZINE ILLUSTRATION FOR AN ARTICLE ABOUT A WRITER

PUBLICATION: N/A

ART DIRECTION: ALDO BUSCALFERRI, VENTIQUATTRO

DIMENSIONS: 21 1/4 X 12 1/4 IN 540 X 310 MM

MEDIA: ACRYLIC ON PAPER

ARTIST REPRESENTATION: COSTUME 3 PIÈCES (FR,UK) / MARLENA AGENCY (USA)

CONTACT: CONTACT@COSTUME3PIECES.COM / MARLENA@MARLENAAGENCY.COM

URL: WWW.COSTUME3PIECES.COM / WWW.MARLENAAGENCY.COM

shg★
174 rivington nyc

CHRIS RUBINO (USA) *facing page*
TITLE: SUGARHEAD QUARTERS
BRIEF: POSTCARD PROMOTING THE OPENING
OF THE NEW YORK BOUTIQUE
PUBLICATION: N/A
ART DIRECTION: SUGARHEAD QUARTERS
DIMENSIONS: 4 X 6 IN 102 X 152 MM
MEDIA: PEN AND INK, DIGITAL COLOR
ARTIST REPRESENTATION: ART DEPARTMENT
CONTACT: STEPHANIEP@ART-DEPT.COM
URL: WWW.ART-DEPT.COM

MARGUERITE SAUVAGE (FRANCE) *left*
TITLE: MUSIC TASTES
BRIEF: PERSONAL PIECE PORTRAYING DIFFERENT
WAYS OF LISTENING TO MUSIC, INSPIRED BY 1970S
BILLBOARD STYLE
PUBLICATION: N/A
ART DIRECTION: N/A
DIMENSIONS: 7 7/8 X 11 IN 200 X 280 MM
MEDIA: PENCIL ON PAPER, ADOBE PHOTOSHOP
ARTIST REPRESENTATION: N/A
CONTACT: MARGUERITESAUVAGE@GMAIL.COM
URL: WWW.MARGUERITESAUVAGE.COM

LANGUAGE!

MARCO MARELLA (ITALY) *facing page*
TITLE: LANGUAGE
BRIEF: MAGAZINE COVER ON THE USE
OF THE ENGLISH LANGUAGE
PUBLICATION: NEW YORK CITY VENEZIA
MAGAZINE, ITALY
ART DIRECTION: NEW YORK CITY VENEZIA
MAGAZINE, ITALY
DIMENSIONS: 8 3/8 X 11 IN 213 X 279 MM
MEDIA: MIXED MEDIA
ARTIST REPRESENTATION: LILLA ROGERS
CONTACT: LILLA@LILLAROGERS.COM
URL: WWW.LILLAROGERS.COM

CAROLE HÉNAFF (FRANCE) *below*
TITLE: AUTOBIOGRAPHIE
BRIEF: BOOK ILLUSTRATION
PUBLICATION: POÈTES EN EXIL, ÉDITIONS MANGO
ART DIRECTION: BRIGITTE STEPHAN AND
CHRISTIAN NOBIAL
DIMENSIONS: 11 1/4 X 20 1/8 IN 285 X 510 MM
MEDIA: ACRYLICS ON CARDBOARD
ARTIST REPRESENTATION: MARLENA AGENCY
CONTACT: MARLENA@MARLENAAGENCY.COM
URL: WWW.MARLENAAGENCY.COM

JOSEPH BLAKEY (UK) *above*
TITLE: FLUENT
BRIEF: PERSONAL PIECE
PUBLICATION: N/A
ART DIRECTION: N/A
DIMENSIONS: 5 X 4 3/4 IN 126 X 120 MM
MEDIA: PENCIL, DIGITAL
ARTIST REPRESENTATION: JELLY LONDON
CONTACT: INFO@JELLYLONDON.COM
URL: WWW.JELLYLONDON.COM

CAMPBELL LAIRD (USA)

TITLE: MODU, FRACTURE, AND OPTIK

BRIEF: POSTERS FOR FORD DETROIT INTERNATIONAL JAZZ FESTIVAL

PUBLICATION: N/A

ART DIRECTION: ALEXANDER LOWE, J.WALTER THOMPSON ADVERTISING

DIMENSIONS: 24 X 36 IN 610 X 914 MM

MEDIA: DIGITAL VECTOR ARTWORK

ARTIST REPRESENTATION: N/A

CONTACT: INFO@CAMPBELLAIRDSTUDIO.COM

URL: WWW.CAMPBELLAIRDSTUDIO.COM

25 | FORD DETROIT INTERNATIONAL | Jazz Festival

SEPTEMBER 4-6, 2004

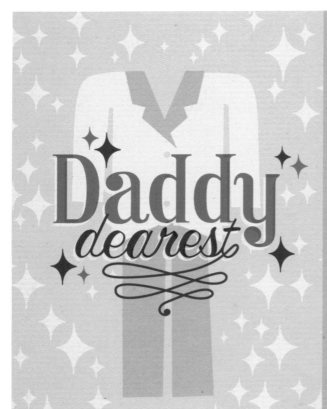

297

JESSICA HISCHE (USA) *facing page*
TITLE: UNEMPLOYED *top*
TITLE: OVERWORKED *bottom*
BRIEF: UNPUBLISHED WORK—TWO OF TEN
"PARENT CARDS" IN A BOARD GAME
PUBLICATION: N/A
ART DIRECTION: N/A
DIMENSIONS: 8 X 5 ½ IN 203 X 140 MM
MEDIA: DIGITAL VECTOR ART AND TEXTURE
ARTIST REPRESENTATION: FRANK STURGES REPS
CONTACT: FRANK@STURGESREPS.COM
URL: WWW.STURGESREPS.COM

DAVID B. MCMACKEN (USA) *left*
TITLE: PRANCER
BRIEF: ADVERTISEMENT ARTWORK
PUBLICATION: N/A
ART DIRECTION: DAN BRUCE, JWT/CH
DIMENSIONS: N/A
MEDIA: ACRYLIC
ARTIST REPRESENTATION: N/A
CONTACT: DAVE@MCMACKENGRAPHICS.COM
URL: WWW.MCMACKENGRAPHICS.COM

YEE TING KUIT (UK) *left*
TITLE: TEA
BRIEF: SELF-PROMOTIONAL PIECE
PUBLICATION: N/A
ART DIRECTION: N/A
DIMENSIONS: 7 ½ X 9 IN 190 X 230 MM
MEDIA: DIGITAL
ARTIST REPRESENTATION: THE ORGANISATION
CONTACT: INFO@ORGANISART.CO.UK
URL: WWW.ORGANISART.CO.UK

AARON LEIGHTON (CANADA) *below*
TITLE: SNOWMEN
BRIEF: SELF-PROMOTIONAL PIECE FOR CHRISTMAS 2006
PUBLICATION: N/A
ART DIRECTION: N/A
DIMENSIONS: 6 ⅜ X 6 ½ IN 163 X 160 MM
MEDIA: INK, DIGITAL COLOR
ARTIST REPRESENTATION: LINDGREN & SMITH
CONTACT: INFO@LSILLUSTRATION.COM
URL: WWW.LINDGRENSMITH.COM

HOWARD BESANÇON–MATIL (NEW ZEALAND) *this page*
TITLE: POSTER FOR BUBBLE FONT
BRIEF: SELF-PROMOTIONAL POSTER
PUBLICATION: N/A
ART DIRECTION: N/A
DIMENSIONS: 16 ½ X 23 ⅜ IN 420 X 594 MM
MEDIA: ADOBE ILLUSTRATOR
ARTIST REPRESENTATION: N/A
CONTACT: HOWARDMATIL@MAC.COM

HOWARD BESANÇON–MATIL (NEW ZEALAND) *previous page*
TITLE: CSS TOUR POSTER
BRIEF: PROMOTIONAL POSTER
PUBLICATION: N/A
ART DIRECTION: N/A
DIMENSIONS: 11 ¾ X 16 ½ IN 297 X 420 MM
MEDIA: ADOBE ILLUSTRATOR
ARTIST REPRESENTATION: N/A
CONTACT: HOWARDMATIL@MAC.COM

TOM GENOWER (UK)
TITLE: EL MORITO! *above left*
TITLE: LA CALAVERA *above right*
BRIEF: CARD IMAGES INSPIRED BY OLD ENAMEL SIGNAGE
FOR "MONSTERS' LOTERIA" GAME AND EXHIBITION
PUBLICATION: N/A
ART DIRECTION: MONSTERS ILLUSTRATION
DIMENSIONS: N/A
MEDIA: DIGITAL
ARTIST REPRESENTATION: MONSTERS ILLUSTRATION
CONTACT: TOMGENOWER@YAHOO.CO.UK
URL: WWW.MONSTERS.CO.UK

CHRIS RUBINO (USA) *facing page*
TITLE: METALLIC FALCONS
BRIEF: SILKSCREEN POSTER ART PROMOTING THE
RELEASE OF AN ALBUM BY THE "METALLIC FALCONS"
PUBLICATION: N/A
ART DIRECTION: VOODOO–EROS
DIMENSIONS: 11 X 17 IN 279 X 432 MM
MEDIA: PEN AND INK, SILKSCREEN
ARTIST REPRESENTATION: ART DEPARTMENT
CONTACT: STEPHANIEP@ART-DEPT.COM
URL: WWW.ART-DEPT.COM

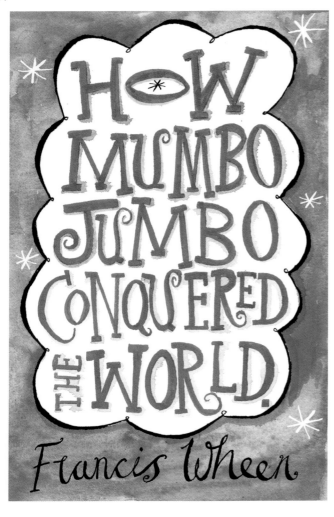

MICHAEL A. HILL (UK) *left*
TITLE: HOW MUMBO JUMBO CONQUERED
THE WORLD
BRIEF: SELF-PROMOTIONAL SAMPLE BOOK JACKET
USING HAND-DRAWN TYPE
PUBLICATION: N/A
ART DIRECTION: N/A
DIMENSIONS: 6 3/4 X 10 5/8 IN 170 X 270 MM
MEDIA: WATERCOLOR, GOUACHE, INK
ARTIST REPRESENTATION: KATE LARKWORTHY
CONTACT: KATE@LARKWORTHY.COM
URL: WWW.LARKWORTHY.COM

ROMAN KLONEK (POLAND) *left*
TITLE: GOOD MORNING
BRIEF: SELF-PROMOTIONAL PIECE
PUBLICATION: N/A
ART DIRECTION: N/A
DIMENSIONS: 19 1/4 X 27 1/8 IN 490 X 690 MM
MEDIA: WOODCUT PRINT
ARTIST REPRESENTATION: FRANK STURGES REPS
CONTACT: FRANK@STURGESREPS.COM
URL: WWW.STURGESREPS.COM

NATE WILLIAMS (USA) *right*
TITLE: ALL TOGETHER NOW
BRIEF: COVER ART FOR A CHILDREN'S CD OF "BEATLES" SONGS
PUBLICATION: N/A
ART DIRECTION: DAVID CALDERLY, V2 RECORDS
DIMENSIONS: 10 X 10 IN 254 X 254 MM
MEDIA: MIXED MEDIA, DIGITAL
ARTIST REPRESENTATION: MAGNET REPS
CONTACT: ART@MAGNETREPS.COM
URL: WWW.MAGNETREPS.COM

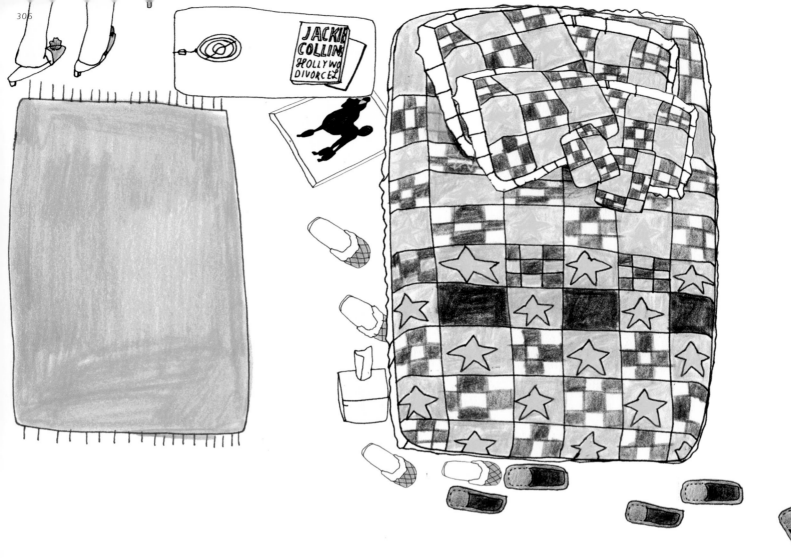

HANNA MELIN (SWEDEN)
TITLE: LOVING BUT NOT SHARING
BRIEF: TO ILLUSTRATE AN ARTICLE ABOUT AN AMERICAN
TREND TO BUILD HOUSES WITH TWO MASTER BEDROOMS,
ONE FOR THE HUSBAND AND ONE FOR THE WIFE
PUBLICATION: THE GUARDIAN G2 SUPPLEMENT, UK
ART DIRECTION: RICHARD TURLEY, THE GUARDIAN, UK
DIMENSIONS: 16 ½ X 11 ¾ IN 420 X 297 MM
MEDIA: MIXED MEDIA
ARTIST REPRESENTATION: PRIVATE VIEW, UK
CONTACT: CREATE@PVUK.COM
URL: WWW.PVUK.COM

OLIVIER KUGLER (GERMANY) *right*
TITLE: ANDY WARHOL
BRIEF: ONE OF A SERIES OF ILLUSTRATIONS
OF 20TH-CENTURY HEROES FOR A BOOKLET
PUBLICATION: N/A
ART DIRECTION: ANN WHATLEY, CONRAN DESIGN
DIMENSIONS: N/A
MEDIA: HAND DRAWN AND DIGITAL
ARTIST REPRESENTATION: ART DEPARTMENT
CONTACT: STEPHANIEP@ART-DEPT.COM
URL: WWW.ART-DEPT.COM

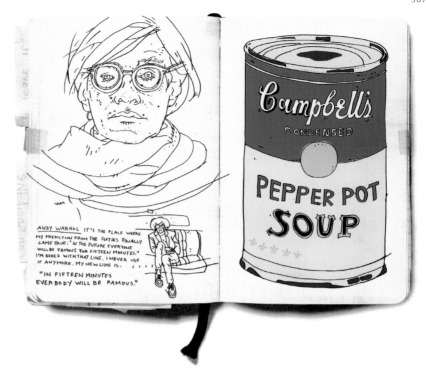

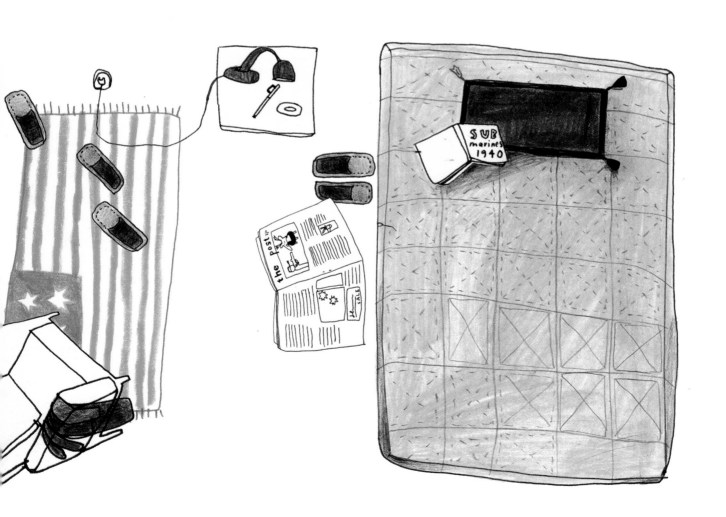

FRANCK OMER (FRANCE) *above*
TITLE: C'EST L'HISTOIRE DE GREGG L'OEUF
BRIEF: COVER ART FOR A CHILDREN'S BOOK, FEATURING
AN ERUPTED VOLCANO, A FLYING EGG, AND A PINK
ELEPHANT PAINTING THE TITLE
PUBLICATION: "C'EST L'HISTOIRE DE GREGG L'OEUF"
ART DIRECTION: EDITIONS COURTES ET LONGUES
DIMENSIONS: 17 3/8 X 9 3/8 IN 440 X 237 MM
MEDIA: TRADITIONAL AND DIGITAL
ARTIST REPRESENTATION: COSTUME 3 PIÈCES
CONTACT: CONTACT@COSTUME3PIECES.COM
URL: WWW.COSTUME3PIECES.COM

BO LUNDBERG (SWEDEN) *facing page*
TITLE: BAREFOOT IN THE PARK
BRIEF: POSTER FOR A BROADWAY PLAY BY NEIL SIMON
PUBLICATION: N/A
ART DIRECTION: JESSICA DISBROW,
GAIL ANDERSON, SPOT CO.
DIMENSIONS: VARIABLE
MEDIA: ADOBE ILLUSTRATOR
ARTIST REPRESENTATION: ART DEPARTMENT
CONTACT: STEPHANIEP@ART-DEPT.COM
URL: WWW.ART-DEPT.COM

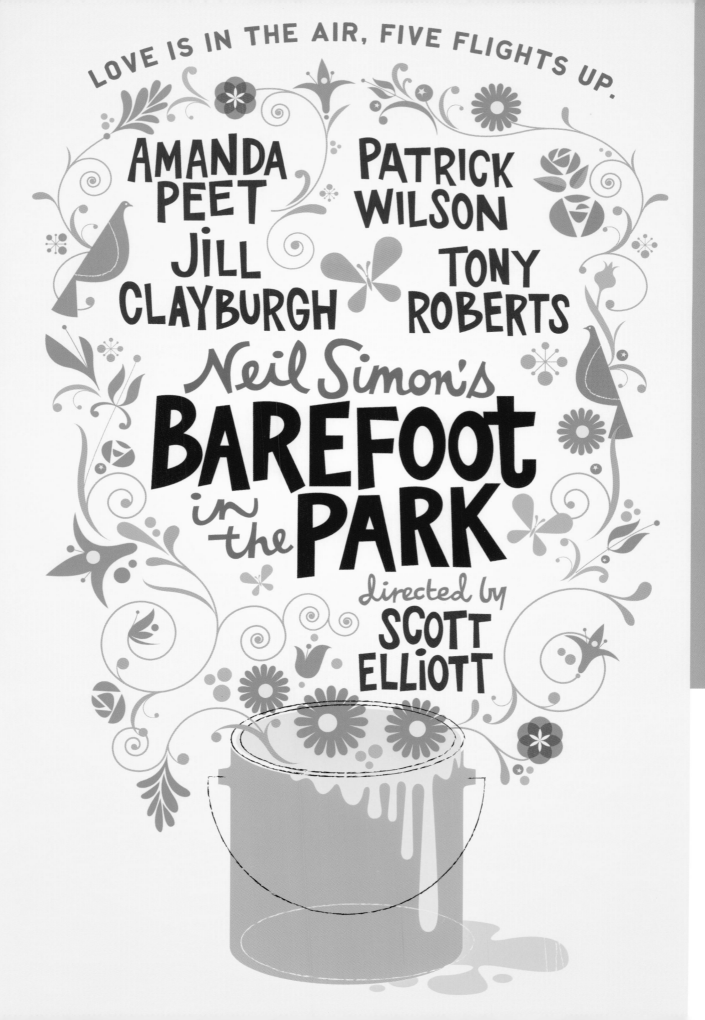

ALLAN DEAS (UK) *above*
TITLE: LOVE FOR SALE
BRIEF: SELF-PROMOTIONAL PIECE, CREATING AN
ALPHABET ON THE THEME OF FASHION
PUBLICATION: N/A
ART DIRECTION: N/A
DIMENSIONS: 7 7/8 X 7 7/8 IN 200 X 200 MM
MEDIA: PEN AND INK, DIGITAL
ARTIST REPRESENTATION: N/A
CONTACT: ALLAN.DEAS@MAC.COM
URL: WWW.ALLANDEAS.COM

HARRIET RUSSELL (UK) *right*
TITLE: THE TRUE AND OUTSTANDING ADVENTURES
OF THE HUNT SISTERS
BRIEF: HAND-LETTERED BOOK COVER
PUBLICATION: "THE TRUE AND OUTSTANDING ADVENTURES
OF THE HUNT SISTERS" BY ELISABETH ROBINSON
ART DIRECTION: KARI BROWNLIE, SIMON & SCHUSTER
DIMENSIONS: 5 3/8 X 8 IN 135 X 204 MM
MEDIA: MIXED MEDIA
ARTIST REPRESENTATION:
CENTRAL ILLUSTRATION AGENCY (CIA)
CONTACT: INFO@CENTRALILLUSTRATION.COM
URL: WWW.CENTRALILLUSTRATION.COM

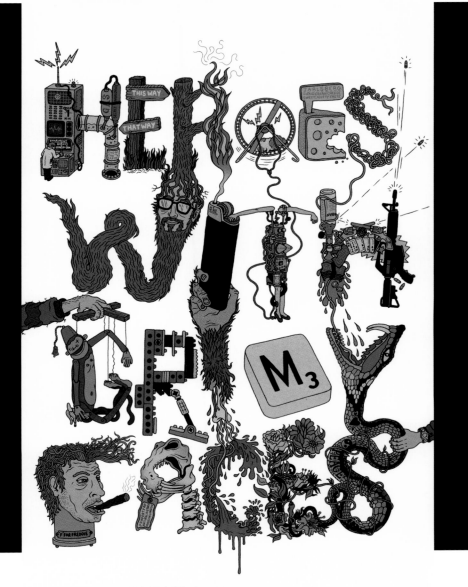

MATT JOHNSTONE (UK) *above*
TITLE: HEROES WITH GRIMY FACES
BRIEF: T-SHIRT DESIGN
PUBLICATION: N/A
ART DIRECTION: N/A
DIMENSIONS: 11 ¾ X 16 ½ IN 297 X 420 MM
MEDIA: DIGITAL
ARTIST REPRESENTATION: JELLY LONDON
CONTACT: INFO@JELLYLONDON.COM
URL: WWW.JELLYLONDON.COM

SCOTT KENNEDY (NEW ZEALAND) *facing page*
TITLE: JARGON
BRIEF: TO ILLUSTRATE A BORE SPOUTING BUSINESS JARGON
PUBLICATION: FAIRFAX NEWSPAPER SUNDAY SUPPLEMENT
ART DIRECTION: SUE THOMAS, FAIRFAX NEWSPAPER
DIMENSIONS: 10 5/8 X 12 1/4 IN 270 X 310 MM
MEDIA: DIGITAL
ARTIST REPRESENTATION: THREE EYES LTD.
CONTACT: THREEEYES@PARADISE.NET.NZ
URL: WWW.THREEEYES.CO.NZ

OLIVIER KUGLER (GERMANY) *below*
TITLE: A FOREIGN AFFAIR
BRIEF: BOOK JACKET ILLUSTRATION
PUBLICATION: "A FOREIGN AFFAIR," EBURY PRESS
ART DIRECTION: DAVID ELDRIDGE, TWO ASSOCIATES
FOR EBURY PRESS
DIMENSIONS: N/A
MEDIA: HAND DRAWN AND DIGITAL
ARTIST REPRESENTATION: ART DEPARTMENT
CONTACT: STEPHANIEP@ART-DEPT.COM
URL: WWW.ART-DEPT.COM

JEFF FINLEY (USA) *overleaf*
TITLE: FERGIE
BRIEF: DESIGN FOR A LOGO-BASED T-SHIRT FOR
RECORDING ARTIST FERGIE. THE THEMES INCLUDED
"JUICY," "CANDY," "DELICIOUS," AND "TASTY"
PUBLICATION: N/A
ART DIRECTION: GO MEDIA
DIMENSIONS: 15 5/8 X 11 1/8 IN 396 X 284 MM
MEDIA: ADOBE ILLUSTRATOR
ARTIST REPRESENTATION: BERNSTEIN & ANDRIULLI (USA)
CONTACT: LOUISA@BA-REPS.COM
URL: WWW.BA-REPS.COM

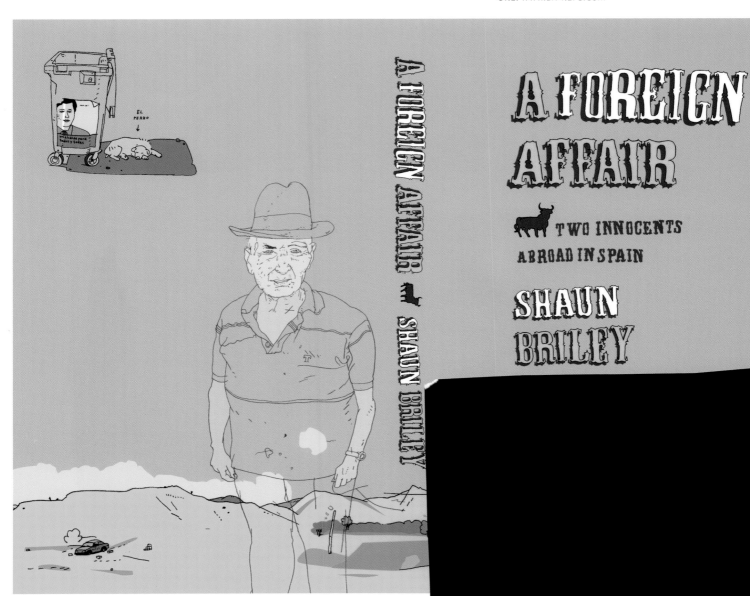

CHRIS ANDREWS (UK)
TITLE: VALENTINES
BRIEF: SELF-PROMOTIONAL IMAGE CREATED FOR VALENTINE'S DAY
PUBLICATION: N/A
ART DIRECTION: N/A
DIMENSIONS: 11 ¼ X 11 ¼ IN 286 X 286 MM
MEDIA: PAINT
ARTIST REPRESENTATION: EASTWING
CONTACT: ANDREA@EASTWING.CO.UK
URL: WWW.EASTWING.CO.UK

index

RICHARD WILKINSON *10*

DAMIEN WEIGHILL *12*

ANNIKA WESTER *12*

MARLENA ZUBER *13*

MARTINA WITTE *13*

CHARLES WILKIN *14*

PAUL WILLOUGHBY *14*

TOM BAGSHAW *15*

KARIN ÅKESSON *16*

MARILINE FIORI *17*

MARGUERITE SAUVAGE *18*

GEORGINA FEARNS *18*

CHARLES WILKIN *19*

PIETER VAN EENOGE *20*

LISA YARDLEY *21*

RALPH *22*

GIANLUCA FOLÌ *23*

JOANNA WALSH *24*

JUSTINE BECKETT *25*

SUZANNE BARRETT *26*

KATIE WOOD *26*

PIETER VAN EENOGE *26*

TRACY WALKER *27*

BARBARA SPOETTEL *28*

ADRIAN VALENCIA *29*

PAULA MCNAMARA *29*

JASON STAVROU *30*

DAN TAYLOR *31*

GORDON WIEBE *31*

GEOFF WESTBY *31*

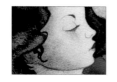

DANIELA
JAGLENKA TERRAZZINI *32*

LOUISA ST. PIERRE *32*

EROTIC DRAGON *33*

KARINE FAOU *34*

SIEGELBAUM *35*

NICK DEWAR *36*

HANNA MELIN *37*

PIETER
VAN EENOGE *37*

PHILIPPE NEUMAGER *38*

OWEN SHERWOOD *38*

KIM ROSEN *39*

MARLENA ZUBER *40*

BJORN RUNE LIE *40*

VIDHA SAUMYA *41*

RENAUD PERRIN *42*

VALERIA PETRONE *43*

SUSAN
ESTELLE KWAS *43*

BELLA PILAR *44*

EMILIANO PONZI *44*

ERIC GIRIAT *45*

SUSAN MCKENNA *45*

ANJA KROENCKE *46-47*

ILANA KOHN *48*

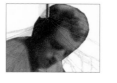

MARK LAZENBY *48*

MARCO MARELLA *49*

SUSAN FARRINGTON *49*

MAYUMI FUJIMOTO *50*

LEIF PARSONS *50*

OLIVIER KUGLER *51*

GISELLE POTTER *52*

ERIC GIRIAT *53*

MARTIN HAAKE *53*

SCOTT CHAMBERS *54*

CECILY LANG *55*

ALEXANDRA HIGLETT *55*

DANIEL HASKETT *56*

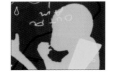
CHRIS KEEGAN *56*

JESSIE FORD *57*

CLEMENTINE HOPE *58*

GUSTAF VON ARBIN *58*

ADAM GRAFF *59*

JOAQUIN GONZALES *60*

LAURE FOURNIER *60*

GEZ FRY *61*

JOHN JAY CABUAY *62*

REINHARD SCHLEINING *62-63*

MARIA CARDELLI *63*

MARIA CARDELLI *64*

JASON BROOKS *64*

JOHN JAY CABUAY *65*

MATT CROFT *66*

PAUL BOMMER *66*

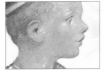
GÉRARD DUBOIS *67*

ADRIAN D'ALIMONTE *68*

SCOTT KENNEDY *69*

PAUL BOMMER *69*

OLAF HAJEK *70*

JONATHAN CROFT *71*

SCOTT CHAMBERS *71*

INGI ERLINGSSON *72*

STÉPHANE GAMAIN *73*

MARLENA ZUBER *74*

DORIS HÉMAR *75*

CARINE ABRAHAM *76*

KIM ROSEN *78*

REBECCA BRADLEY *79*

BRIAN GRIMWOOD *79*

BEN HASLER *80*

REILLY *80-81*

MARIA RAYMONDSDOTTER *81*

AMELIE HEGARDT *82*

J. DAVID MCKENNEY *82*

ANJA KROENCKE *83*

SARAH BEETSON *84*

DANIEL F. BIRCH *85*

WALSHWORKS *85*

RUSS TUDOR *85*

A. SKWISH *85*

320

DAVID HUMPHRIES 86

RINA DONNERSMARCK 87

ESTHER WATSON 87

AMELIE HEGARDT 88-89

KERASCOËT 90

OLIVIER GOKA 91

MIKE LAUGHEAD 91

TOM GENOWER 92

DANIEL HASKETT 93

VICKY WOODGATE 93

BONNIE DAIN 94

GUSTAF VON ARBIN 94

IZAK ZENOU 95

NELLY DIMITRANOVA 96

JOY GOSNEY 97

KEVIN MCBRIDE 97

RICK TULKA 97

AMELIE HEGARDT 98

ESTHER WATSON 99

REBECCA BRADLEY 99

AARON BIHARI 100

JULIA BRECKENREID 101

ANDY WARD 101

AGNES DECOURCHELLE 102

RACHEL GOSLIN 103

MIKAEL KANGAS 104

JIM LAURENCE 105

GREG STEVENSON 105

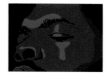
CHRIS RUBINO 105

SARAJO FRIEDEN 106

GISELLE POTTER 107

JITESH PATEL 107

ALEXANDRA COMPAIN-TISSIER 108

PAULA SANZ CABALLERO 109

LOUISE WALLACE 109

AIMEE LEVY 109

GREG STEVENSON 110

MARTINA WITTE 111

STEVEN TABBUTT 111

MONIKA ROE 112

MAYUMI FUJIMOTO 113

ROBERT CLYDE ANDERSON 113

MARGUERITE SAUVAGE 114-115

KALANI LEE 114

STANLEY CHOW 115

SERGE SEIDLITZ 116

DAN TAYLOR 117

ROMAN KLONEK 117

CASSANDRE MONTORIOL 118

BONNIE DAIN 118

TRACY WALKER 119

TIM TOMKINSON 120

MARGARET LEE 120-121

JASON STAVROU 121

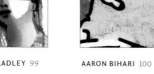

BO LUNDBERG *122*

REILLY *122-123*

DAVID NAVASCUES *123*

DANIEL HASKETT *124*

ADAM OSGOOD *124*

LUKE WILSON *125*

SHAWN BARBER *125*

RINA DONNERSMARCK *126*

RICH LILLASH *128*

AARON LEIGHTON *128*

PAUL BOMMER *129*

CECILY LANG *130*

IAN PHILLIPS *130*

OWEN SHERWOOD *131*

SCOTT CHAMBERS *132*

GAVIN REECE *133*

HOLLY WALES *133*

BRITTA STENHOUSE *134*

JENNY WREN *134*

TRACY WALKER *135*

BRITTA STENHOUSE *135*

ANSON LIAW *136*

MASAKI RYO *137*

ANNIKA WESTER *137*

ANSON LIAW *137*

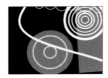
SEAN SIMS *138*

JOANNA WALSH *139*

TRINA DALZIEL *139*

MARY KILVERT *140*

CLEMENTINE HOPE *140*

AGNES DECOURCHELLE *141*

MARY KILVERT *142*

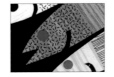
GEORGINA HOUNSOME *142*

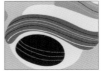

MELVYN EVANS *143*

SAM WILSON *143*

YEE TING KUIT *144*

MARIKO JESSE *146*

JUDY STEVENS *146*

ILOVEDUST *147*

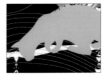

KARINE FAOU *148*

JOSEF GAST *149*

FRÉDÉRIC PÉAULT *149*

TRISHA KRAUSS *150*

AGNESE BICOCCHI *150*

JANELL GENOVESE *150*

REBECCA BRADLEY *151*

BELLA PILAR *151*

PAUL BOMMER *152*

WALSHWORKS *152*

ANNE SMITH *153*

JOJO ENSSLIN *154*

GUNNLAUG MOEN HEMBERY *155*

NADIA BERKANE *155*

HOLLY WALES *156*

LEE WOODGATE *157*

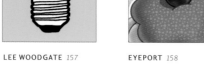

EYEPORT *158*

HELEN DARDIK *158*

BELINDA PEARCE *159*

GINA TRIPLETT &
MATT CURTIUS *160*

CHARLES WILKIN *161*

MARTINA WITTE *162*

DAVID NAVASCUES *164*

FRÉDÉRIC PÉAULT *165*

LIZZIE GARDINER *165*

JO GOODBERRY *166*

ANDREW BYLO *166*

ANN BOYAJIAN *167*

TIM TOMKINSON *168*

CAROLINE TOMLINSON *169*

JOHN SPENCER *170*

JUDY STEVENS *170*

ALEXANDRA
HIGLETT *170*

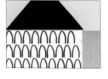

LISA DEJOHN *171*

WALSHWORKS *171*

SYLVIE PINSONNEAUX *172*

LINDA KETELHUT *172-173*

STÉPHANE GAMAIN *173*

LINDA KETELHUT *173*

LINDA KETELHUT *174*

JONATHAN CROFT *174*

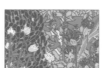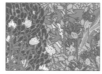

JOANNA WALSH *175*

STEFAN G. BUCHER *175*

ALLAN DEAS *176*

BO LUNDBERG *177*

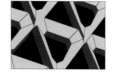

REILLY *178*

PAUL JACKSON *179*

DAN TAYLOR *179*

REILLY *180*

OWEN SHERWOOD *180*

PHILIPPE LECHIEN *181*

PABLO BERNASCONI *181*

KEVIN MCBRIDE *182*

KEVIN MCBRIDE *182*

JASON STAVROU *182*

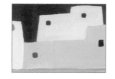

CAROLE HÉNAFF *183*

CHLOÉ POIZAT *184*

GINA TRIPLETT &
MATT CURTIUS *184*

SARAH PERKINS *184*

MANDY PRITTY *185*

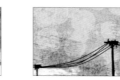

CHLOÉ POIZAT *185*

GINA TRIPLETT &
MATT CURTIUS *186*

OLAF HAJEK *186*

GIANPAOLO PAGNI *187*

CHRIS ANDREWS *188*

GARY EMBURY *188*

YEE TING KUIT *189*

JONATHAN CROFT *190*

MARY KILVERT *190*

 ROMAN KLONEK *191*

 NADIA BERKANE *192*

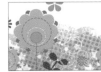 YEE TING KUIT *192*

 RINA DONNERSMARCK *193*

 CHRIS RUBINO *194*

 JUDY STEVENS *194*

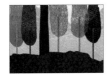 GEORGINA HOUNSOME *195*

 KEITH HERBERT *196*

 BARBARA SPOETTEL *197*

 CHRIS KEEGAN *197*

 ROBIN CHEVALIER *198*

 JOSH COCHRAN *198*

 MELVYN EVANS *199*

 SIMON SPILSBURY *199*

 ALEXANDRA HIGLETT *200*

 GINA TRIPLETT & MATT CURTIUS *200*

 CHRISTOPHER HADJINICOLA *201*

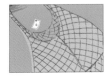 TRINA DALZIEL *202*

 VINCENT BALAS *202-203*

 SERGE SEIDLITZ *202-203*

 MIKAEL KANGAS *204-205*

 STEVEN TABBUTT *206*

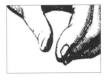 NOBBY SPROUTS *208*

 MATTHEW LEBARON *208*

 CASSANDRE MONTORIOL *209*

 OLIVER BARRETT *210*

 SÉVERINE SCAGLIA *210*

 DAVE BAIN *211*

 JESSICA HISCHE *212*

 SUSANNE SAENGER *212*

 STEPHAN BRITT *212*

 REILLY *213*

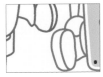 MARK BLADE *213*

 KRISTIAN RUSSELL *214*

 BEN HASLER *214*

 KERRY ROPER *215*

 SILJA GÖTZ *216*

 JONATHAN BURTON *217*

 VALERIA PETRONE *217*

 GÉRARD DUBOIS *217*

 NATE WILLIAMS *218*

 PABLO PICYK *218*

 NATE WILLIAMS *219*

 BEN CHALLENOR *219*

 ROBIN CHEVALIER *220*

 ROBIN CHEVALIER *220*

 EMILIANO PONZI *220*

 COLE GERST *221*

 STEPHEN LEDWIDGE *222*

     THOMAS KUHLENBECK *223*

  DAVID HUMPHRIES *223*

DANIEL CHANG *223*

 KERASCOËT *224*

COLE GERST *224*

OLAF HAJEK 224

GEORGINA HOUNSOME 225

LUCY DAVEY 225

MARK LAZENBY 226

CAROLE HÉNAFF 226

TRAVIS LAMPE 227

MATT LEE 227

DANIEL CHANG 227

SILJA GÖTZ 228

ANNE HORST 228

ADAM GRAFF 229

JO BIRD 229

LIZZIE COLLCUTT 230

MARK LAZENBY 231

JOSEPH DANIEL FIEDLER 231

GÉRARD DUBOIS 231

AKA 232

KUMKUM NOODLES 233

ALEXANDER BLUE 233

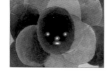

GORDON WIEBE 234

FRAZER HUDSON 234

TOMASZ WALENTA 235

MARIE LAFRANCE 236

BEPPE GIACOBBE 236

LAURENCE WHITELEY 237

A. RICHARD ALLEN 237

ANNE HORST 238

MARIE LAFRANCE 239

ALEXANDRA HIGLETT 239

STEPHEN LEDWIDGE 239

MARK TODD 240

VIKTORIA FOMINA 241

ROB HARE 241

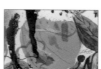 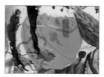

MARK TODD 241

FRANCK OMER 243

NICKY ACKLAND-SNOW 242

FRAZER HUDSON 243

HOLLY WALES 243

KRISTIAN RUSSELL 244

PAUL ZWOLAK 244

KERRY ROPER 244

GARY NEILL 245

GARY NEILL 245

CHRIS RUBINO 246

DAVE BAIN 246-247

JONATHAN BALL 247

ESTHER WATSON 247

IAN PHILLIPS 248

MARK LAZENBY 248

JULIETTE BORDA 249

SÉVERINE SCAGLIA 250-251

CARINE ABRAHAM 250-251

CARINE ABRAHAM 251

MATT JOHNSTONE 252

OLIVIER LATYK 254

SERGE SEIDLITZ 256

LIZZIE GARDINER 256

GEMMA ROBINSON 257

MATT JOHNSTONE 258

SERGE SEIDLITZ 259

SERGE SEIDLITZ 259

MATT JOHNSTONE 260

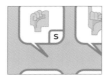

ADRIAN D'ALIMONTE 260

LEE WOODGATE 261

RACHEL ROSS 262

JANELL GENOVESE 262

MARIKO JESSE 263

ANDREW FOSTER 264

ROBIN HURSTHOUSE 265

GLYN BREWERTON 266

MARTIN HAAKE 266

PATRICK BATEMAN 267

JESSICA HISCHE 268

A. SKWISH 269

DAVID ATKINSON 270

MICHAEL A. HILL 270

FRED VAN DEELEN 271

ANDY WARD 271

SUSAN MCKENNA 272

ANNE SMITH 273

SUSY PILGRIM-WATERS 273

JOY GOSNEY 273

SARAJO FRIEDEN 274-275

LEIF PARSONS 276

KATHERINE BAXTER 277

MARY KILVERT 278

MARTIN HAAKE 278

LUCY TRUMAN 279

SUSANNE SAENGER 280

ANDY WARD 282

ANDREW FOSTER 283

CHARLES WILKIN 283

EKATERINA SILINA 284

EMILIANO PONZI 285

TRISHA KRAUSS 286

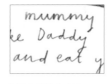

HANNA MELIN 287

GIANPAOLO PAGNI 288-289

CHRIS RUBINO 290

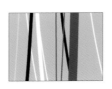

MARGUERITE SAUVAGE 291

MARCO MARELLA 292

JOSEPH BLAKEY 293

CAROLE HÉNAFF 293

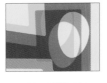

CAMPBELL LAIRD 294

CAMPBELL LAIRD 294

CAMPBELL LAIRD 295

JESSICA HISCHE 296

JESSICA HISCHE 296

DAVID B. MCMACKEN 297

YEE TING KUIT 298

AARON LEIGHTON 299

HOWARD
BESANÇON-MATIL 300

HOWARD
BESANÇON-MATIL 301

TOM GENOWER 302

TOM GENOWER 302

CHRIS RUBINO 303

MICHAEL A. HILL 304

ROMAN KLONEK 304

NATE WILLIAMS 305

HANNA MELIN 306-307

OLIVIER KUGLER 307

FRANCK OMER 307

BO LUNDBERG 309

ALLAN DEAS 310

HARRIET RUSSELL 310

MATT JOHNSTONE 311

SCOTT KENNEDY 312

OLIVIER KUGLER 313

JEFF FINLEY 314-375

CHRIS ANDREWS 316

HOWARD
BESANÇON-MATIL 327

MARIA
RAYMONDSDOTTER 329

GUSTAF VON ARBIN 332

ROB HARE 334

HOWARD BESANÇON–MATIL (NEW ZEALAND)
TITLE: CRYSTAL HEALING
BRIEF: SELF-PROMOTIONAL PIECE
PUBLICATION: N/A
ART DIRECTION: N/A
DIMENSIONS: 16 ½ X 23 ⅜ IN 420 X 594 MM
MEDIA: ADOBE ILLUSTRATOR
ARTIST REPRESENTATION: N/A
CONTACT: HOWARDMATIL@MAC.COM

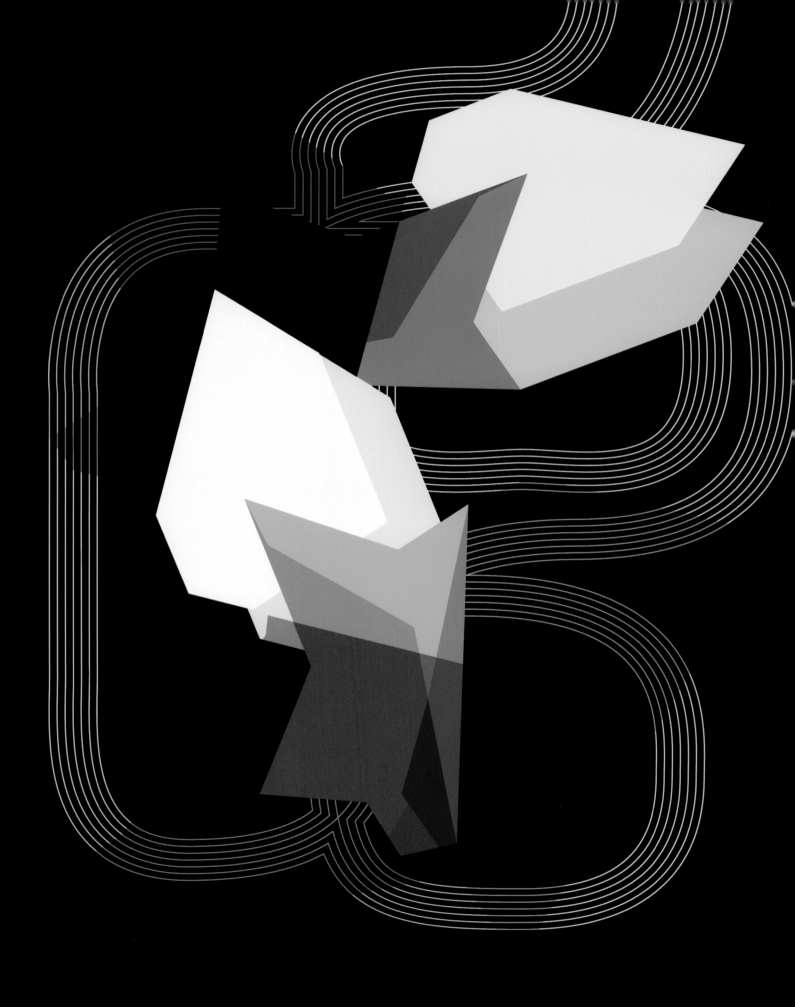

index

MARIA RAYMONDSDOTTER (SWEDEN)
TITLE: PARTY TRICKS
BRIEF: TO ILLUSTRATE AN ARTICLE ABOUT PARTY TRICKS
PUBLICATION: TATLER MAGAZINE, UK
ART DIRECTION: TATLER MAGAZINE, UK
DIMENSIONS: N/A
MEDIA: INK AND DIGITAL
ARTIST REPRESENTATION: CENTRAL ILLUSTRATION AGENCY (CIA)
CONTACT: INFO@CENTRALILLUSTRATION.COM
URL: WWW.CENTRALILLUSTRATION.COM

agents

ANNA GOODSON MANAGEMENT
TEL: +1 514 482 0488
FAX: +1 514 482 0686
EMAIL: INFO@AGOODSON.COM
EMAIL: ANNA@AGOODSON.COM
URL: WWW.AGOODSON.COM

ART DEPARTMENT
ILLUSTRATION DIVISION
420 WEST 24TH STREET, #1F
NEW YORK, NY 10011
USA
TEL: +1 212 243 2103
FAX: +1 212 243 2104
EMAIL: ILLUSTRATION@ART-DEPT.COM
EMAIL: STEPHANIEP@ART-DEPT.COM
URL: WWW.ART-DEPT.COM

ARTS COUNSEL, INC.
853 BROADWAY, SUITE 606
NEW YORK, NY 10003
USA
TEL: +1 212 777 6777
FAX: +1 212 995 5585
EMAIL: INFO@ARTSCOUNSELINC.COM
URL: WWW.ARTSCOUNSELINC.COM

THE ARTWORKS
40 FRITH STREET
LONDON W1D 5LN
UK
TEL: +44 (0) 20 7734 3333
FAX: +44 (0) 20 7734 3484
EMAIL: STEPH@THEARTWORKSINC.COM
URL: WWW.THEARTWORKSINC.COM

BERNSTEIN & ANDRIULLI
58 WEST 40TH STREET
NEW YORK, NY 10018
USA
TEL: +1 212 682 1490
FAX: +1 212 286 1890
EMAIL: LOUISA@BA-REPS.COM
URL: WWW.BA-REPS.COM

BIG ACTIVE
UNIT 6.01 THE TEA BUILDING
56 SHOREDITCH HIGH STREET
LONDON, E1 6JJ
UK
TEL: +44 (0) 20 7739 5601
FAX: +44 (0) 20 7739 7479
EMAIL: TIM@BIGACTIVE.COM
URL: WWW.BIGACTIVE.COM

CENTRAL ILLUSTRATION AGENCY (CIA)
URL: WWW.CENTRALILLUSTRATION.COM

UK
36 WELLINGTON STREET
COVENT GARDEN
LONDON WC2E 7BD
TEL: +44 (0) 20 7240 8925
FAX: +44 (0) 20 7836 1177
EMAIL: INFO@CENTRALILLUSTRATION.COM

FRANCE
HUGO WEINBERG
32 PLACE SAINT GEORGES
PARIS 75009
FRANCE
TEL: +33 (1) 49 95 93 69
EMAIL: H.WEINBERG@WANADOO.FR

USA
PLEASE SEE BERNSTEIN & ANDRIULLI

GUSTAF VON ARBIN (SWEDEN)
TITLE: SMOKER
BRIEF: DRAWING FOR AN ANIMATED FILM, PART OF A PROJECT
ENTITLED "DAYTRIPS," EXHIBITED IN STOCKHOLM, SWEDEN.
PUBLICATION: N/A
ART DIRECTION: N/A
DIMENSIONS: 11 1/8 X 15 5/8 IN 282 X 396 MM
MEDIA: BLACK INK AND CUT-OUT PAPER
ARTIST REPRESENTATION: ART DEPARTMENT
CONTACT: STEPHANIEP@ART-DEPT.COM
URL: WWW.ART-DEPT.COM

CHEZ ANTOINE ILLUSTRATION MANAGEMENT
45 RUE VOLTA
75003 PARIS
FRANCE
TEL: +33 (1) 42 78 07 72
TEL: +33 (0) 609 88 09 44
EMAIL: INFO@CHEZANTOINE.COM
URL: WWW.CHEZANTOINE.COM

COSTUME 3 PIÈCES
URL: WWW.COSTUME3PIECES.COM

FRANCE
1 CITÉ PARADIS
75010 PARIS
TEL: +33 (1) 42 47 10 10
EMAIL: CONTACT@COSTUME3PIECES.COM

UK
298 WESTBOURNE GROVE
LONDON W11 2PS
TEL: +44 (0) 20 7229 6846
EMAIL: TIPHAINE@COSTUME3PIECES.COM

CWC INTERNATIONAL
611 BROADWAY, SUITE 730
NEW YORK, NY 10012
USA
TEL: +1 646 486 6586
FAX: +1 646 486 7622
EMAIL: AGENT@CWC-I.COM
URL: WWW.CWC-I.COM

DÉBUT ART
30 TOTTENHAM ST
LONDON W1T 4RJ
UK
TEL: +44 (0) 20 7636 1064
FAX: +44 (0) 20 7580 7017
EMAIL: INFO@DEBUTART.COM
URL: WWW.DEBUTART.COM

EASTWING
99 CHASE SIDE
ENFIELD
LONDON EN2 6NL
UK
TEL: +44 (0) 20 8367 6760
TEL: +44 (0) 20 8367 6730
EMAIL: ANDREA@EASTWING.CO.UK
URL: WWW.EASTWING.CO.UK

EYE CANDY ILLUSTRATION AGENCY
PEPPERPOT CORNER, MANOR YARD
BLITHBURY ROAD, HAMSTALL RIDWARE
STAFFORDSHIRE WS15 3RS
UK
EMAIL: INFO@EYECANDY.CO.UK
URL: WWW.EYECANDY.CO.UK

LONDON
TEL: +44 (0) 20 8291 0729

NEW YORK
TEL: +1 212 710 1378

FOLIO
10 GATE STREET
LONDON WC2A 3HP
UK
TEL: +44 (0) 20 7242 9562
FAX: +44 (0) 20 7242 1816
EMAIL: ALL@FOLIOART.CO.UK
URL: WWW.FOLIOART.CO.UK

FRANK STURGES REPS
TEL: +1 740 369 9702
EMAIL: FRANK@STURGESREPS.COM
URL: WWW.STURGESREPS.COM

FRIEND AND JOHNSON
443 GREENWICH STREET #6J
NEW YORK, NY 10013
USA
TEL: +1 212 337 0055
FAX: +1 212 367 7098
EMAIL: SFRIEND@FRIENDANDJOHNSON.COM
EMAIL: BJOHNSON@FRIENDANDJOHNSON.COM
URL: WWW.FRIENDANDJOHNSON.COM

I2I ART
EMAIL: INFO@I2IART.COM
URL: WWW.I2IART.COM

NORTH AMERICA
TEL: 1 888 277 7200 (TOLL FREE)
TEL: +1 416 505 9522
FAX: +1 416 504 0400

UK
TEL: 08081011247 (TOLL FREE)

ILLUSTRATION WEB (EUROPE)
2 BROOKS COURT
CRINGLE STREET
LONDON SW8 5BX
UK
TEL: +44 (0) 20 7720 5202
EMAIL: TEAM@ILLUSTRATIONWEB.COM
URL: WWW.ILLUSTRATIONWEB.COM

THE INKSHED ILLUSTRATION AGENCY
99 CHASE SIDE
ENFIELD
LONDON EN2 6NL
UK
TEL: + 44 (0) 20 8367 4545
FAX: + 44 (0) 20 8367 6730
EMAIL: ABBY@INKSHED.CO.UK
URL: WWW.INKSHED.CO.UK

KATE LARKWORTHY ARTIST REPRESENTATION
350 CENTRAL PARK WEST #13D
NEW YORK, NY 10025
USA
TEL: +1 212 531 1722
FAX: +1 212 531 1739
EMAIL: KATE@LARKWORTHY.COM
URL: WWW.LARKWORTHY.COM

KOMBINATROTWEISS
KAISERSTRASSE 69
FRANKFURT AM MAIN 60329
GERMANY
TEL: +49 69 264 88 625

FAX: +49 69 264 88 627
EMAIL: INFO@KOMBINATROTWEISS.DE
URL: WWW.KOMBINATROTWEISS.DE

LILLA ROGERS STUDIO
6 PARKER ROAD
ARLINGTON, MA 02474
USA
TEL: +1 781 641 2787
FAX: +1 781 641 2244
EMAIL: LILLA@LILLAROGERS.COM
URL: WWW.LILLAROGERS.COM

LINDGREN & SMITH
630 NINTH AVENUE
NEW YORK, NY 10036
USA
EMAIL: INFO@LSILLUSTRATION.COM
URL: WWW.LINDGRENSMITH.COM

NEW YORK
TEL: +1 212 397 7330

SAN FRANCISCO
TEL: +1 415 788 8552

MAGNET REPS
1685 H STREET, #219
BLAINE, WA 98230
USA
EMAIL: ART@MAGNETREPS.COM
URL: WWW.MAGNETREPS.COM

LOS ANGELES
TEL: +1 866 390 5656

VANCOUVER
TEL: +1 604 990 9775

MAPS ILLUSTRATED
42 BARNMEAD ROAD
BECKENHAM
KENT BR3 1JE
UK
TEL: +44 (0) 20 8776 7984
EMAIL: MAIL@MAPSILLUSTRATED.COM
URL: WWW.MAPSILLUSTRATED.COM

MARLENA AGENCY
322 EWING STREET
PRINCETON, NJ 08540
USA
TEL: +1 609 252 9405
EMAIL: MARLENA@MARLENAAGENCY.COM
URL: WWW.MARLENAAGENCY.COM

MORGAN GAYNIN INC.
194 THIRD AVENUE
NEW YORK, NY 10003
USA
TEL: +1 212 475 0440
FAX: +1 212 353 8538
EMAIL: INFO@MORGANGAYNIN.COM
URL: WWW.MORGANGAYNIN.COM

NEW DIVISION
5 RISBOROUGH STREET
LONDON SE1 0HF
UK

TEL: +44 (0) 20 7593 0505
FAX: +44 (0) 20 7593 0501
EMAIL: INFO@NEWDIVISION.COM
URL: WWW.NEWDIVISION.COM

NB ILLUSTRATION
40 BOWLING GREEN LANE
CLERKENWELL
LONDON EC1R ONE
UK
TEL: +44 (0) 20 7278 9131
FAX: +44 (0) 20 7278 9121
EMAIL: INFO@NBILLUSTRATION.CO.UK
URL: WWW.NBILLUSTRATION.CO.UK

THE ORGANISATION
69 CALEDONIAN ROAD
LONDON N1 9BT
UK
TEL: +44 (0) 20 7833 8268
FAX: +44 (0) 20 7833 8269
EMAIL: INFO@ORGANISART.CO.UK
URL: WWW.ORGANISART.CO.UK

PIART ART & DESIGN AGENCY
NARODNAY 14/2
MOSCOW 117 152
RUSSIA
TEL: +7 495 912 08 99
FAX: +7 495 912 08 99
EMAIL: PIART2000@PIART.ORG
URL: WWW.PIART.ORG

PRIVATE VIEW, UK
17A SWAN HILL
SHREWSBURY, SHROPSHIRE
SY1 1NL
UK
TEL: +44 (0) 1743 350355
EMAIL: CREATE@PVUK.COM
URL: WWW.PVUK.COM

SHANNON ASSOCIATES
EMAIL: INFORMATION@SHANNONASSOCIATES.COM
URL: WWW.SHANNONASSOCIATES.COM

NEW YORK
630 9TH AVENUE SUITE 707
NEW YORK, NY 10036
USA
TEL: +1 212 333 2551

LOS ANGELES
TEL: +1 323 874 5700

ORLANDO
TEL: +1 917 408 9964

CHICAGO
TEL: +1 312 364 0244

MINNEAPOLIS
TEL: +1 612 338 3733

TORONTO
TEL: +1 416 279 1113

UK
30 GAP ROAD
LONDON SW19 8JG
UK
TEL: +44 (0) 20 8543 7085

SYNERGY
URL: WWW.SYNERGYART.CO.UK

UK
52-54 TURNMILL STREET
LONDON EC1M 5SH
TEL: +44 (0) 20 7251 4300
FAX: +44 (0) 20 7251 4302
EMAIL: INFO@SYNERGYART.CO.UK

AUSTRALIA
6 THORNTON STREET
SYDNEY 2094
TEL: +61 (0) 406 768812
EMAIL: FRANCES@SYNERGYART.CO.UK

TAIKO AND ASSOCIATES
#202 4-3-26 KOMABA
MEGURO-KU
TOKYO 153-0041
JAPAN
TEL: +81 03 5790 2334
FAX: +81 03 5790 2335
EMAIL: TAIKO@UA-NET.COM
URL: WWW.UA-NET.COM/TAIKO

THREE EYES LTD.
127 BREAKER BAY RD
SEATOUN
WELLINGTON 2066
NEW ZEALAND
TEL: +64 4 939 4541
FAX: +64 4 939 4540
EMAIL: THREEEYES@PARADISE.NET.NZ
URL: WWW.THREEEYES.CO.NZ

TRAFFIC CREATIVE MANAGEMENT
20 WEST 22ND STREET
SUITE 1602
NEW YORK, NY 10010
USA
TEL: +1 212 255 3965
FAX: +1 212 255 8918
EMAIL: INFO@TRAFFICNYC.COM
URL: WWW.TRAFFICNYC.COM

AGENCE VIRGINIE
10 RUE SAINT-NICOLAS
75012 PARIS
FRANCE
TEL +33 (0)1 5698 0708
EMAIL: VIRGINIE@VIRGINIE.FR
URL: WWW.VIRGINIE.FR

WANDA NOWAK CREATIVE ILLUSTRATORS' AGENCY
231 EAST 76TH STREET, SUITE 5D
NEW YORK, NY 1002
USA
TEL: +1 212 535 0438
FAX: +1 212 535 1624
EMAIL: WANDA@WANDANOW.COM
URL: WWW.WANDANOW.COM

ROB HARE (UK)
TITLE: THOUGHTS
BRIEF: PERSONAL WORK
PUBLICATION: N/A
ART DIRECTION: N/A
DIMENSIONS: 7 1/8 X 9 1/2 IN 180 X 240 MM
MEDIA: DIGITAL
ARTIST REPRESENTATION: JELLY LONDON
CONTACT: INFO@JELLYLONDON.COM
URL: WWW.JELLYLONDON.COM

page 1
HOWARD BESANÇON–MATIL (NEW ZEALAND)
TITLE: NIGHTMARE STEAK
BRIEF: OPEN BRIEF ILLUSTRATION FOR AN
"UNCHRISTMASSY" CHRISTMAS T-SHIRT DESIGN
PUBLICATION: N/A
ART DIRECTION: N/A
DIMENSIONS: 8 ¼ X 11 ¾ IN 210 X 297 MM
MEDIA: ADOBE ILLUSTRATOR
ARTIST REPRESENTATION: N/A
CONTACT: HOWARDMATIL@MAC.COM

page 2
MENISHA (FRANCE)
TITLE: LA SOLITUDE
BRIEF: PERSONAL PIECE
PUBLICATION: N/A
ART DIRECTION: N/A
DIMENSIONS: 8 ¼ X 11 ¾ IN 210 X 297 MM
MEDIA: MIXED MEDIA
ARTIST REPRESENTATION: CHEZ ANTOINE
CONTACT: INFO@CHEZANTOINE.COM
URL: WWW.CHEZANTOINE.COM

page 3
STEPHEN LEDWIDGE (IRELAND)
TITLE: MOBILE MUSIC
BRIEF: ILLUSTRATION BASED ON THE THEME
OF "MUSIC" FOR ORANGE MOBILE PHONES
PUBLICATION: N/A
ART DIRECTION: ORANGE / NYC
DIMENSIONS: N/A
MEDIA: ACRYLIC AND PENCIL
ARTIST REPRESENTATION: ANNA GOODSON MANAGEMENT
CONTACT: INFO@AGOODSON.COM
URL: WWW.AGOODSON.COM

page 5
GIANLUCA FOLÌ (ITALY)
TITLE: COWGIRL
BRIEF: SELF-PROMOTIONAL PIECE
PUBLICATION: N/A
ART DIRECTION: N/A
DIMENSIONS: N/A
MEDIA: PENCIL, WATERCOLOR
ARTIST REPRESENTATION: ANNA GOODSON MANAGEMENT
CONTACT: INFO@AGOODSON.COM
URL: WWW.AGOODSON.COM

detail, right, and endpapers
KARIN ÅKESSON (SWEDEN)
TITLE: SLEEP, WE WILL WAKE YOU UP TO A NEW DAY
BRIEF: POSTER ARTWORK
PUBLICATION: N/A
ART DIRECTION: N/A
DIMENSIONS: 14 X 9 ½ IN 356 X 242 MM
MEDIA: MIXED MEDIA
ARTIST REPRESENTATION: EYE CANDY ILLUSTRATION AGENCY
CONTACT: INFO@EYECANDY.CO.UK
URL: WWW.EYECANDY.CO.UK